Progress Chart

This chart lists all the topics in the book. Once you have completed each page, stick a star in the correct box below.

Page	Topic	Star	Page	Topic	Star	Page	Topic	Star
2	Numbers		13	Ordering decimals		24	Word problems	
3	Place value		14	Adding		25	Word problems	
4	Multiplying by 10		15	Adding		26	Problems with measures	
5	Ordering		16	Subtracting		27	Telling time	
6	Rounding		17	Subtracting		28	Telling time	
7	Polygons		18	Choosing the operation		29	Tables and graphs	
8	Identifying patterns		19	Multiplying		30	Necessary information	
9	Odds and evens		20	Multiplying		31	Number pairs	
10	Addition fact families		21	Dividing		32	2 times table	
11	Fractions		22	Dividing		33	Multiplying by 2	
12	Fractions		23	Choosing the operation		34	Dividing by 2	

When you have completed
the progress chart in this book, fill in
the certificate at the back.

Math
made easy

Grade 3
ages 8-9
Workbook

Author and Consultant
Sean McArdle

LONDON • NEW YORK • SYDNEY • MOSCOW • DELHI

Numbers

Write the number in words.

4,567   *Four thousand, five hundred sixty-seven*

Write the number in standard form.

Two thousand, four hundred eighty-six.   *2,486*

Write each number in words.

7,285

3,926

8,143

4,538

Write the numbers in standard form.

Two thousand, six hundred
forty-seven.

Six thousand, one hundred
fifty-eight.

Five thousand, two hundred
seventy-three.

Seven thousand, three
hundred eighty-two.

Nine thousand, five hundred
sixty-one.

Eight thousand, seven
hundred twenty-four.

Write each number in words.

7,207

4,046

5,008

8,309

Write the numbers in standard form.

Three thousand
twenty-one.

Five thousand, two hundred
seven.

Eight thousand two.

Place value

12,645 is the same as:
1 ten thousand, 2 thousands, 6 hundreds, 4 tens, 5 ones
or
12,645 is the same as 10,000 + 2,000 + 600 + 40 + 5

Write the correct number in the space.

7,945 = 7,000 + 900 + 40 + 5   6,312 = 6,000 +   + 10 + 2

4,749 = 4,000 + 700 +   + 9   5,263 = 5,000 + 200 +   + 3

8,294 = 8,000 +   + 90 + 4   13,742 = 10,000 + 3,000 +   + 40 + 2

2,176 = 2,000 +   + 70 + 6   17,375 = 10,000 +   + 300 + 70 + 5

7,264 =   + 200 + 60 + 4   14,286 =   + 4,000 + 200 + 80 + 6

Write the number that is the same as:

Six thousand, two hundred eighty-four

Twelve thousand, one hundred sixty-nine

Fifteen thousand, eight hundred seventy-two

Two thousand sixty-six

Seventeen thousand, four hundred twenty-seven

Nine thousand forty-three

Sixteen thousand, two hundred ten

Twenty-one thousand three

Eleven thousand eleven

Thirteen thousand thirty-eight

Look at these numbers: 6 8 3 0 7

Arrange these digits to make the largest number you can.

Arrange these digits to make the smallest number you can.

Multiplying by 10

Multiply each number by 10.

7   70   12   120   3   30   13   130

Multiply each of these numbers by 10.

6	14	12	17	20
9	15	13	2	23
1	19	24	28	22
5	3	26	11	25

Multiply each of these numbers by 10.

20	17	12	14	6
23	2	13	15	9
22	28	24	19	1
25	11	26	3	5

Multiply each of these numbers by 10.

56	48	67	39	82
69	32	74	57	43
95	63	55	77	40

Multiply each of these numbers by 10.

38	67	48	56	74
32	69	82	63	95
43	57	99	40	77

Ordering

Write these numbers in order, from smallest to largest.

4,675	3,830	8,390	2,617
2,617	3,830	4,675	8,390

Write these numbers in order, from smallest to largest.

1,574	4,683	7,847	2,563				
7,473	2,670	5,371	8,421				
8,389	3,726	7,995	1,843				
3,562	7,264	8,923	5,674				
6,853	4,567	5,684	2,557				
3,241	3,785	9,538	7,647				

Write these numbers in order, from smallest to largest.

5,705	6,390	4,903	2,704				
3,067	2,809	6,330	5,035				
4,207	7,380	5,005	3,027				
8,045	3,028	7,036	1,006				
9,004	3,075	6,003	3,800				

Write these numbers in order, from smallest to largest.

5,780	365	968	1,089				
7,890	4,078	678	999				
4,950	1,230	845	1,002				
8,004	4,800	840	3,980				
679	375	5,078	3,001				

Rounding

What is 132 rounded to the nearest ten?

```
100      110      120      130      140      150      160      170      180
|_____|_____|_____|_____|_____|_____|_____|_____|
                            ↑
```

132 rounded to the nearest 10 is 130 .

Round each number to the nearest ten.

247 _____   306 _____   493 _____   733 _____

834 _____   651 _____   379 _____   215

Round each number to the nearest ten.

```
120    130    140    150    160    170    180    190    200
|_____|        _____
                              ↑
```

```
320    330    340    350    360    370    380    390    400
|_____|        _____
               ↑
```

```
220    230    240    250    260    270    280    290    300
|_____|        _____
                      ↑
```

```
480    490    500    510    520    530    540    550    560
|_____|        _____
                                            ↑
```

```
700    710    720    730    740    750    760    770    780
|_____|        _____
               ↑
```

```
60     70     80     90     100    110    120    130    140
|_____|        _____
                      ↑
```

```
450    460    470    480    490    500    510    520    530
|_____|        _____
                      ↑
```

```
170    180    190    200    210    220    230    240    250
|_____|        _____
                                            ↑
```

```
640    650    660    670    680    690    700    710    720
|_____|        _____
                                     ↑
```

```
500    510    520    530    540    550    560    570    580
|_____|        _____
               ↑
```

Polygons

Match the polygon with a solid figure.

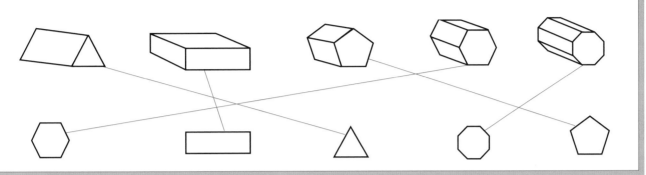

Circle the octagon.

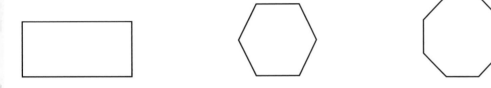

Circle the rectangle.

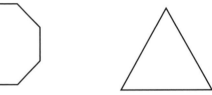

Match the polygon to the solid object in which it appears.

hexagon   octagon   rectangle   pentagon   triangle

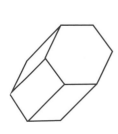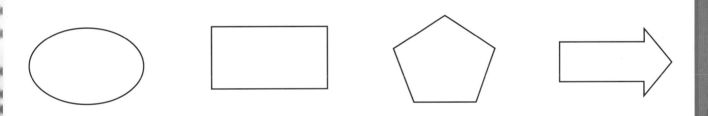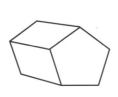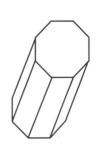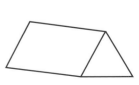

Identifying patterns

Continue each pattern.

0	6	12	18	24	30
0	7	14	21	28	35
60	52	44	36	28	20

Continue each pattern.

3	9	15	21
2	9	16	23
1	9	17	25
7	15	23	31
7	13	19	25
7	12	17	22

Continue each pattern.

71	65	59	53
90	82	74	66
56	49	42	35
72	66	60	54
96	88	80	72
48	42	36	30

Continue each pattern.

36	43					85
61	55				25	19
0	7	14				49
7	14					56
4	12		36			

Odds and evens

Multiply the odd number by the odd number.   7 x 5 = 35

Multiply the even number by the even number.   6 x 8 = 48

Multiply the odd number by the odd number.

5 x 7 =	3 x 9 =	1 x 5 =	3 x 5 =
7 x 3 =	9 x 7 =	7 x 1 =	7 x 7 =
3 x 3 =	3 x 1 =	5 x 9 =	1 x 1 =
5 x 3 =	9 x 9 =	5 x 5 =	7 x 9 =

What do you notice about the numbers in your answer boxes?

_____

Multiply the even number by the even number.

2 x 8 =	6 x 4 =	6 x 10 =	2 x 6 =
4 x 4 =	8 x 2 =	6 x 8 =	6 x 6 =
4 x 6 =	10 x 4 =	4 x 8 =	12 x 12 =
2 x 2 =	8 x 6 =	6 x 2 =	10 x 10 =

What do you notice about the numbers in your answer boxes?

_____

Multiply the odd number by the even number.

3 x 6 =	10 x 5 =	7 x 8 =	2 x 9 =
4 x 7 =	3 x 10 =	4 x 9 =	10 x 7 =
5 x 8 =	6 x 9 =	8 x 5 =	8 x 7 =
9 x 6 =	6 x 3 =	9 x 4 =	10 x 3 =

What do you notice about the numbers in your answer boxes?

_____

Addition fact families

Circle the number sentence that is in the same fact family.

$12 - 5 = 7$
$5 + 7 = 12$ 　　　$12 - 4 = 8$ 　　　(7 + 5 = 12) 　　　$12 + 12 = 24$

$10 - 8 = 2$
$8 + 2 = 10$ 　　　$8 - 6 = 2$ 　　　(2 + 8 = 10) 　　　$8 - 2 = 6$

Circle the number sentence that is in the same fact family.

$7 + 8 = 15$
$8 + 7 = 15$ 　　　$7 + 5 = 12$ 　　　$15 - 8 = 7$ 　　　$8 - 7 = 1$

$17 - 6 = 11$
$11 + 6 = 17$ 　　　$17 - 11 = 6$ 　　　$17 + 6 = 23$ 　　　$5 + 6 = 11$

$14 - 5 = 9$
$14 - 9 = 5$ 　　　$9 - 3 = 6$ 　　　$14 + 9 = 23$ 　　　$5 + 9 = 14$

$9 + 7 = 16$
$7 + 9 = 16$ 　　　$16 - 9 = 7$ 　　　$16 + 7 = 23$ 　　　$9 - 7 = 2$

$19 - 9 = 10$
$19 - 10 = 9$ 　　　$9 + 3 = 12$ 　　　$9 + 10 = 19$ 　　　$18 - 8 = 10$

$4 + 7 = 11$
$11 - 4 = 7$ 　　　$11 + 4 = 15$ 　　　$7 + 4 = 11$ 　　　$7 + 7 = 14$

Write the fact family for each group of numbers.

5, 6, 11 　　　　　　6, 10, 4 　　　　　　5, 13, 8

Fractions

Write the fraction for the part that is shaded.

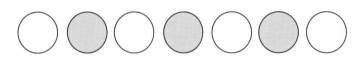

How many shaded circles? 3

How many circles? 8

So, the fraction of circles shaded = $\frac{3}{8}$ $\frac{\text{numerator}}{\text{denominator}}$

Circle the fraction that shows the part that is shaded.

 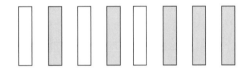

$\frac{2}{5}$ $\frac{2}{3}$ $\frac{3}{5}$ $\frac{3}{4}$ $\frac{4}{7}$ $\frac{3}{7}$

Write the fraction for the part that is shaded.

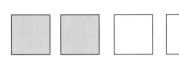   

—   —   —

   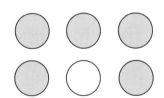   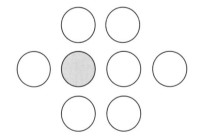

—   —   —

   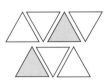   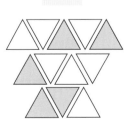

—   —   —

Fractions

Color $\frac{3}{4}$ of each shape.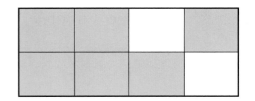

Color $\frac{2}{3}$ of each shape.

 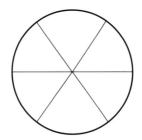 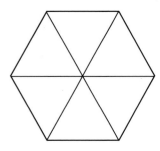

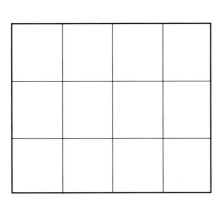 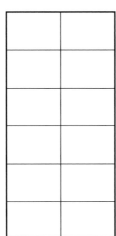 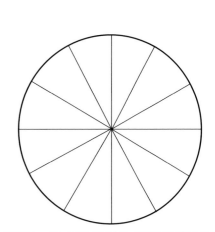

Color $\frac{3}{4}$ of each shape.

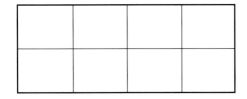 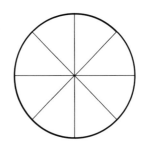 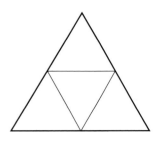

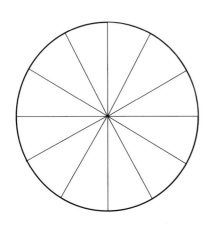 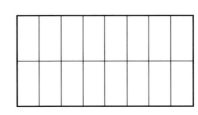 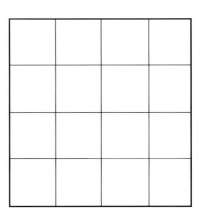

Ordering decimals

Put these decimals in order from smallest to largest.

0.6   0.3   0.7   0.5   0.9   *0.3*   *0.5*   *0.6*   *0.7*   *0.9*

Put these decimals in order from smallest to largest.

0.2	0.8	0.5	0.1	0.9					
0.4	0.2	0.1	0.7	0.6					
0.6	0.3	0.2	0.9	0.1					
0.5	0.6	0.1	0.4	0.2					
0.3	0.5	0.7	0.9	0.6					

Put these decimals in order from smallest to largest.

1.6	1.2	1.9	1.5	1.8					
1.3	1.1	1.7	1.9	1.5					
1.7	1.8	1.1	1.3	1.9					
1.5	1.6	1.9	1.2	1.4					
1.8	1.4	1.2	1.0	1.9					

Put these decimals in order from smallest to largest.

2.8	2.0	2.3	2.5	2.7					
3.7	3.4	3.9	3.6	3.2					
4.2	7.5	2.6	1.4	3.5					
2.8	3.4	4.6	1.8	2.3					
5.3	4.8	2.9	1.9	3.5					

Adding

Write the answer between the lines.

```
  34          28          75
+ 42        + 11        + 14
─────       ─────       ─────
  76          39          89
```

Write the answer between the lines.

```
  24          36          45          61
+ 14        + 23        + 13        + 17
─────       ─────       ─────       ─────


  63          71          48          53
+ 14        + 16        + 10        + 16
─────       ─────       ─────       ─────


  60          46          54          83
+ 36        + 21        + 33        +  6
─────       ─────       ─────       ─────


  28          53          74          38
+ 31        + 36        + 25        + 21
─────       ─────       ─────       ─────


  57          65          79          47
+ 22        + 14        + 10        + 12
─────       ─────       ─────       ─────


  35          46          57          68
+ 13        + 22        + 31        + 40
─────       ─────       ─────       ─────


  44          53          26          62
+ 25        + 34        + 33        + 17
─────       ─────       ─────       ─────


  50          47          66          45
+ 37        + 11        + 22        + 32
─────       ─────       ─────       ─────
```

Adding

Write the answer between the lines.

```
   15          25          55
 + 20        + 40        +  5
   35          65          60
```

Write the answer between the lines.

```
   50          70          90          20
 + 25        + 15        +  5        + 45
 _____      _____      _____      _____


   65          25          35          85
 + 30        + 40        + 50        + 10
 _____      _____      _____      _____


   30          60          55          75
 + 25        + 35        + 30        + 20
 _____      _____      _____      _____


   25          45          65          15
 + 15        +  5        + 25        + 15
 _____      _____      _____      _____


   75          15          35          45
 + 10        + 25        + 25        + 15
 _____      _____      _____      _____


   65          45           5          55
 + 35        + 25        + 65        + 35
 _____      _____      _____      _____


   35          45          15          75
 + 45        + 35        + 30        +  5
 _____      _____      _____      _____


    5          50          45          80
 + 95        + 35        + 45        + 15
 _____      _____      _____      _____
```

Subtracting

Write the answer between the lines.

$$36 - 14 = \underline{22}$$ $$25 - 13 = \underline{12}$$ $$57 - 26 = \underline{31}$$

Write the answer between the lines.

27 − 14	35 − 12	47 − 32	63 − 20
54 − 23	38 − 16	47 − 12	56 − 21
44 − 32	57 − 24	65 − 32	78 − 35
66 − 26	75 − 35	84 − 64	93 − 33
87 − 34	76 − 45	67 − 33	49 − 28
56 − 35	73 − 40	47 − 25	54 − 32
79 − 38	45 − 21	76 − 43	75 − 12
43 − 30	55 − 12	67 − 33	53 − 12

Subtracting

Write the answer between the lines.

36 − 28	41 − 35	53 − 46	65 − 47
44 − 27	35 − 18	62 − 24	73 − 44
56 − 46	37 − 18	43 − 26	68 − 49
34 − 12	45 − 18	63 − 46	37 − 15
60 − 43	47 − 24	63 − 40	86 − 29
73 − 34	56 − 47	48 − 36	80 − 45
54 − 38	70 − 45	37 − 18	53 − 26
34 − 18	71 − 44	25 − 17	83 − 29

Choosing the operation

Write either + or – in the box to make each problem correct.

15 + 25 = 40   30 – 8 = 22   50 – 25 = 25

Write either + or – in the box to make each problem correct.

45 _____ 12 = 33   48 _____ 14 = 34   31 _____ 15 = 46

17 _____ 13 = 30   60 _____ 35 = 25   70 _____ 35 = 35

27 _____ 15 = 12   26 _____ 18 = 44   50 _____ 12 = 62

65 _____ 25 = 40   80 _____ 35 = 45   63 _____ 23 = 40

Write either + or – in the box to make each problem correct.

12 yd _____ 5 yd = 27 yd   34 ft _____ 18 ft = 16 ft

29 cm _____ 17 cm = 12 cm   42 in. _____ 20 in. = 62 in.

28 in. _____ 28 in. = 56 in.   60 cm _____ 15 cm = 45 cm

40 ft _____ 8 ft = 32 ft   90 cm _____ 35 cm = 55 cm

28 cm _____ 15 cm = 43 cm   70 yd _____ 29 yd = 41 yd

90 in. _____ 12 in. = 78 in.   28 m _____ 21 m = 49 m

Write the answer in the box.

I start with 12 apples and end up with 18 apples. How many have I added or subtracted?

A number is added to 14 and the result is 20. What number has been added?

I start with 14 pens. I finish up with 9 pens. How many pens have I lost or gained?

I take a number away from 30 and have 12 left. What number did I take away?

Multiplying

Solve the problems.

```
  12          51          30          35
x  2        x  3        x  4        x  2
----        ----        ----        ----
  24         153         120          70
```

Solve the problems.

```
  11          13          14          12
x   4       x   3       x   2       x   4
----        ----        ----        ----


  32          23          41          33
x   4       x   3       x   4       x   2
----        ----        ----        ----


  30          40          12          24
x   3       x   2       x   3       x   2
----        ----        ----        ----
```

Solve the problems.

```
  23          32          41          44
x   2       x   3       x   3       x   2
----        ----        ----        ----


  21          22          30          50
x   4       x   4       x   2       x   2
----        ----        ----        ----


  14          25          42          34
x   1       x   2       x   2       x   2
----        ----        ----        ----


  16          13          24          31
x   1       x   2       x   3       x   3
----        ----        ----        ----


  14          15          22          32
x   3       x   3       x   3       x   2
----        ----        ----        ----
```

Multiplying

Solve each problem.

$16 \times 4 = (10 \times 4) + (6 \times 4)$
$\qquad = 40 + 24$
$\qquad = 64$

$$\begin{array}{r} 10 \\ \times\ 4 \\ \hline 40 \end{array} \qquad \begin{array}{r} 6 \\ \times\ 4 \\ \hline 24 \end{array}$$

$40 + 24 = 64$

Solve each problem.

18 x 4	15 x 6
17 x 5	14 x 7
19 x 3	16 x 6
23 x 4	26 x 5
24 x 6	27 x 4
32 x 7	34 x 4

Dividing

Write the answer to each division problem.

$27 \div 4 = \boxed{6\,r\,3}$ $36 \div 10 = \boxed{3\,r\,6}$ $\begin{array}{r} 7\,r\,3 \\ 5\overline{)38} \\ -35 \\ \hline 3 \end{array}$

Write the answer to each division problem.

$43 \div 10 =$ $31 \div 4 =$ $19 \div 2 =$ $42 \div 5 =$

$27 \div 10 =$ $42 \div 4 =$ $21 \div 2 =$ $35 \div 5 =$

$61 \div 10 =$ $26 \div 4 =$ $17 \div 2 =$ $46 \div 5 =$

$90 \div 10 =$ $47 \div 4 =$ $13 \div 2 =$ $29 \div 5 =$

Write the answer in the box.

$5\overline{)27}$ $3\overline{)15}$ $4\overline{)23}$ $2\overline{)17}$ $3\overline{)21}$

$2\overline{)8}$ $10\overline{)77}$ $5\overline{)31}$ $3\overline{)33}$ $2\overline{)11}$

Write the answer in the box.

What is the remainder when 15 is divided by 2?

How many groups of 3 are there in 21 and what is the remainder?

Divide 27 by 3.

How many groups of 5 are there in 45?

What is the remainder when 63 is divided by 10?

How many groups of 4 are there in 26?

Dividing

Write the answer to each division problem.

$14 \div 3 = 4\,r\,2$ $18 \div 5 = 3\,r\,3$ $2\overline{)9}$ with $\dfrac{4\,r\,1}{\begin{array}{r}9\\ -8\\ \hline 1\end{array}}$

Write the answer in the box.

$17 \div 3 =$	$24 \div 5 =$	$17 \div 10 =$	$29 \div 4 =$
$13 \div 3 =$	$19 \div 5 =$	$58 \div 10 =$	$36 \div 4 =$
$24 \div 3 =$	$37 \div 5 =$	$44 \div 10 =$	$18 \div 4 =$
$31 \div 3 =$	$29 \div 5 =$	$80 \div 10 =$	$24 \div 4 =$

Write the answer in the box.

$3\overline{)16}$ $5\overline{)17}$ $10\overline{)41}$ $4\overline{)12}$ $3\overline{)25}$

$3\overline{)9}$ $5\overline{)14}$ $10\overline{)64}$ $4\overline{)20}$ $10\overline{)69}$

Write the answer in the box.

What is the remainder when 36 is divided by 10?

How many whole sets of 3 are there in 16?

How many sets of 4 are there in 30 and what is the remainder?

What is the remainder when 44 is divided by 40?

Divide 26 by 3.

Divide 40 by 6.

Choosing the operation

Write either x or ÷ in the box to make the product correct.

12 ÷ 2 = 6   12 × 2 = 24   10 ÷ 2 = 5

Write either x or ÷ in the box to make the product correct.

18 ☐ 3 = 6	20 ☐ 10 = 2	6 ☐ 3 = 18
2 ☐ 9 = 18	20 ☐ 2 = 10	12 ☐ 4 = 3
12 ☐ 10 = 120	24 ☐ 3 = 8	30 ☐ 10 = 3
27 ☐ 3 = 9	18 ☐ 3 = 6	14 ☐ 2 = 28
16 ☐ 4 = 4	24 ☐ 4 = 6	30 ☐ 3 = 10
3 ☐ 8 = 24	5 ☐ 10 = 50	6 ☐ 2 = 3

Write either x or ÷ in the box to make the product correct.

27 cm ☐ 3 = 9 cm	40 in. ☐ 10 = 4 in.	15 cm ☐ 3 = 5 cm
18 in. ☐ 2 = 9 in.	4 m ☐ 5 = 20 m	10 cm ☐ 4 = 40 cm
30 in. ☐ 10 = 3 in.	50 ft ☐ 5 = 10 ft	60 in. ☐ 2 = 30 in.
5 yd ☐ 8 = 40 yd	4 cm ☐ 2 = 2 cm	4 m ☐ 2 = 8 m
20 cm ☐ 10 = 2 cm	20 in. ☐ 4 = 5 in.	20 cm ☐ 2 = 40 cm
12 m ☐ 2 = 6 m	1 ft ☐ 10 = 10 ft	4 yd ☐ 3 = 12 yd

Write the answer in the box.

Which number multiplied by 3 equals 24? ☐

Which number divided by 10 equals 7? ☐

Which number divided by 8 equals 5? ☐

Which number multiplied by 6 equals 6? ☐

Which number multiplied by 9 equals 36? ☐

Which number multiplied by 5 equals 30? ☐

Word problems

Write the answer in the box.

I multiply a number by 6 and the answer is 24.

What number did I begin with?   4

Write the answer in the box.

A number multiplied by 7 equals 35. What is the number?

I divide a number by 10 and the answer is 3. What number did I divide?

I multiply a number by 4 and the answer is 20. What is the number I multiplied?

After dividing a piece of wood into four equal sections, each section is 4 in. long. How long was the piece of wood I started with?

A number multiplied by 6 gives the answer 24. What is the number?

Some money is divided into five equal amounts. Each amount is 10 cents. How much money was there before it was divided?

I multiply a number by 9 and the result is 45. What number was multiplied?

A number divided by 6 is 3. What number was divided?

Three children share 18 peanuts equally among themselves. How many peanuts does each child receive?

A number divided by 4 is 8. What is the number?

I multiply a number by 6 and the answer is 30. What is the number?

Four sets of a number equal 16. What is the number?

A number divided by 5 is 5. What is the number?

A child divides a number by 8 and gets 2. What number was divided?

Three groups of a number equal 27. What is the number?

I multiply a number by 10 and the result is 100. What is the number?

Word problems

Write the answer in the box.

A child is given four dimes. How much money does she have altogether? 40¢

Write the answer in the box.

A box contains 6 eggs. How many boxes would I need to buy to have 18 eggs?

A boy is given three bags of candy. There are 20 pieces in each bag. How many pieces of candy does the boy have in total?

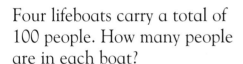

Four lifeboats carry a total of 100 people. How many people are in each boat?

A shepherd had 200 sheep but 70 were lost in a snowstorm. How many sheep does the shepherd have left?

Three women win the lottery and share $900 equally among themselves. How much does each woman receive?

A truck contains 50 barrels of oil. It delivers 27 barrels to one garage. How many barrels are left on the truck?

Andrej has a collection of 150 baseball cards. He sells 30 of them to a friend. How many cards does he have left?

When Peter multiplies his apartment number by 3, the result is 75. What is his apartment number?

One photograph costs $1.80. How much will two photographs cost?

A dog buries 20 bones on Monday, 30 bones on Tuesday, and 40 bones on Wednesday. How many bones has the dog buried altogether?

A car trip is supposed to be 70 miles long but the car breaks down half-way. How far has the car gone when it breaks down?

A teacher has 32 children in her class. 13 children are out with the flu. How many children are left in class?

Problems with measures

Which would be the best unit to use
for the length of a worm?

inch

Choose the most appropriate unit for the measurements below.

| yard | gallon | mile | ounce | foot | pound | inch |

Write the best unit for each of the following.

The length of a garden path.

The weight of a brick.

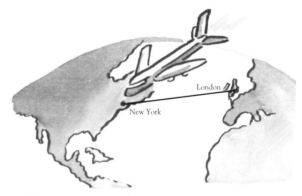

The distance from
London to New York.

The weight of a thimble.

The length of a tortoise.

The capacity of a bucket.

Telling time

What time is shown by these clocks?

  28 minutes to 7

 14 minutes past 3

What time is shown by these clocks?

Telling time

Draw the time on each clock face.
Twenty-six minutes past four.

Draw the time on each clock face.

Twelve minutes to eight

Twenty to nine

Seventeen minutes past four

Eleven minutes to six

Twenty-seven minutes
past twelve

Tables and graphs

Look at this bar graph.

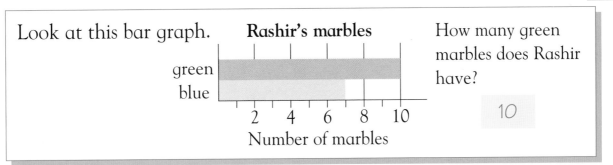

Rashir's marbles

green
blue

2 4 6 8 10
Number of marbles

How many green marbles does Rashir have?

10

Look at this bar graph.

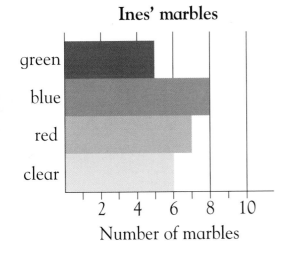

Ines' marbles

green
blue
red
clear

2 4 6 8 10
Number of marbles

How many green marbles does Ines have?

Ines has 7 marbles of which colour?

How many clear marbles does Ines have?

Of which colour does Ines have the most marbles?

How many marbles does Ines have altogether?

Complete the table.

Favorite pets

Pets	tally marks	total
hamsters	⅟⅟⅟⅟ | |	
mice		4
gerbils	| | |	
rats		5

Number of children

How many more children have hamsters than have rats?

Which animal is owned by 4 children?

Necessary information

Write the missing information you need to have to answer the question.

Tim wants to buy juice for his friends. Each box of juice costs 79¢. How much will it cost in all?

You need to know *the number of friends for whom Tim is buying juice.*

Write the missing information you need to have to answer the question.

On Saturday, 367 people saw the first of five movies playing at the local theater. How many people went to the movies on Saturday?

You need to know

Patsy has $5.25. She wants to buy a soda for $1.00. She also wants a sandwich. Does she have enough money?

You need to know

Seashells cost 35¢, 50¢, or 75¢ depending upon their size. Sara bought four shells that had the same price. How much money did she spend?

You need to know

Martina divided her class into 5 teams of students. How many students were on each team?

You need to know

Katya made sandwiches for her mother, her father, her three brothers and her sisters. She also made herself a sandwich. How many sandwiches did she make?

You need to know

Carl bought two paperback books for $6.99 each. He spent 35¢ on a pen and $1.75 on a notepad. How much money did he have left?

You need to know

Number pairs

Write the number pairs of the letter A.

A = (2,1)

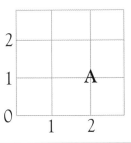

Look at this grid and write the number pairs of each letter.

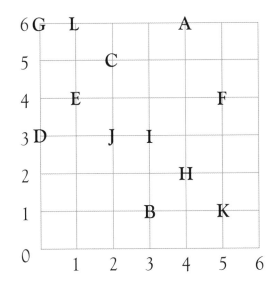

A =   G =

B =   H =

C =   I =

D =   J =

E =   K =

F =   L =

Use the grid to write the number pairs.

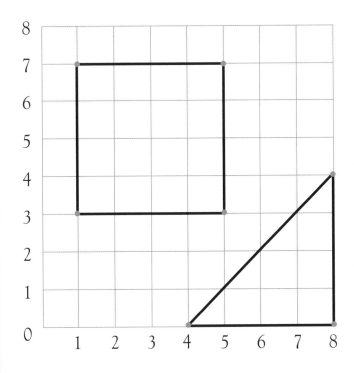

Write the number pairs of each corner of the square.

Write the number pairs of each corner of the triangle.

2 times table

Count in 2s, color, and find a pattern.

1	2	3	4	5
6	7	8	9	10
11	12	13	14	15
16	17	18	19	20
21	22	23	24	25

Write the answers.

1 x 2 = 2   2 x 2 = ☐   3 x 2 = ☐   4 x 2 = ☐

5 x 2 = ☐   6 x 2 = ☐   7 x 2 = ☐   8 x 2 = ☐

9 x 2 = ☐   10 x 2 = ☐

How many ears?

 5 sets of 2   5 x 2 = 10 ears

 ☐ sets of 2   ☐ x ☐ = ☐ ears

 ☐ sets of 2   ☐ x ☐ = ☐ ears

 ☐ sets of 2   ☐ x ☐ = ☐ ears

Multiplying by 2

Write the problems.

 How many pairs of feet?

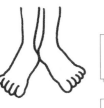  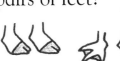

2 sets of 2 = 4

2 x 2 = 4

How many pairs of feet?

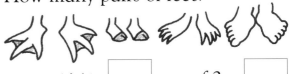

[ ] sets of 2 = [ ]

[ ] x [ ] = [ ]

How many pairs of feet?

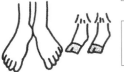 

[ ] sets of 2 = [ ]

[ ] x [ ] = [ ]

How many pairs of feet?

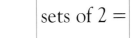

 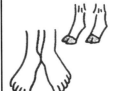

[ ] sets of 2 = [ ]

[ ] x [ ] = [ ]

How many pairs of feet?

[ ] sets of 2 = [ ]

[ ] x [ ] = [ ]

How many pairs of feet?

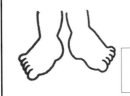

[ ] set of 2 = [ ]

[ ] x [ ] = [ ]

Draw different pictures to go with these problems.

8 x 2 = 16	10 x 2 = 20

Dividing by 2

Share the eggs equally between the nests.

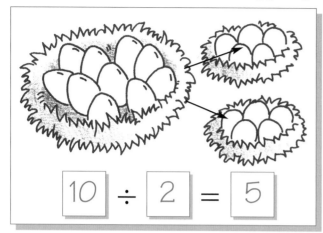

$$\boxed{10} \div \boxed{2} = \boxed{5}$$

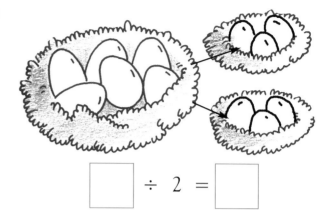

$$\boxed{} \div 2 = \boxed{}$$

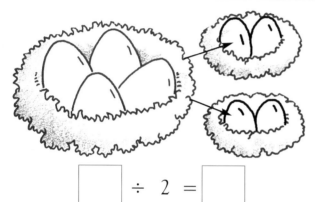

$$\boxed{} \div 2 = \boxed{}$$

$$\boxed{} \div 2 = \boxed{}$$

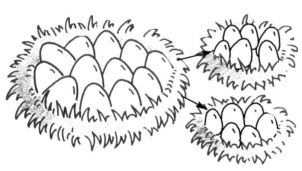

$$\boxed{} \div 2 = \boxed{}$$

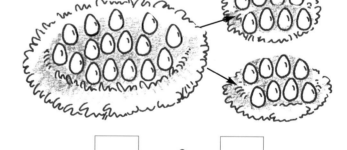

$$\boxed{} \div 2 = \boxed{}$$

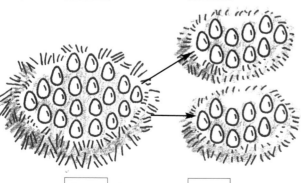

$$\boxed{} \div 2 = \boxed{}$$

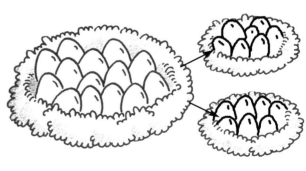

$$\boxed{} \div 2 = \boxed{}$$

Using the 2 times table

Write the problems to match the stamps.

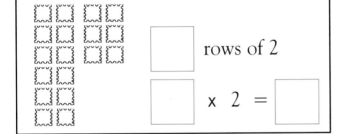

6 rows of 2

6 x 2 = 12

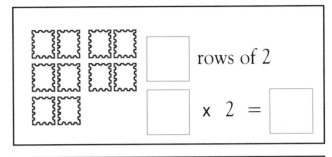

rows of 2

x 2 =

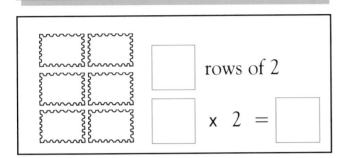

rows of 2

x 2 =

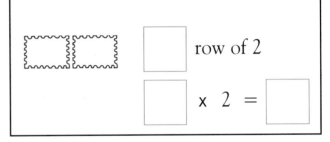

rows of 2

x 2 =

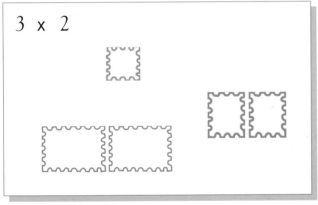

rows of 2

x 2 =

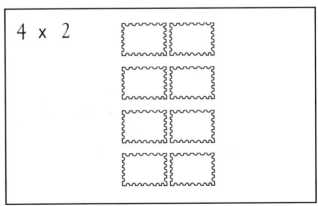

row of 2

x 2 =

Draw the stamps to match these problems.

3 x 2

4 x 2

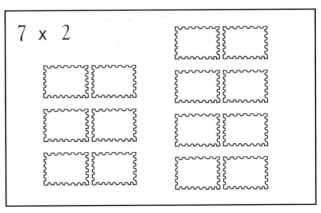

2 x 2

7 x 2

Using the 2 times table

Each face stands for 2. Join each set of faces to the correct number.

2

6

8

10

12

14

16

20

Using the 2 times table

How many eyes?

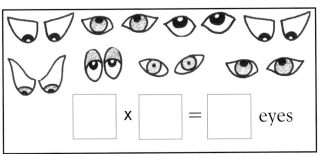

3 x 2 = 6 eyes

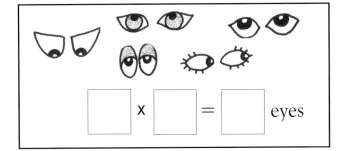

☐ x ☐ = ☐ eyes

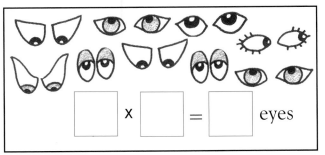

☐ x ☐ = ☐ eyes

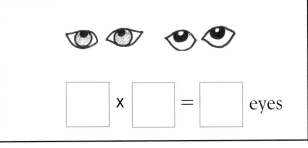

☐ x ☐ = ☐ eyes

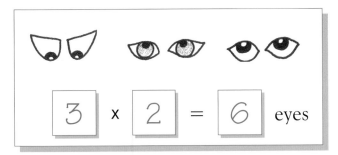

☐ x ☐ = ☐ eyes

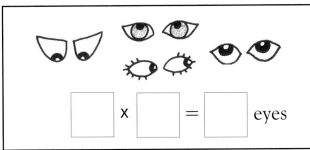

☐ x ☐ = ☐ eyes

Draw your own pictures to match these number sentences.

2 x 2 = 4

10 x 2 = 20

3 x 2 = 6

7 x 2 = 14

5 times table

Count in 5s, color, and find a pattern.

1	2	3	4	5	6	7	8	9	10
11	12	13	14	15	16	17	18	19	20
21	22	23	24	25	26	27	28	29	30
31	32	33	34	35	36	37	38	39	40
41	42	43	44	45	46	47	48	49	50
51	52	53	54	55	56	57	58	59	60
61	62	63	64	65	66	67	68	69	70
71	72	73	74	75	76	77	78	79	80
81	82	83	84	85	86	87	88	89	90
91	92	93	94	95	96	97	98	99	100

Write the answers.

1 x 5 = 5 2 x 5 = ☐   3 x 5 = ☐   4 x 5 = ☐

5 x 5 = ☐   6 x 5 = ☐   7 x 5 = ☐   8 x 5 = ☐

10 x 5 = ☐   9 x 5 = ☐

How many candies?

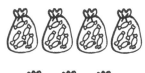 4 sets of 5 4 x 5 = 20 candies

 ☐ sets of 5   ☐ x ☐ = ☐ candies

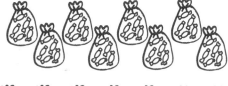 ☐ sets of 5   ☐ x ☐ = ☐ candies

 ☐ sets of 5   ☐ x ☐ = ☐ candies

Multiplying by 5

Draw a ring around rows of 5. Complete the problem.

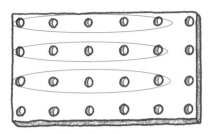

3 x 5 = 15

Draw a ring around rows of 5. Complete the problem.

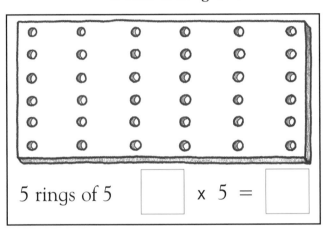

5 rings of 5   ☐ x 5 = ☐

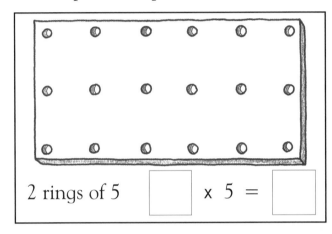

2 rings of 5   ☐ x 5 = ☐

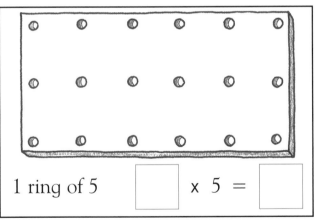

1 ring of 5   ☐ x 5 = ☐

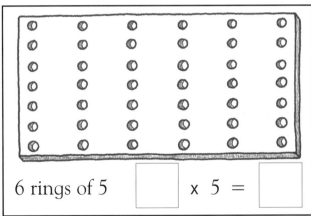

6 rings of 5   ☐ x 5 = ☐

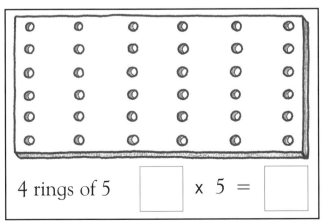

4 rings of 5   ☐ x 5 = ☐

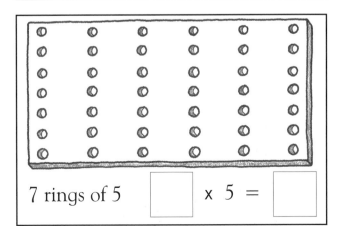

7 rings of 5   ☐ x 5 = ☐

Dividing by 5

Write a number sentence to show how many cubes are in each stack.

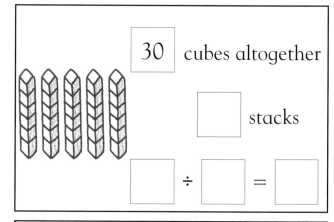

15 cubes altogether

5 stacks

15 ÷ 5 = 3

Write a number sentence to show how many cubes are in each stack.

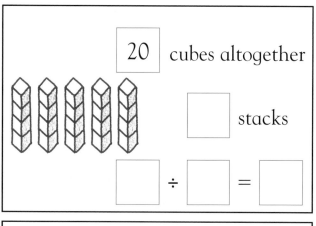

20 cubes altogether

☐ stacks

☐ ÷ ☐ = ☐

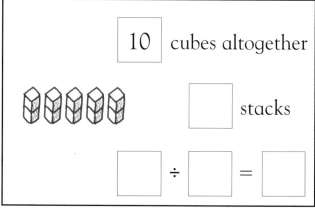

30 cubes altogether

☐ stacks

☐ ÷ ☐ = ☐

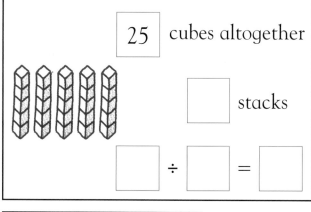

25 cubes altogether

☐ stacks

☐ ÷ ☐ = ☐

10 cubes altogether

☐ stacks

☐ ÷ ☐ = ☐

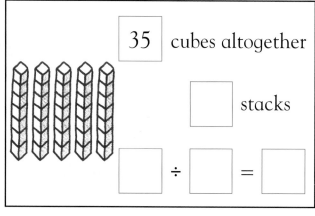

35 cubes altogether

☐ stacks

☐ ÷ ☐ = ☐

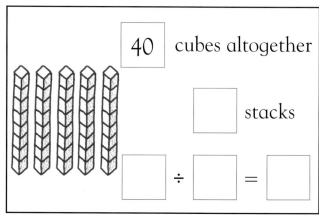

40 cubes altogether

☐ stacks

☐ ÷ ☐ = ☐

Using the 5 times table

Write the number that is hiding under the star.

 x 5 = 20

Write the number that is hiding under the star.

 x 5 = 10   3 x 5 =

 x 5 = 25   1 x 5 =

 x 5 = 50   8 x 5 =

 x 5 = 45   0 x 5 =

 x 5 = 35   6 x 5 =

Using the 5 times table

Each frog stands for 5. Join each set of frogs to the correct number.

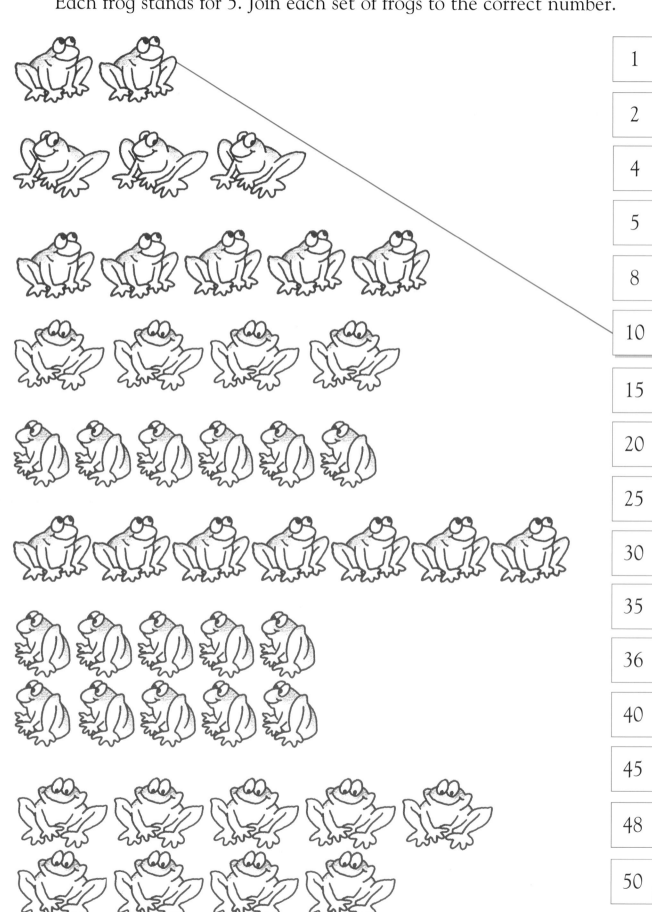

1

2

4

5

8

10

15

20

25

30

35

36

40

45

48

50

Using the 5 times table

How many altogether?

Georgia had 7 cats. Each cat had 5 kittens.
How many kittens were there altogether?

$\boxed{7}$ x $\boxed{5}$ = $\boxed{35}$ kittens

How many altogether?

Charlie had 6 boxes. He had 5 trains
in each box. How many trains did
he have altogether?

$\boxed{}$ x $\boxed{}$ = $\boxed{}$ trains

Zoe had 3 jackets. Each jacket
had 5 buttons. How many
buttons were there altogether?

$\boxed{}$ x $\boxed{}$ = $\boxed{}$ buttons

Yan had 8 fish tanks. Each tank had
5 fish in it. How many fish were
there altogether?

$\boxed{}$ x $\boxed{}$ = $\boxed{}$ fish

How many in each?

Joe had 45 pencils and 5 pencil cases.
How many pencils were in each case?

$\boxed{45}$ ÷ $\boxed{5}$ = $\boxed{9}$ pencils

How many in each?

Heather had 10 mice and 5 cages.
How many mice were in each cage?

$\boxed{}$ ÷ $\boxed{}$ = $\boxed{}$ mice

Shannon had 35 candies in 5 bags.
How many candies were in each bag?

$\boxed{}$ ÷ $\boxed{}$ = $\boxed{}$ candies

Mark put 25 seeds into 5 pots.
How many seeds were in each pot?

$\boxed{}$ ÷ $\boxed{}$ = $\boxed{}$ seeds

43

10 times table

Count in 10s, color, and find a pattern.

1	2	3	4	5	6	7	8	9	10
11	12	13	14	15	16	17	18	19	20
21	22	23	24	25	26	27	28	29	30
31	32	33	34	35	36	37	38	39	40
41	42	43	44	45	46	47	48	49	50
51	52	53	54	55	56	57	58	59	60
61	62	63	64	65	66	67	68	69	70
71	72	73	74	75	76	77	78	79	80
81	82	83	84	85	86	87	88	89	90
91	92	93	94	95	96	97	98	99	100

Write the answers.

1 x 10 = 10   2 x 10 = ☐   3 x 10 = ☐   4 x 10 = ☐

5 x 10 = ☐   6 x 10 = ☐   7 x 10 = ☐   8 x 10 = ☐

10 x 10 = ☐   9 x 10 = ☐

Each box contains 10 crayons. How many crayons are there altogether?

   2 sets of 10   2 x 10 = 20 crayons

      ☐ sets of 10   ☐ x ☐ = ☐ crayons

      ☐ sets of 10   ☐ x ☐ = ☐ crayons

    ☐ sets of 10   ☐ x ☐ = ☐ crayons

Multiplying and dividing

Each pod contains 10 peas. How many peas are there altogether?

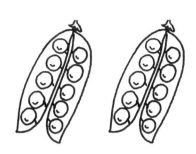

How many pods? 2

2 x 10 = 20 peas

Write how many peas.

 How many pods? ☐

 ☐ x 10 = ☐ peas

 How many pods? ☐

 ☐ x ☐ = ☐ peas

 How many pods? ☐

 ☐ x ☐ = ☐ peas

 How many pods? ☐

 ☐ x ☐ = ☐ peas

---

How many pods did the peas come from?

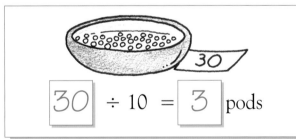

30 ÷ 10 = 3 pods

Write how many pods.

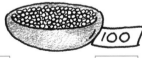

☐ ÷ 10 = ☐ pod

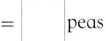

☐ ÷ 10 = ☐ pods

☐ ÷ 10 = ☐ pods

☐ ÷ 10 = ☐ pods

Dividing by 10

One dollar is worth the same as ten dimes.

How many dollars are there?

30 dimes

$30 \div 10 = \$ 3$

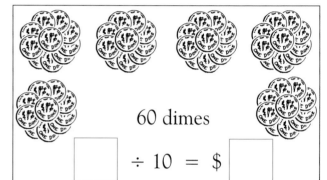

60 dimes

$\boxed{} \div 10 = \$ \boxed{}$

40 dimes

$\boxed{} \div 10 = \$ \boxed{}$

50 dimes

$\boxed{} \div 10 = \$ \boxed{}$

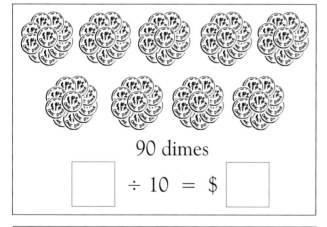

90 dimes

$\boxed{} \div 10 = \$ \boxed{}$

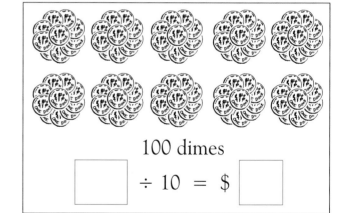

100 dimes

$\boxed{} \div 10 = \$ \boxed{}$

10 dimes

$\boxed{} \div 10 = \$ \boxed{}$

20 dimes

$\boxed{} \div 10 = \$ \boxed{}$

Using the 10 times table

How many altogether?

The squirrels had 4 food dens. Each den had 10 acorns. How many acorns were there altogether?

| 4 | x | 10 | = | 40 | acorns |

How many altogether?

The monkeys had 6 trees. There were 10 bananas in each tree. How many bananas did they have altogether?

| | x | | = | | bananas |

The frogs had 2 ponds. Each pond had 10 lily pads. How many lily pads were there altogether?

| | x | | = | | lily pads |

The snakes had 5 nests. Each nest had 10 eggs in it. How many eggs were there altogether?

| | x | | = | | eggs |

The lions had 7 cubs. Each cub already had 10 teeth. How many teeth did the cubs have altogether?

| | x | | = | | teeth |

How many in each?

The crows had 40 eggs and 10 nests. How many eggs were in each nest?

| 40 | ÷ | 10 | = | 4 | eggs |

How many in each?

There were 90 mice living in 10 nests. How many mice were in each nest?

| | ÷ | | = | | mice |

There were 60 foxes hiding in 10 dens. How many foxes were in each den?

| | ÷ | | = | | foxes |

Using the 10 times table

Match each dog to the right bone.

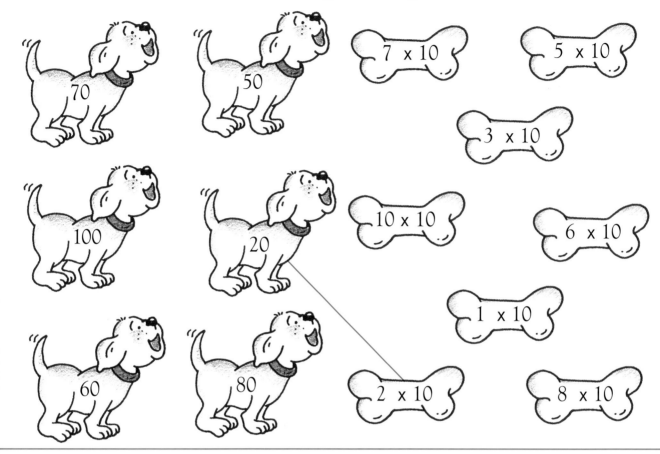

Match each mouse to the right cheese.

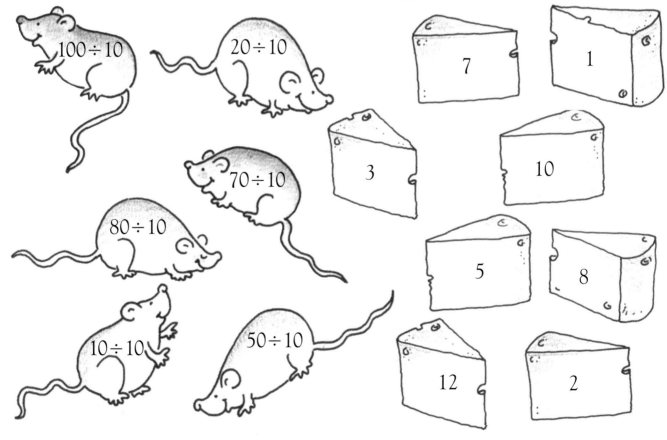

Using the 10 times table

Write in the missing numbers.

$3 \times 10 = 30$
$10 \times 3 = 30$
$30 \div 3 = 10$
$30 \div 10 = 3$

$5 \times 10 = 50$
$\boxed{} \times \boxed{} = 50$
$50 \div \boxed{} = 5$
$50 \div \boxed{} = 10$

$7 \times 10 = 70$
$\boxed{} \times \boxed{} = \boxed{}$
$\boxed{} \div \boxed{} = \boxed{}$
$\boxed{} \div \boxed{} = \boxed{}$

$9 \times 10 = 90$
$\boxed{} \times \boxed{} = \boxed{}$
$\boxed{} \div \boxed{} = \boxed{}$
$\boxed{} \div \boxed{} = \boxed{}$

$2 \times 10 = 20$
$\boxed{} \times \boxed{} = \boxed{}$
$\boxed{} \div \boxed{} = \boxed{}$
$\boxed{} \div \boxed{} = \boxed{}$

$4 \times 10 = 40$
$\boxed{} \times \boxed{} = \boxed{}$
$\boxed{} \div \boxed{} = \boxed{}$
$\boxed{} \div \boxed{} = \boxed{}$

$8 \times 10 = 80$
$\boxed{} \times \boxed{} = \boxed{}$
$\boxed{} \div \boxed{} = \boxed{}$
$\boxed{} \div \boxed{} = \boxed{}$

$6 \times 10 = 60$
$\boxed{} \times \boxed{} = \boxed{}$
$\boxed{} \div \boxed{} = \boxed{}$
$\boxed{} \div \boxed{} = \boxed{}$

3 times table

Count in 3s, color, and find a pattern.

1	2	3	4	5
6	7	8	9	10
11	12	13	14	15
16	17	18	19	20
21	22	23	24	25

Write the answers.

1 x 3 = [3]   2 x 3 = [ ]   3 x 3 = [ ]   4 x 3 = [ ]   5 x 3 = [ ]

How many flowers?

   [2] sets of 3   [2] x [3] = [6]

   [ ] sets of 3   [ ] x [ ] = [ ]

   [ ] sets of 3   [ ] x [ ] = [ ]

   [ ] sets of 3   [ ] x [ ] = [ ]

Multiplying by 3

Write the number sentences to match the pictures.

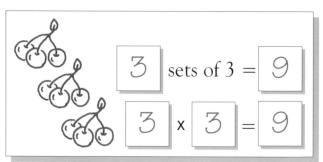 3 sets of 3 = 9

3 x 3 = 9

 4 sets of 3 = ☐

☐ x ☐ = ☐

 ☐ sets of 3 = ☐

☐ x ☐ = ☐

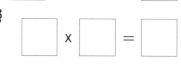 ☐ sets of 3 = ☐

☐ x ☐ = ☐

 ☐ sets of 3 = ☐

☐ x ☐ = ☐

 ☐ set of 3 = ☐

☐ x ☐ = ☐

Draw your own pictures to match these number sentences.

5 x 3 = 15

2 x 3 = 6

3 x 3 = 9

4 x 3 = 12

Dividing by 3

Divide the money equally among the purses.
Write a problem to show what you have done.
You might find it easier to change all the money into 1¢ coins.

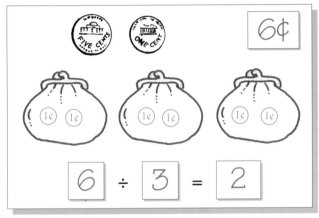

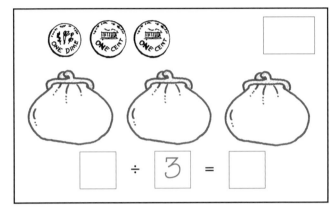

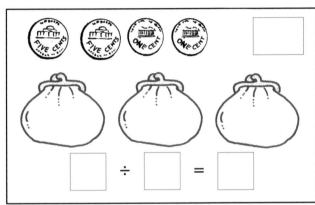

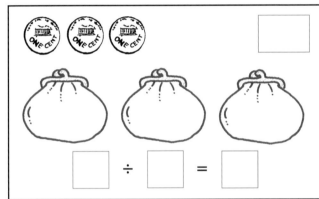

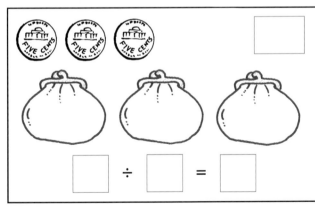

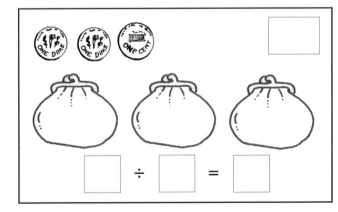

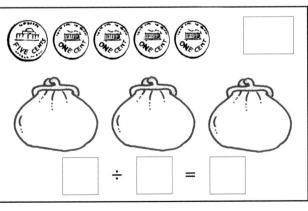

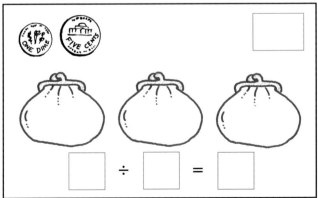

4 times table

Count in 4s, color, and find a pattern.

1	2	3	4	5
6	7	8	9	10
11	12	13	14	15
16	17	18	19	20
21	22	23	24	25

Write the answers.

1 x 4 = $\boxed{4}$ 2 x 4 = $\boxed{}$ 3 x 4 = $\boxed{}$ 4 x 4 = $\boxed{}$ 5 x 4 = $\boxed{}$

How many flowers?

 $\boxed{4}$ sets of 4 $\boxed{4}$ x $\boxed{4}$ = $\boxed{16}$

 $\boxed{}$ sets of 4 $\boxed{}$ x $\boxed{}$ = $\boxed{}$

 $\boxed{}$ sets of 4 $\boxed{}$ x $\boxed{}$ = $\boxed{}$

 $\boxed{}$ sets of 4 $\boxed{}$ x $\boxed{}$ = $\boxed{}$

Write number sentences to match the pictures.

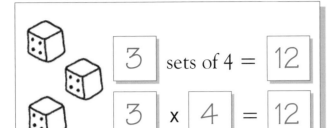 3 sets of 4 = 12

3 x 4 = 12

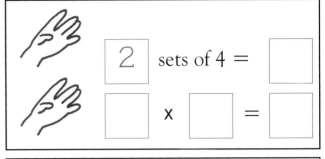 2 sets of 4 =

☐ x ☐ = ☐

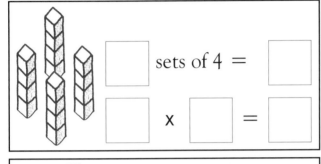 ☐ sets of 4 = ☐

☐ x ☐ = ☐

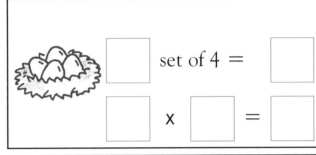 ☐ set of 4 = ☐

☐ x ☐ = ☐

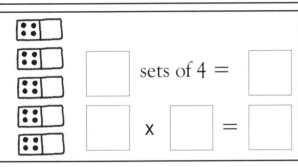 ☐ sets of 4 = ☐

☐ x ☐ = ☐

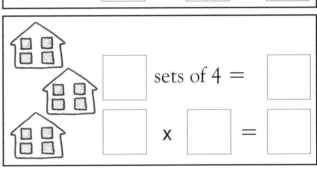 ☐ sets of 4 = ☐

☐ x ☐ = ☐

Draw different pictures to match these number sentences.

2 x 4 = 8

4 x 4 = 16

5 x 4 = 20

3 x 4 = 12

Dividing by 4

How many on each plate?

There are 4 children. How many things will each child have?
Draw the objects in the circles.

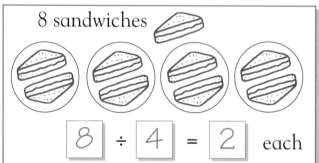

8 sandwiches

$$8 \div 4 = 2 \text{ each}$$

12 cookies

$$\boxed{} \div \boxed{4} = \boxed{} \text{ each}$$

4 drinks

$$\boxed{} \div \boxed{} = \boxed{} \text{ each}$$

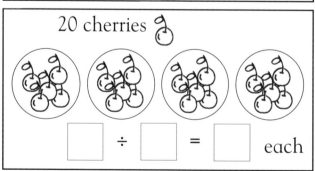

20 cherries

$$\boxed{} \div \boxed{} = \boxed{} \text{ each}$$

16 cupcakes

$$\boxed{} \div \boxed{} = \boxed{} \text{ each}$$

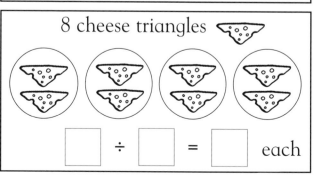

8 cheese triangles

$$\boxed{} \div \boxed{} = \boxed{} \text{ each}$$

Mixed tables

How many pegs are there in each pegboard?

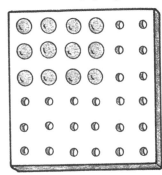

| 3 | rows of | 4 |

3 x 4 = 12

How many pegs are there in each pegboard?

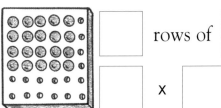   ☐ rows of ☐   ☐ x ☐ = ☐

   ☐ rows of ☐   ☐ x ☐ = ☐

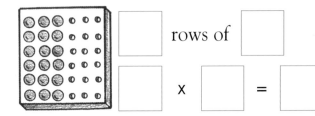   ☐ rows of ☐   ☐ x ☐ = ☐

   ☐ rows of ☐   ☐ x ☐ = ☐

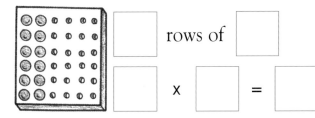   ☐ rows of ☐   ☐ x ☐ = ☐

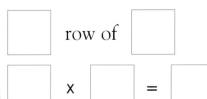   ☐ row of ☐   ☐ x ☐ = ☐

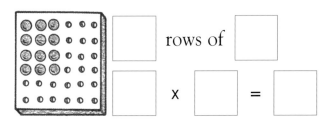   ☐ rows of ☐   ☐ x ☐ = ☐

☐ rows of ☐   ☐ x ☐ = ☐

Mixed tables

Divide the 12 pennies equally. Draw the coins
and write the problem to show how many each person gets.

12 ÷ 3 = 4

4 ¢ each

☐ ÷ ☐ = ☐

☐ ¢ each

☐ ÷ ☐ = ☐

☐ ¢ each

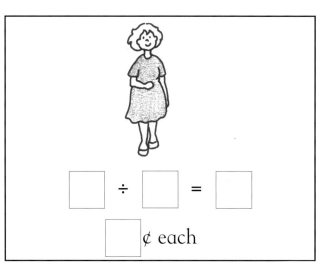

☐ ÷ ☐ = ☐

☐ ¢ each

☐ ÷ ☐ = ☐

☐ ¢ each

Mixed tables

How much will they get paid?

Price List for Jobs
Dust bedroom	3¢
Feed rabbit	2¢
Put toys away	6¢
Fetch newspaper	5¢
Walk dog	10¢

Write a problem to show how much money
Joe and Jasmine will get for these jobs.

Feed 4 rabbits  $4 \times 2¢ = 8¢$

Dust 2 bedrooms $\square \times \square = \square ¢$

Walk the dog 4 times $\square \times \square = \square ¢$

Put the toys away 3 times $\square \times \square = \square ¢$

Fetch the newspaper 5 times $\square \times \square = \square ¢$

How much will they get for these jobs?
Use the space to work out the problems.

Dust 3 bedrooms and walk
the dog twice

$\square + \square = \square ¢$

Feed the rabbit 10 times and
put the toys away twice

$\square + \square = \square ¢$

Mixed tables

Write the numbers that the raindrops are hiding.

4   x   ⟨5⟩   =   20

20   ÷   4   =   ⟨5⟩

2 x 4 = ◯

◯ ÷ 2 = 4

1 x ◯ = 3

◯ x 3 = 6

6 ÷ 3 = ◯

3 x ◯ = 3

45 ÷ 5 = ◯

5 x ◯ = 45

8 x 2 = ◯

16 ÷ 2 = ◯

60 ÷ ◯ = 6

10 x ◯ = 60

◯ x 4 = 12

12 ÷ 4 = ◯

7 x 5 = ◯

◯ ÷ 5 = 7

5 x ◯ = 50

50 ÷ ◯ = 5

59

Mixed tables

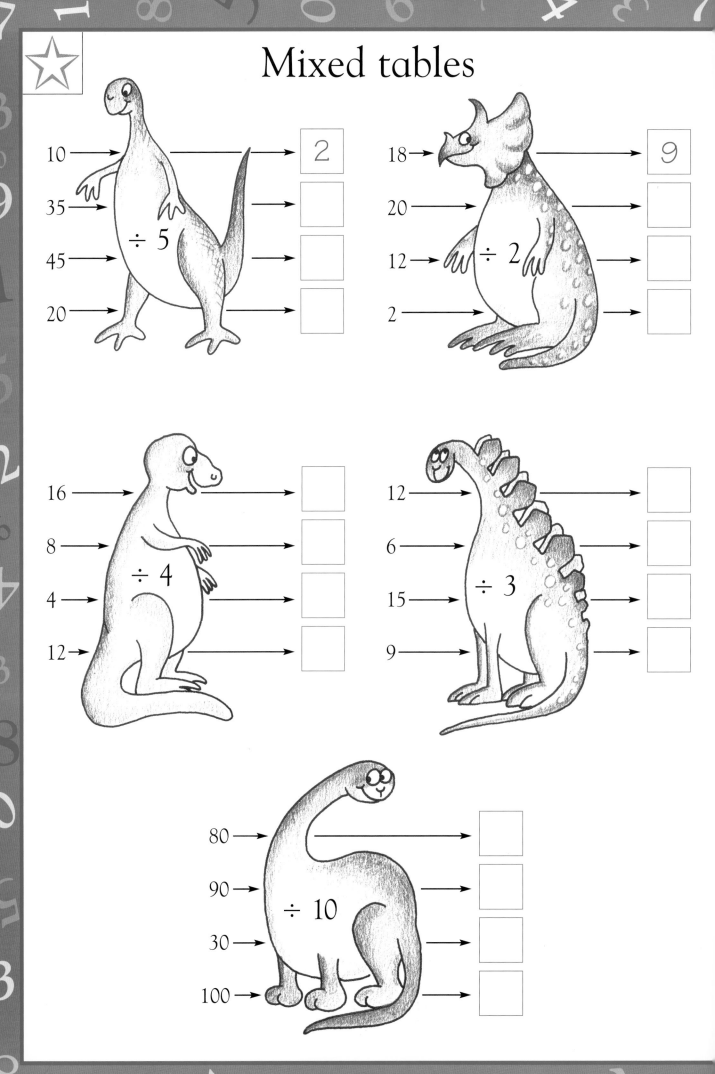

$10 \longrightarrow$ $\boxed{2}$
$35 \longrightarrow$ $\div 5$ $\boxed{}$
$45 \longrightarrow$ $\boxed{}$
$20 \longrightarrow$ $\boxed{}$

$18 \longrightarrow$ $\boxed{9}$
$20 \longrightarrow$ $\div 2$ $\boxed{}$
$12 \longrightarrow$ $\boxed{}$
$2 \longrightarrow$ $\boxed{}$

$16 \longrightarrow$ $\boxed{}$
$8 \longrightarrow$ $\div 4$ $\boxed{}$
$4 \longrightarrow$ $\boxed{}$
$12 \longrightarrow$ $\boxed{}$

$12 \longrightarrow$ $\boxed{}$
$6 \longrightarrow$ $\div 3$ $\boxed{}$
$15 \longrightarrow$ $\boxed{}$
$9 \longrightarrow$ $\boxed{}$

$80 \longrightarrow$ $\boxed{}$
$90 \longrightarrow$ $\div 10$ $\boxed{}$
$30 \longrightarrow$ $\boxed{}$
$100 \longrightarrow$ $\boxed{}$

Mixed tables

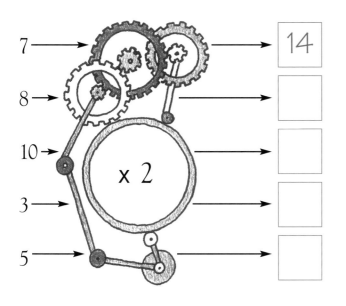

7 → 14

8 →

10 → x 2

3 →

5 →

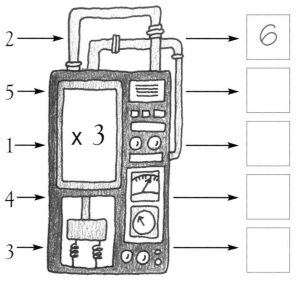

2 → 6

5 →

1 → x 3

4 →

3 →

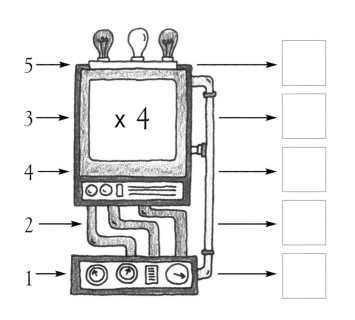

5 →

3 → x 4

4 →

2 →

1 →

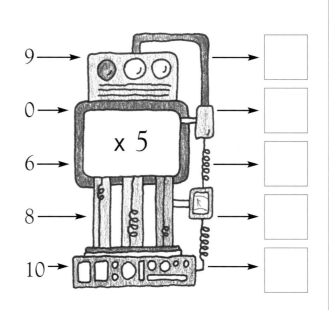

9 →

0 →

6 → x 5

8 →

10 →

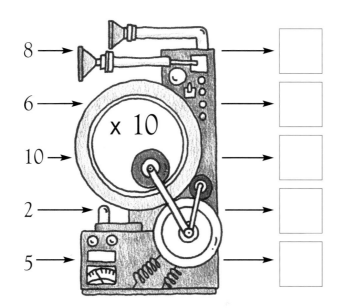

8 →

6 →

10 → x 10

2 →

5 →

Mixed tables

Work out how many.

Legs on 1 monster $\boxed{1}$ x $\boxed{3}$ = $\boxed{3}$ legs

Work out how many.

Buttons on 6 monsters $\boxed{}$ x $\boxed{}$ = $\boxed{}$ buttons

Eyes on 6 monsters $\boxed{}$ x $\boxed{}$ = $\boxed{}$ eyes

Hands on 9 monsters $\boxed{}$ x $\boxed{}$ = $\boxed{}$ hands

Noses on 7 monsters $\boxed{}$ x $\boxed{}$ = $\boxed{}$ noses

Legs on 4 monsters $\boxed{}$ x $\boxed{}$ = $\boxed{}$ legs

Eyes on 3 monsters $\boxed{}$ x $\boxed{}$ = $\boxed{}$ eyes

Arms on 8 monsters $\boxed{}$ x $\boxed{}$ = $\boxed{}$ arms

Buttons on 10 monsters $\boxed{}$ x $\boxed{}$ = $\boxed{}$ buttons

Number pairs

Put an X at (3,2).

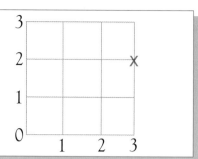

Put an X on this grid at each of these number pairs:

(1,1) (1,9) (3,9) (3,6) (7,6) (7,9) (9,9) (9,1) (7,1) (7,4) (3,4) (3,1) (1,1)

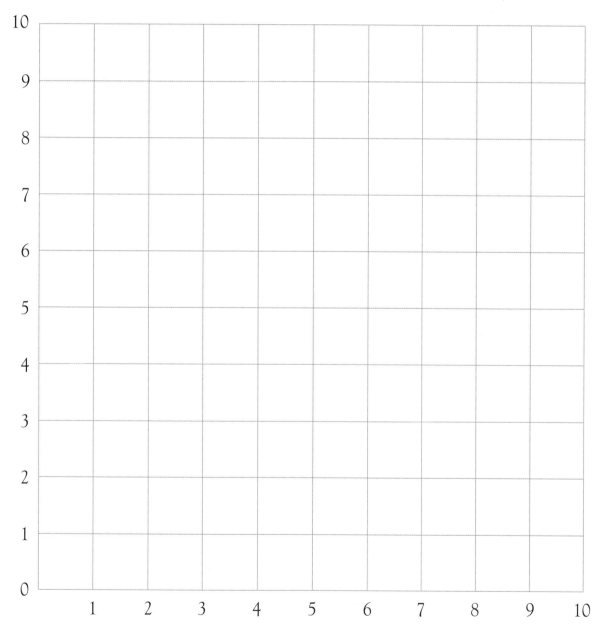

Join the Xs in the same order.

Which capital letter have you drawn?

Logic problems

Read the clues to find the secret number.

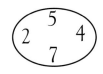

3 4 5 6 7 8

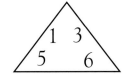

It is in both the rectangle and the circle.

It is not in the triangle. It is greater than 5.

What number is it?   7

Read the clues to find the secret number.

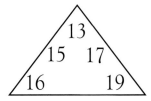

| 13 |
| 15 17 |
| 16   19 |

| 12   15 |
| 11   14 |
| 13 |

| 21   20   16 |
| 12   14   18 |

It is not in the square. It is an even number.

It is greater than any number in the triangle.

What number is it?

| 10   11 |
| 16   18 |
| 12   13 |

| 14 |
| 13   15 |
| 19   20 |

| 16   18   19 |
| 20   21 |

It is in the square and the circle.

It is greater than 10 and less than 16. It is an odd number.

What number is it?

It is in the triangle.

It is not an even number.

It is in the rectangle and the square.

What number is it?

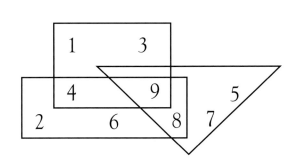

Dividing

Write the answer in the box.

$60 \div 10 =$ [6]

$$10 \overline{)80} \quad 8$$

$20 \div 10 =$ [2]

Write the answer in the box.

$50 \div 10 =$	$80 \div 10 =$	$10 \div 10 =$
$120 \div 10 =$	$60 \div 10 =$	$190 \div 10 =$
$230 \div 10 =$	$40 \div 10 =$	$160 \div 10 =$
$30 \div 10 =$	$300 \div 10 =$	$330 \div 10 =$
$70 \div 10 =$	$390 \div 10 =$	$560 \div 10 =$
$90 \div 10 =$	$420 \div 10 =$	$850 \div 10 =$

Write the answer in the box.

$10 \overline{)60}$	$10 \overline{)90}$	$10 \overline{)120}$	$10 \overline{)70}$
$10 \overline{)10}$	$10 \overline{)200}$	$10 \overline{)40}$	$10 \overline{)260}$
$10 \overline{)370}$	$10 \overline{)410}$	$10 \overline{)560}$	$10 \overline{)630}$
$10 \overline{)690}$	$10 \overline{)800}$	$10 \overline{)850}$	$10 \overline{)900}$

Write the answer in the box.

$1{,}630 \div 10 =$	$2{,}480 \div 10 =$	$2{,}700 \div 10 =$
$3{,}040 \div 10 =$	$6{,}000 \div 10 =$	$3{,}980 \div 10 =$
$4{,}500 \div 10 =$	$2{,}000 \div 10 =$	$4{,}020 \div 10 =$
$5{,}320 \div 10 =$	$6{,}800 \div 10 =$	$8{,}000 \div 10 =$

Rounding

Round each amount to the nearest whole unit.

$1.70	$2.80	1.30 m	1.50 m
$2.00	$3.00	1.00 m	2.00 m

Round each amount to the nearest dollar.

$1.45	$4.10	$7.25	$2.65
$4.15	$6.35	$8.90	$4.70
$5.60	$8.25	$7.40	$2.90
$12.75	$6.20	$13.80	$12.65
$11.65	$0.80	$17.75	$18.25

Round each amount to the nearest meter.

1.45 m	2.60 m	1.15 m	5.65 m
3.35 m	7.70 m	8.35 m	2.25 m
4.70 m	2.90 m	6.05 m	2.45 m
7.30 m	4.05 m	6.55 m	3.80 m
2.95 m	1.60 m	9.25 m	6.45 m

Round each amount to the nearest whole unit.

$3.50	4.50 m	1.50 m	$6.50
6.50 m	$0.50	$10.50	12.50 m
20.50 m	$3.50	5.50 m	$7.50

Congruency

Figures that are the same size and shape are congruent.
Are these figures congruent?

yes   no   no   yes

Circle the congruent figures.

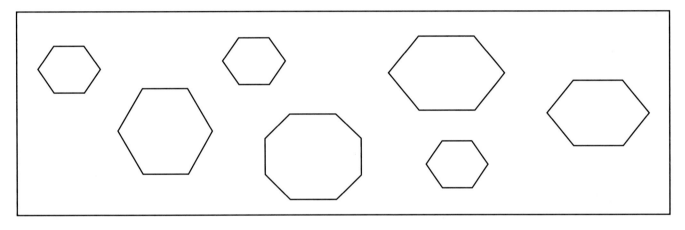

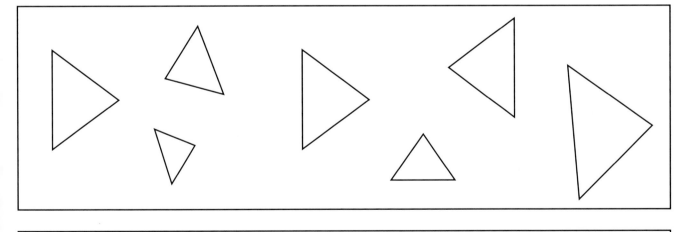

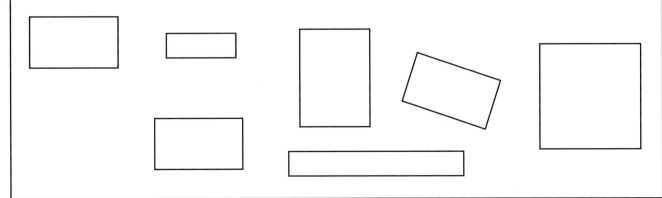

Identifying patterns

Complete each pattern.

48	42	36	30	24	18	12	6
44	41	38	35	32	29	26	23

Complete each pattern.

21	19	17					
38	34	30					
36	31	26					
55	50	45					
42	37	32					
52	48	44					
62	57	52					
35	31	27					
41	39	37					
38	33	28					
42	36	30					
50	44	38					
63	57	51					
37	34	31					
58	53	48					
78	70	62					
67	60	53					

Odds and evens

Write the answer in the box.

3 + 3 = 6   4 + 6 = 10   7 + 3 = 10   2 + 6 = 8

Add the even numbers to the even numbers.

4 + 8 =	12 + 6 =	10 + 6 =	8 + 14 =
20 + 14 =	14 + 12 =	16 + 10 =	30 + 20 =
14 + 16 =	18 + 6 =	22 + 8 =	20 + 40 =

What do you notice about each answer? _____

Add the odd numbers to the odd numbers.

7 + 9 =	5 + 7 =	11 + 5 =	9 + 5 =
7 + 7 =	9 + 3 =	15 + 5 =	13 + 7 =
11 + 3 =	17 + 9 =	15 + 9 =	13 + 15 =

What do you notice about each answer? _____

Add the odd numbers to the even numbers.

3 + 8 =	9 + 12 =	5 + 18 =	7 + 14 =
11 + 4 =	13 + 10 =	15 + 6 =	21 + 4 =
7 + 20 =	13 + 30 =	11 + 12 =	17 + 6 =

What do you notice about each answer? _____

Add the even numbers to the odd numbers.

6 + 7 =	8 + 5 =	10 + 9 =	2 + 17 =
10 + 29 =	14 + 3 =	8 + 13 =	12 + 5 =
14 + 7 =	8 + 51 =	16 + 9 =	30 + 17 =

What do you notice about each answer? _____

Probability

Look at the marbles in the bag.

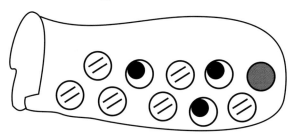

This kind of marble is least likely to be picked from the bag.

This kind of marble is most likely to be picked from the bag.

Look at this table.

Kinds of beads in grab bag

metal	glass	clay	wood	plastic
9	12	2	5	1

Which kind of bead is the least likely to be picked?

Which kind of bead is the most likely to be picked?

Look at the chart.

Marbles in the bag

COLOR	TALLIES
Red	卌
Blue	|||
Purple	卌 ||
Green	卌

Which color marble
is most likely to be picked?

Which color marble
is least likely to be picked?

Which color marble is as likely
to be picked as a green marble?

Place value

What is the value of each of the numbers in 573?

The value of 5 in 573 is 500 or five hundred

The value of 7 in 573 is 70 or seventy

The value of 3 in 573 is 3 or three

What is the value of 4 in these numbers? Write using number and words.

34	142	4,906	12,412

547,902	7,462	13,034	6,140

Circle each number with a 5 having the value of fifty.

457,682   67,954   870,534   575,555

Circle each number with a 4 having the value of four hundred.

457,482   67,954   870,434   544,985

Write increases or decreases and by how much.

Change the 2 in 24 to 3. The value of the number _____ by _____

Change the 6 in 86 to 3. The value of the number _____ by _____

Change the 1 in 17 to 9. The value of the number _____ by _____

Change the 9 in 921 to 8. The value of the number _____ by _____

Change the 7 in 276 to 9. The value of the number _____ by _____

Change the 5 in 5,247 to 1. The value of the number _____ by _____

Fractions

Write the answer in the box.

$1\frac{1}{2} + \frac{1}{4} = \boxed{1\frac{3}{4}}$ $2\frac{1}{2} + 3\frac{1}{2} = \boxed{6}$ $1\frac{1}{4} + 2\frac{1}{2} = \boxed{3\frac{3}{4}}$

Write the answer in the box.

$2\frac{1}{4} + 1\frac{1}{4} = \boxed{}$ $1\frac{1}{2} + 1\frac{1}{2} = \boxed{}$ $1\frac{1}{4} + \frac{1}{4} = \boxed{}$

$3\frac{1}{2} + 1 = \boxed{}$ $3\frac{1}{2} + 1\frac{1}{4} = \boxed{}$ $2\frac{1}{4} + 4 = \boxed{}$

$4\frac{1}{2} + 1\frac{1}{4} = \boxed{}$ $2\frac{1}{2} + 1\frac{1}{2} = \boxed{}$ $5 + 1\frac{1}{2} = \boxed{}$

$3\frac{1}{4} + 1\frac{1}{2} = \boxed{}$ $2 + 3\frac{1}{2} = \boxed{}$ $7 + \frac{1}{2} = \boxed{}$

$3 + \frac{1}{4} = \boxed{}$ $4\frac{1}{4} + \frac{1}{4} = \boxed{}$ $5 + 4\frac{1}{2} = \boxed{}$

Write the answer in the box.

$1\frac{1}{3} + 2\frac{1}{3} = \boxed{}$ $3\frac{1}{3} + 4\frac{2}{3} = \boxed{}$ $1\frac{2}{3} + 5 = \boxed{}$

$3\frac{2}{3} + 2 = \boxed{}$ $4\frac{1}{3} + 1\frac{2}{3} = \boxed{}$ $2\frac{2}{3} + 1\frac{2}{3} = \boxed{}$

$1\frac{2}{3} + 1\frac{2}{3} = \boxed{}$ $4\frac{1}{3} + 2\frac{1}{3} = \boxed{}$ $3 + 2\frac{1}{3} = \boxed{}$

$6 + 2\frac{2}{3} = \boxed{}$ $2\frac{1}{3} + 3\frac{2}{3} = \boxed{}$ $3\frac{1}{3} + 1\frac{1}{3} = \boxed{}$

$5\frac{2}{3} + 2\frac{2}{3} = \boxed{}$ $7 + \frac{1}{3} = \boxed{}$ $2\frac{2}{3} + 5\frac{2}{3} = \boxed{}$

Write the answer in the box.

$2\frac{1}{5} + 2\frac{2}{5} = \boxed{}$ $3\frac{1}{5} + 2\frac{3}{5} = \boxed{}$ $1\frac{4}{5} + 6 = \boxed{}$

$3\frac{1}{5} + 3\frac{2}{5} = \boxed{}$ $4 + 2\frac{2}{5} = \boxed{}$ $5\frac{3}{5} + 1\frac{1}{5} = \boxed{}$

$\frac{3}{5} + \frac{3}{5} = \boxed{}$ $3\frac{2}{5} + \frac{4}{5} = \boxed{}$ $3\frac{2}{5} + \frac{2}{5} = \boxed{}$

Part of a whole

Write the fraction that shows the shaded part.

How many parts are shaded? 3 parts

How many parts in all? 4 parts

The shaded part is $\frac{3}{4}$

Circle the fraction that shows the shaded part.

$\frac{1}{2}$ $\frac{1}{3}$ $\frac{1}{4}$

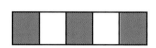

$\frac{2}{5}$ $\frac{3}{4}$ $\frac{3}{5}$

$\frac{7}{8}$ $\frac{1}{6}$ $\frac{4}{5}$

Write the fraction that shows the shaded part.

   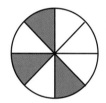   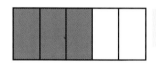

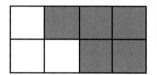   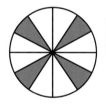   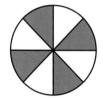

   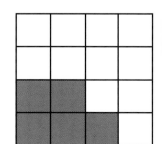   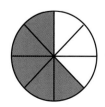

Decimals

Write these decimals in order, from least to greatest.

0.35   0.4   0.25   0.15   0.2   0.15   0.2   0.25   0.35   0.4

Write each row of decimals in order, from least to greatest.

0.41	0.48	0.42	0.45	0.40
1.45	1.75	1.35	1.80	1.40
4.23	4.73	4.83	4.13	4.93
6.28	6.48	6.98	6.08	6.18
4.34	3.34	8.34	2.34	7.34
2.16	3.65	4.64	5.38	1.37
5.31	2.85	4.97	6.35	1.44
8.32	6.17	9.32	7.43	2.38
5.98	4.06	3.07	2.38	6.27

Write each row of decimals in order, from least to greatest.

2.67	5.28	1.73	4.92	2.56
7.27	4.94	2.91	4.38	5.68
8.27	4.56	8.42	9.28	8.44
1.37	1.94	2.36	3.16	4.21
4.36	7.27	5.25	6.28	5.29
3.34	2.63	4.13	3.21	4.28
7.35	6.48	7.21	6.22	4.46
5.45	4.97	5.21	4.89	5.03

Fractions and decimals

Write each fraction as a decimal.

$1\frac{1}{10}$ = 1.1 $\qquad$ $1\frac{2}{10}$ = 1.2 $\qquad$ $1\frac{7}{10}$ = 1.7

Write each decimal as a fraction.

2.5 = $2\frac{1}{2}$ $\qquad$ 1.7 = $1\frac{7}{10}$ $\qquad$ 3.2 = $3\frac{2}{10}$

Write each fraction as a decimal.

$2\frac{1}{2}$ $\qquad$ $3\frac{1}{10}$ $\qquad$ $4\frac{3}{10}$ $\qquad$ $1\frac{1}{2}$

$5\frac{1}{10}$ $\qquad$ $2\frac{3}{10}$ $\qquad$ $8\frac{1}{10}$ $\qquad$ $5\frac{1}{2}$

$7\frac{8}{10}$ $\qquad$ $2\frac{4}{10}$ $\qquad$ $6\frac{1}{2}$ $\qquad$ $8\frac{1}{2}$

$7\frac{6}{10}$ $\qquad$ $9\frac{1}{2}$ $\qquad$ $6\frac{7}{10}$ $\qquad$ $10\frac{1}{2}$

Write each decimal as a fraction.

3.2 $\qquad$ 4.5 $\qquad$ 1.7 $\qquad$ 1.2

6.5 $\qquad$ 2.7 $\qquad$ 5.2 $\qquad$ 5.5

7.2 $\qquad$ 8.5 $\qquad$ 9.7 $\qquad$ 10.2

11.5 $\qquad$ 12.7 $\qquad$ 13.2 $\qquad$ 14.5

15.7 $\qquad$ 16.2 $\qquad$ 17.5 $\qquad$ 18.7

Write each fraction as a decimal.

$\frac{1}{2}$ = $\qquad$ $\frac{2}{10}$ = $\qquad$ $\frac{3}{10}$ =

Write each decimal as a fraction.

0.5 = $\qquad$ 0.2 = $\qquad$ 0.7 =

Adding

Write the answer between the lines.

```
  1              1              1
 46            57            48
+ 25          + 24          + 24
─────         ─────         ─────
 71            81            72
```

Write the answer between the lines.

```
  26           37           48           59           25
+ 15         + 16         + 14         + 12         + 15
────         ────         ────         ────         ────


  38           25           36           43           27
+ 15         + 16         + 17         + 19         + 15
────         ────         ────         ────         ────


  56           18           28           47           58
+ 17         + 14         + 14         + 26         + 15
────         ────         ────         ────         ────


  27           19           23           57           68
+ 14         + 14         + 16         + 15         + 13
────         ────         ────         ────         ────


  26           34           13           18           25
+ 35         + 48         + 27         + 32         + 45
────         ────         ────         ────         ────


  17           33           29           32           23
+ 44         + 58         + 53         + 53         + 48
────         ────         ────         ────         ────
```

Adding

Write the answer between the lines.

```
  1
  45          66          43
+ 15        + 23        + 18
------      ------      ------
  60          89          61
```

Write the answer between the lines.

```
  17          23          45          62          38
+ 13        + 17        + 25        + 18        + 12
------      ------      ------      ------      ------
```

```
  25          37          42          50          30
+ 25        + 23        + 28        + 37        + 48
------      ------      ------      ------      ------
```

```
  46          74          42          67          37
+ 34        + 16        + 38        + 23        + 43
------      ------      ------      ------      ------
```

```
  54          38          47          83          31
+ 46        + 32        + 43        + 17        + 39
------      ------      ------      ------      ------
```

```
  76          68          73          55          74
+ 24        + 32        + 27        + 45        + 26
------      ------      ------      ------      ------
```

```
  73          48          49          28          65
+ 16        + 33        + 42        + 26        + 45
------      ------      ------      ------      ------
```

Subtracting

Write the answer between the lines.

$$
\begin{array}{r} 38 \\ -\ 23 \\ \hline 15 \end{array}
\qquad
\begin{array}{r} 42 \\ -\ 20 \\ \hline 22 \end{array}
\qquad
\begin{array}{r} 64 \\ -\ 34 \\ \hline 30 \end{array}
$$

Write the answer between the lines.

$$
\begin{array}{r} 45 \\ -\ 23 \\ \hline \end{array}
\qquad
\begin{array}{r} 27 \\ -\ 14 \\ \hline \end{array}
\qquad
\begin{array}{r} 53 \\ -\ 20 \\ \hline \end{array}
\qquad
\begin{array}{r} 85 \\ -\ 41 \\ \hline \end{array}
\qquad
\begin{array}{r} 47 \\ -\ 25 \\ \hline \end{array}
$$

$$
\begin{array}{r} 29 \\ -\ 16 \\ \hline \end{array}
\qquad
\begin{array}{r} 53 \\ -\ 12 \\ \hline \end{array}
\qquad
\begin{array}{r} 82 \\ -\ 40 \\ \hline \end{array}
\qquad
\begin{array}{r} 37 \\ -\ 26 \\ \hline \end{array}
\qquad
\begin{array}{r} 44 \\ -\ 31 \\ \hline \end{array}
$$

$$
\begin{array}{r} 63 \\ -\ 21 \\ \hline \end{array}
\qquad
\begin{array}{r} 74 \\ -\ 32 \\ \hline \end{array}
\qquad
\begin{array}{r} 47 \\ -\ 36 \\ \hline \end{array}
\qquad
\begin{array}{r} 63 \\ -\ 42 \\ \hline \end{array}
\qquad
\begin{array}{r} 76 \\ -\ 35 \\ \hline \end{array}
$$

$$
\begin{array}{r} 85 \\ -\ 42 \\ \hline \end{array}
\qquad
\begin{array}{r} 83 \\ -\ 41 \\ \hline \end{array}
\qquad
\begin{array}{r} 95 \\ -\ 35 \\ \hline \end{array}
\qquad
\begin{array}{r} 67 \\ -\ 53 \\ \hline \end{array}
\qquad
\begin{array}{r} 86 \\ -\ 45 \\ \hline \end{array}
$$

$$
\begin{array}{r} 65 \\ -\ 35 \\ \hline \end{array}
\qquad
\begin{array}{r} 74 \\ -\ 54 \\ \hline \end{array}
\qquad
\begin{array}{r} 86 \\ -\ 66 \\ \hline \end{array}
\qquad
\begin{array}{r} 96 \\ -\ 86 \\ \hline \end{array}
\qquad
\begin{array}{r} 67 \\ -\ 17 \\ \hline \end{array}
$$

$$
\begin{array}{r} 59 \\ -\ 39 \\ \hline \end{array}
\qquad
\begin{array}{r} 48 \\ -\ 27 \\ \hline \end{array}
\qquad
\begin{array}{r} 46 \\ -\ 32 \\ \hline \end{array}
\qquad
\begin{array}{r} 78 \\ -\ 47 \\ \hline \end{array}
\qquad
\begin{array}{r} 67 \\ -\ 56 \\ \hline \end{array}
$$

Subtracting

Write the answer between the lines.

```
  3 13            4 14            5 11
  4̷3̷             5̷4̷             6̷1̷
-  27          -  28          -  43
  ____           ____           ____
   16             26             18
```

Write the answer between the lines.

45 − 28	36 − 18	42 − 17	50 − 45	62 − 17
43 − 29	74 − 47	90 − 37	65 − 48	63 − 49
57 − 39	64 − 48	62 − 34	78 − 69	36 − 27
54 − 26	68 − 39	50 − 27	38 − 28	44 − 36
31 − 16	43 − 28	70 − 36	53 − 37	46 − 28
90 − 46	50 − 26	54 − 35	66 − 48	90 − 44

Real-life problems

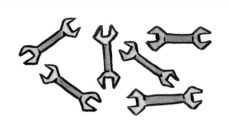

Write the answer in the box.

Sarah has eight wrenches and is given six more.
How many wrenches does she have now?

$8 + 6 = 14$

Write the answer in the box.

Karl has 20 marbles but loses 12 in a game of marbles
contest. How many marbles does he have left?

After buying some candy for 30¢, Naomi still has
65¢ left. How much did she have to begin with?

Billy takes 20 balls out of a barrel
and leaves 15 in the barrel.
How many balls are
there altogether?

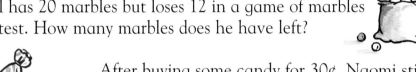

June collected 150 stamps and her father gave her
60 more. How many stamps does June have now?

Angela puts 40 toys in a box that already has 35 toys in it.
How many toys are in the box now?

Patrick leaves 45¢ at home and takes 50¢ with him. How much
money does Patrick have altogether?

Don gives some of his allowance to his sister. He gives his sister
80¢ and has 60¢ left. How much allowance did Don have in the
first place?

Five letters of the alphabet are vowels. How many letters of the
alphabet are not vowels?

Multiplying

Write the answer between the lines.

```
    1
   24          71          1
 x  3        x  6         36
 _____    _____   x  3
   72          426       _____
                          108
```

Write the answer between the lines.

```
   46          28          72          65          76
 x  2        x  2        x  2        x  2        x  2
 _____    _____    _____    _____    _____


   43          75          53          39          55
 x  3        x  3        x  3        x  3        x  3
 _____    _____    _____    _____    _____


   47          28          64          45          62
 x  4        x  4        x  4        x  4        x  4
 _____    _____    _____    _____    _____


   75          72          94          38          64
 x  5        x  5        x  5        x  5        x  5
 _____    _____    _____    _____    _____


   46          73          72          78          94
 x  6        x  6        x  6        x  6        x  6
 _____    _____    _____    _____    _____


   85          48          93          37          55
 x  7        x  7        x  7        x  7        x  7
 _____    _____    _____    _____    _____
```

Multiplying

Write the answer between the lines.

```
    28             64             85             28             83
x    8         x    8         x    8         x    8         x    8
```

```
    43             94             52             93             46
x    9         x    9         x    9         x    9         x    9
```

```
    53             74             84             83             49
x    4         x    4         x    4         x    4         x    4
```

```
    39             38             29             47             57
x    5         x    5         x    5         x    5         x    5
```

```
    29             59             39             69             79
x    4         x    5         x    6         x    7         x    8
```

```
    46             36             96             26             56
x    4         x    5         x    6         x    7         x    8
```

Dividing

Write the answer in the box.

65 ÷ 8 = **8 r 1**   34 ÷ 7 = **4 r 6**   37 ÷ 9 = **4 r 1**

Write the answer in the box.

26 ÷ 6 =   34 ÷ 6 =   63 ÷ 6 =

42 ÷ 6 =   38 ÷ 6 =   54 ÷ 6 =

19 ÷ 6 =   25 ÷ 6 =   30 ÷ 6 =

21 ÷ 6 =   33 ÷ 6 =   44 ÷ 6 =

57 ÷ 7 =   46 ÷ 7 =   52 ÷ 7 =

38 ÷ 7 =   28 ÷ 7 =   64 ÷ 7 =

39 ÷ 7 =   35 ÷ 7 =   24 ÷ 7 =

63 ÷ 7 =   82 ÷ 7 =   64 ÷ 7 =

43 ÷ 8 =   53 ÷ 8 =   73 ÷ 8 =

52 ÷ 8 =   78 ÷ 8 =   46 ÷ 8 =

54 ÷ 8 =   32 ÷ 8 =   51 ÷ 8 =

49 ÷ 8 =   37 ÷ 8 =   44 ÷ 8 =

64 ÷ 9 =   73 ÷ 9 =   38 ÷ 9 =

63 ÷ 9 =   37 ÷ 9 =   40 ÷ 9 =

45 ÷ 9 =   22 ÷ 9 =   43 ÷ 9 =

51 ÷ 9 =   48 ÷ 9 =   70 ÷ 9 =

Dividing

Write the answer above the line.

```
 5 r 2          4 r 1          6 r 2
6) 32          7) 29          9) 56
   30             28             54
    2              1              2
```

Write the answer in the box above the line.

```
6) 45          6) 37          6) 27          6) 41          6) 38
   42             36             24             36             36
    3              1              3              5              2
```

```
7) 34          7) 42          7) 74          7) 36          7) 41
   28             42             70             35             35
    6              0              4              1              6
```

```
8) 37          8) 29          8) 44          8) 73          8) 39
   32             24             40             72             32
    5              5              4              1              7
```

```
9) 20          9) 34          9) 44          9) 74          9) 38
   18             27             36             72             36
    2              7              8              2              2
```

Choosing the operation

Write either x or ÷ in the box.

4 ⊠ 9 = 36   24 ÷ 4 = 6   80 ÷ 8 = 10

Write either x or ÷ in the box.

9 ☐ 7 = 63   8 ☐ 6 = 48   54 ☐ 9 = 6

5 ☐ 8 = 40   30 ☐ 6 = 5   49 ☐ 7 = 7

36 ☐ 4 = 9   45 ☐ 9 = 5   7 ☐ 8 = 56

48 ☐ 6 = 8   7 ☐ 9 = 63   27 ☐ 3 = 9

4 ☐ 6 = 24   24 ☐ 8 = 3   81 ☐ 9 = 9

8 ☐ 8 = 64   28 ☐ 7 = 4   48 ☐ 8 = 6

63 ☐ 7 = 9   30 ☐ 5 = 6   3 ☐ 8 = 24

6 ☐ 8 = 48   40 ☐ 8 = 5   56 ☐ 7 = 8

54 ☐ 6 = 9   18 ☐ 3 = 6   64 ☐ 8 = 8

16 ☐ 8 = 2   21 ☐ 7 = 3   28 ☐ 4 = 7

27 ☐ 9 = 3   80 ☐ 10 = 8   70 ☐ 7 = 10

8 ☐ 7 = 56   4 ☐ 9 = 36   5 ☐ 9 = 45

20 ☐ 6 = 120   700 ☐ 7 = 100   8 ☐ 8 = 1

100 ☐ 5 = 20   400 ☐ 8 = 50   84 ☐ 7 = 12

42 ☐ 6 = 7   600 ☐ 100 = 6   9 ☐ 9 = 1

5 ☐ 5 = 25   100 ☐ 10 = 10   6 ☐ 6 = 1

Real-life problems

Write the answer in the box.
A number multiplied by 8 is 56.
What is the number?

7

I divide a number by 9 and the result is 6.
What is the number?

54

Write the answer in the box.

A number multiplied by 6 is 42.
What is the number?

I divide a number by 4 and the
result is 7. What is the number?

I divide a number by 8 and the
result is 6. What number did I
begin with?

A number multiplied by itself
gives the answer 25. What is
the number?

I divide a number by 7 and the
result is 7. What number did I
begin with?

A number multiplied by itself
gives the answer 49. What is
the number?

I multiply a number by 7 and
I end up with 56. What number
did I begin with?

Seven times a number is 63.
What is the number?

What do I have to multiply 8
by to get the result 72?

Nine times a number is 81.
What is the number?

When 6 is multiplied by a
number the result is 42. What
number was 6 multiplied by?

A number divided by 8 gives
the answer 10. What was the
starting number?

I multiply a number by 9 and
end up with 45. What number
did I multiply?

I multiply a number by 9 and
the result is 81. What number
did I begin with?

Real-life problems

Solve the problem. Write the answer in the box.

A jump rope is supposed to be 1.30 m long but 35 cm has been cut off. How much of the skipping rope is left?

0.95 m

$$\begin{array}{r} \overset{12}{\cancel{1}}\overset{0\ \cancel{2}\ 10}{\cancel{.}\cancel{3}\cancel{0}}\text{ m} \\ -\ 0.35\text{ m} \\ \hline 0.95\text{ m} \end{array}$$

Solve the problem. Write the answer in the box.

Mario is given three cans of juice. Each can contains 425 ml. How much does Mario have altogether?

Trang sees these toys on sale in a store window. She buys two of the toys and pays $10.10. Which toys does Trang buy?

A school playground is 145 m long. 68 m are used by the 3rd grade children and the rest by the 4th grade children. How much space is used by the 4th grade children?

Mary buys a box of chocolates that costs $7.85. She pays for the chocolates with a ten dollar bill. How much change should she receive?

A box of tea contains 350 grams. Half of the tea has been used. How much of the tea is left?

Real-life problems

Solve the problem. Write the answer in the box.

A boy weighs 15 lb more than his sister.
His sister weighs 72 lb. How much does the brother weigh?

87 lb

$$\begin{array}{r} 72 \\ + 15 \\ \hline 87 \end{array}$$

Solve the problem. Write the answer in the box.

Two bags of cement weigh a total of
150 kg. One bag weighs 80 kg.
How much does the other bag weigh?

There are 44 bars of chocolate in
each box. How many bars will
there be in 7 boxes?

One box contains 186 tissues.
How many tissues will there be
in 4 boxes?

Dean's older sister weighs 95 lb,
and he is 13 lb lighter than her.
How much does Dean weigh?

A boy has a bottle of lemonade that
contains 2 liters. He drinks 465 ml.
How much lemonade is left?

Kitchen countertops can be
measured in millimeters.
How long is 1.50 m in mm?

Problems using time

Write the answer in the box.

What time will it be in 15 minutes?

5:50

Write the answer in the box.

What time will it be in 45 minutes?

What time was it 2 hours ago?

What time was it ten minutes ago?

Write the answer in the box.

What time will it be in half an hour?

What time will it be in 45 minutes?

What time was it half an hour ago?

Write the answer in the box.

What time was it half an hour ago?

How many hours until 12:30?

What time was it 45 minutes ago?

Charts

	Period 1	Period 2	Period 3	Period 4
Monday	Math	English	History	Design Technology
Tuesday	Math	English	Spanish	Gym
Wednesday	Math	English	Science	Science
Thursday	Math	English	Art	Art
Friday	English	Gym	Science	Music

A.M.   P.M.

Write the answer in the box.

What subject does the class have last period on Tuesday?

How many periods of Math does the class have?

When does the class have an afternoon of Art?

How many periods of English does the class have?

What subject comes before Music?

Which day is the Spanish lesson?

Which subject is taught third period on Monday?

What is the last lesson on Friday morning?

When is Science?

What subject is taught second period on Thursday?

Symmetry

The dotted line is a mirror line. Complete each shape.

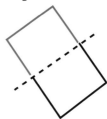 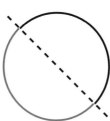

Complete each shape.

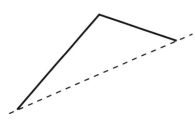

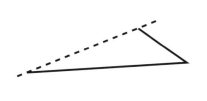

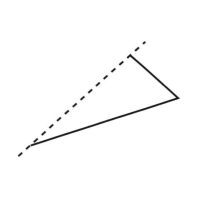

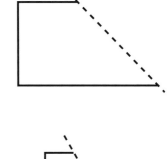

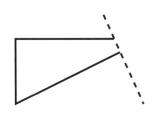

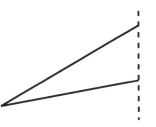

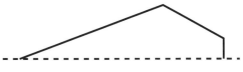

3-dimensional shapes

Draw a small circle around each vertex in this shape.

Draw a small circle around each vertex in these shapes.

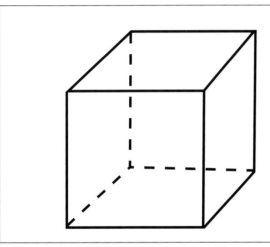

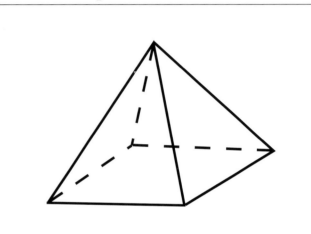

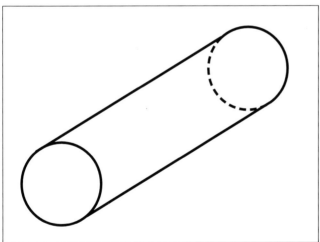

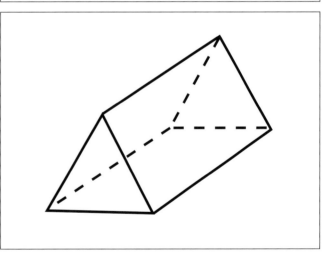

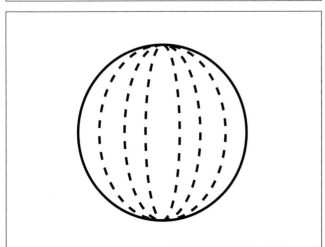

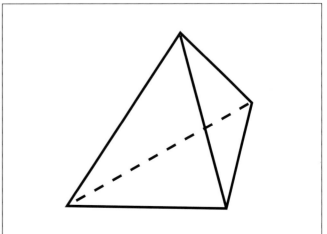

Number pairs

Look at this grid.

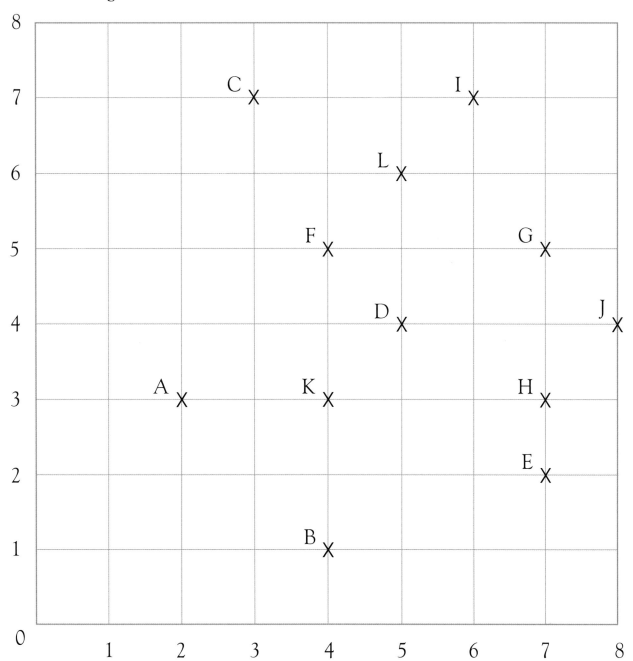

Write the number pairs of the X by each letter.

A = 2, 3   D =   G =   J =

B =   E =   H =   K =

C =   F =   I =   L =

Adding and subtracting

Add 100 to 356.

456

Add 100 to 2,376.

2,476

Subtract 100 from 5,324.

5,224

Subtract 100 from 7,296.

7,196

Add 100 to each number.

376	795	646	585
286	57	4,312	5,634
12	4,789	724	3,803

Add 100 to each number.

485	607	37	843
3,587	7,056	5,045	2,707
5,897	9,564	5,499	9,001

Subtract 100 from each number.

364	729	477	765
103	146	1,203	599
100	5,745	3,178	6,107

Subtract 100 from each number.

4,734	8,610	5,307	9,362
2,675	4,907	8,445	1,401
1,400	5,638	6,832	4,256

Dividing by 10

Divide 90 by 10.	Divide 3,400 by 10.
9	340

Divide each number by 10.

60		80		10		50	
100		150		230		300	
210		170		20		260	
40		360		590		730	
420		380		820		540	

Multiply each number by 10.

30		70		90		10	
60		80		11		140	
170		190		230		280	
380		410		840		940	
600		100		750		560	

Divide each number by 10.

700		2,300		4,100		3,650	
6,480		7,080		3,540		2,030	
1,030		9,670		6,320		1,400	
300		900		1,020		3,660	
20		18,000		13,600		17,890	

Length

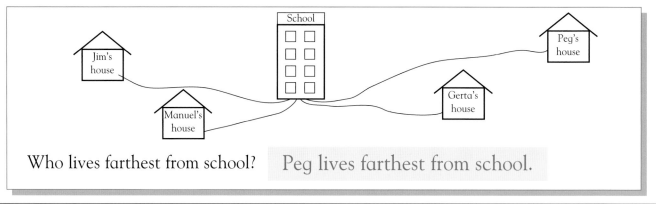

Who lives farthest from school?   Peg lives farthest from school.

Look at this map.

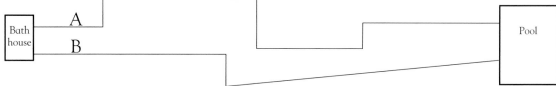

Which route between the bath house and the pool is shorter, A or B?

Look at this map.

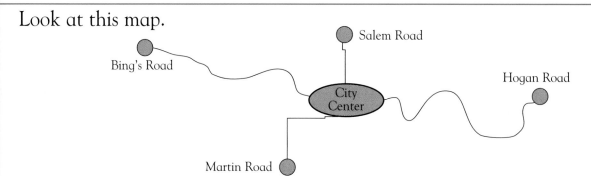

Is the Bing's Road to City Center
longer or shorter than the Martin Road?

Which road to City Center is longest?

Which road to City Center is shorter than the Martin Road?

Look at this picture.

Lucy

Kenny

Marta

Tim

Whose ribbon is longest?

Whose ribbon is shorter than Tim's ribbon?

Whose ribbon is about the same length as Tim's ribbon?

Identifying patterns

Continue each pattern.

12	23	34	45	56			
9	21	33	45	57			
32	43	54	65	76			
2	14	26	38	50			
2	13	24	35	46			
6	18	30	42	54			
3	8	13	18	23			
12	24	36	48	60			

Continue each pattern.

78	67	56	45	34			
94	82	70	58	46			
88	77	66	55	44			
96	84	72	60	48			
7	18	29	40	51			
14	26	38	50	62			
8	19	30	41	52			
10	22	34	46	58			

Properties of polygons

Circle the polygon that has 4 sides of the same length.

Circle the polygon described.

The 3 sides are all the same length.

Exactly 2 pairs of sides are parallel.

Exactly 1 pair of sides is parallel.

All the sides are of equal length and each side is parallel to one other side.

Each of the sides is a different length.

Has 6 sides of equal length.

Square numbers

This square has two rows
and two columns. It is 2 x 2.

How many dots are there?   4

Draw a picture like the one above to show each of these numbers.

3 x 3

How many
dots are there?

4 x 4

How many
dots are there?

5 x 5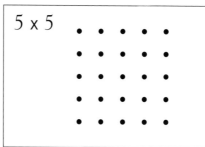

How many
dots are there?

6 x 6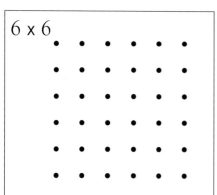

How many
dots are there?

7 x 7

How many
dots are there?

8 x 8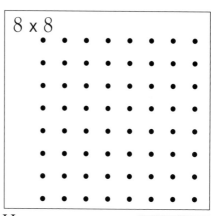

How many
dots are there?

9 x 9

How many dots are there?

10 x 10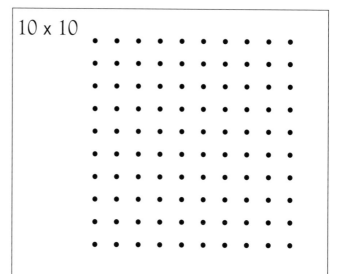

How many dots are there?

Fractions and decimals

Write each fraction as a decimal.

$\frac{1}{2}$ = 0.5 $\frac{1}{10}$ = 0.1

Write this decimal as a fraction.

$0.25 = \frac{25}{100} = \frac{1}{4}$

Write each fraction as a decimal.

$\frac{1}{10}$ $\frac{1}{2}$ $\frac{3}{10}$ $\frac{5}{10}$

$\frac{2}{10}$ $\frac{9}{10}$ $\frac{6}{10}$ $\frac{1}{10}$

$\frac{8}{10}$ $\frac{3}{10}$ $\frac{4}{10}$ $\frac{5}{10}$

$\frac{6}{10}$ $\frac{7}{10}$ $\frac{8}{10}$ $\frac{9}{10}$

Write each decimal as a fraction.

0.8   0.5   0.3   0.4

0.25   0.7   0.2   0.75

0.2   0.6   0.5   0.8

0.1   0.4   0.6   0.9

Write the answer in the box.

Which two of the fractions above are the same as 0.5?

Which two of the fractions above are the same as 0.8?

Which two of the fractions above are the same as 0.6?

Which two of the fractions above are the same as 0.2?

Which two of the fractions above are the same as 0.4?

Fractions of shapes

Shade $\frac{3}{5}$ of each shape.

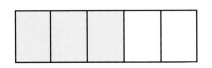

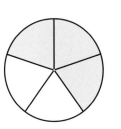

Shade $\frac{4}{5}$ of each shape.

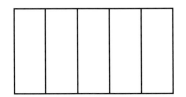

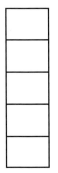

Shade $\frac{8}{10}$ of each shape.

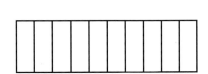

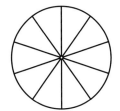

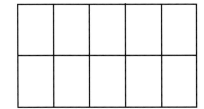

Shade the fraction of each shape.

$\frac{4}{10}$

$\frac{8}{10}$

$\frac{3}{10}$

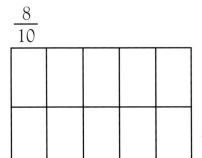

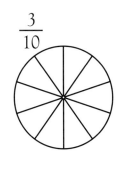

$\frac{7}{10}$

$\frac{6}{10}$

$\frac{9}{10}$

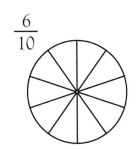

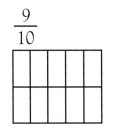

Comparing fractions

In each pair, circle the fraction with the greater value.

$\left(\dfrac{1}{2}\right)$ or $\dfrac{1}{5}$ $\qquad\qquad$ $\dfrac{3}{8}$ or $\left(\dfrac{5}{8}\right)$

In each pair, circle the fraction with the greater value.

$\dfrac{1}{4}$ or $\dfrac{1}{3}$ $\qquad$ $\dfrac{1}{5}$ or $\dfrac{1}{6}$ $\qquad$ $\dfrac{1}{8}$ or $\dfrac{1}{3}$ $\qquad$ $\dfrac{1}{4}$ or $\dfrac{1}{7}$

$\dfrac{1}{2}$ or $\dfrac{1}{3}$ $\qquad$ $\dfrac{1}{12}$ or $\dfrac{1}{2}$ $\qquad$ $\dfrac{1}{3}$ or $\dfrac{1}{9}$ $\qquad$ $\dfrac{1}{10}$ or $\dfrac{1}{100}$

$\dfrac{1}{3}$ or $\dfrac{2}{3}$ $\qquad$ $\dfrac{3}{7}$ or $\dfrac{5}{7}$ $\qquad$ $\dfrac{2}{5}$ or $\dfrac{1}{5}$ $\qquad$ $\dfrac{1}{4}$ or $\dfrac{3}{4}$

$\dfrac{4}{9}$ or $\dfrac{3}{9}$ $\qquad$ $\dfrac{1}{12}$ or $\dfrac{2}{12}$ $\qquad$ $\dfrac{6}{10}$ or $\dfrac{3}{10}$ $\qquad$ $\dfrac{1}{6}$ or $\dfrac{5}{6}$

In each pair, circle the fraction with the greater value.

$1\dfrac{3}{4}$ or $1\dfrac{2}{5}$ $\qquad$ $1\dfrac{1}{2}$ or $1\dfrac{1}{3}$ $\qquad$ $3\dfrac{1}{6}$ or $2\dfrac{1}{3}$ $\qquad$ $2\dfrac{1}{4}$ or $2\dfrac{3}{4}$

$2\dfrac{5}{8}$ or $2\dfrac{3}{8}$ $\qquad$ $1\dfrac{1}{4}$ or $1\dfrac{1}{9}$ $\qquad$ $6\dfrac{2}{3}$ or $4\dfrac{2}{3}$ $\qquad$ $5\dfrac{1}{10}$ or $5\dfrac{3}{10}$

$\dfrac{3}{4}$ or $\dfrac{1}{3}$ $\qquad\qquad$ $\dfrac{3}{5}$ or $\dfrac{2}{3}$ $\qquad\qquad$ $\dfrac{5}{6}$ or $\dfrac{3}{4}$

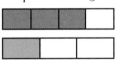  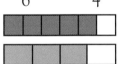

$3\dfrac{1}{2}$ or $3\dfrac{2}{3}$ $\qquad\qquad\qquad\qquad$ $4\dfrac{2}{5}$ or $4\dfrac{5}{6}$

  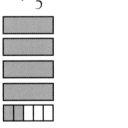

$2\dfrac{6}{10}$ or $2\dfrac{4}{5}$ $\qquad\qquad\qquad\qquad$ $1\dfrac{4}{5}$ or $1\dfrac{4}{6}$

Rounding decimals

Write each amount to the nearest dollar.

$2.67		$3.18		$6.75		$7.43	
$8.28		$8.67		$4.97		$2.43	
$4.66		$8.12		$6.08		$5.40	
$7.02		$6.74		$7.83		$12.78	
$11.64		$10.64		$15.67		$21.37	

Write each length to the nearest meter.

1.76 m		4.32 m		6.75 m		3.84 m	
7.40 m		3.18 m		7.31 m		9.63 m	
5.42 m		12.82 m		18.53 m		16.45 m	
10.53 m		20.65 m		17.45 m		14.32 m	
12.64 m		19.05 m		15.51 m		27.47 m	

Write each amount to the nearest dollar or meter.

3.46 m		$2.50		4.50 m		$7.50	
12.50 m		18.99 m		$12.50		23.50 m	
35.50 m		$61.67		50.50 m		67.50 m	
$45.67		$63.50		$89.78		34.50 m	
$58.50		$21.56		$95.50		64.50 m	

Adding

Write the answer between the lines.

```
        1        1
  67    39    45
+ 32  + 43  + 26
  99    82    71
```

Write the answer between the lines.

```
  43      72      56      28      47
+ 25    + 16    + 14    + 15    + 13
____    ____    ____    ____    ____


  36      54      84      47      54
+ 15    + 17    + 13    + 16    + 19
____    ____    ____    ____    ____


  45      48      64      70      45
+ 15    + 14    + 19    + 14    + 17
____    ____    ____    ____    ____


  18      17      14      18      14
+ 33    + 44    + 56    + 44    + 54
____    ____    ____    ____    ____


  26      45      74      36      81
+ 36    + 34    + 18    + 17    +  8
____    ____    ____    ____    ____


  45      43      57      49      37
+ 35    + 28    + 44    + 37    + 46
____    ____    ____    ____    ____
```

Adding

Write the answer between the lines.

```
   1          1          1
  35 ft      74 ft      46 ft
+ 25 ft    + 18 ft    + 36 ft
─────      ─────      ─────
  60 ft      92 ft      82 ft
```

Write the answer between the lines.

```
  37 ft      56 ft      68 ft      49 ft      28 ft
+ 46 ft    + 36 ft    + 45 ft    + 27 ft    + 36 ft
─────      ─────      ─────      ─────      ─────
```

```
  47 mi      29 mi      56 mi      55 mi      38 mi
+ 44 mi    + 34 mi    + 35 mi    + 37 mi    + 44 mi
─────      ─────      ─────      ─────      ─────
```

```
  65 lb      43 lb      52 lb      47 lb      36 lb
+ 27 lb    + 18 lb    + 17 lb    + 27 lb    + 17 lb
─────      ─────      ─────      ─────      ─────
```

```
  57 oz      48 oz      44 oz      66 oz      43 oz
+ 42 oz    + 24 oz    + 18 oz    + 27 oz    + 29 oz
─────      ─────      ─────      ─────      ─────
```

Write the answer between the lines.

```
   $23.00        $36.00        $75.00        $27.00
+  $18.00     +  $43.00     +  $16.00     +  $38.00
────────      ────────      ────────      ────────
```

Adding

Write the answer between the lines.

```
   12          17          15          12          18
   13          10          13          14          10
+  13        + 11        + 11        + 12        + 11
-----       -----       -----       -----       -----
```

```
   17          19          16          12          19
   26          13          21          25          32
+  12        + 14        + 31        + 33        + 12
-----       -----       -----       -----       -----
```

```
   20          30          40          50          60
   32          26          42          21          14
+  16        + 25        + 25        + 21        +  8
-----       -----       -----       -----       -----
```

```
   25          35          45          55          65
   15          25          15          35          15
+   5        +  5        +  5        +  5        +  5
-----       -----       -----       -----       -----
```

```
   23          34          45          56          67
   45          32          16          16          12
+  32        + 13        +  9        +  7        +  8
-----       -----       -----       -----       -----
```

Subtracting

Write the answer between the lines.

$$\begin{array}{r} 57 \\ -\ 15 \\ \hline 42 \end{array} \qquad \begin{array}{r} {\scriptstyle 3\ 12} \\ \cancel{4}\cancel{2} \\ -\ 16 \\ \hline 26 \end{array} \qquad \begin{array}{r} {\scriptstyle 2\ 16} \\ \cancel{3}\cancel{6} \\ -\ 29 \\ \hline 7 \end{array}$$

Write the answer between the lines.

$$\begin{array}{r} 40 \\ -\ 18 \\ \hline \end{array} \qquad \begin{array}{r} 60 \\ -\ 23 \\ \hline \end{array} \qquad \begin{array}{r} 70 \\ -\ 37 \\ \hline \end{array} \qquad \begin{array}{r} 50 \\ -\ 18 \\ \hline \end{array} \qquad \begin{array}{r} 90 \\ -\ 27 \\ \hline \end{array}$$

$$\begin{array}{r} 41 \\ -\ 14 \\ \hline \end{array} \qquad \begin{array}{r} 62 \\ -\ 15 \\ \hline \end{array} \qquad \begin{array}{r} 85 \\ -\ 37 \\ \hline \end{array} \qquad \begin{array}{r} 64 \\ -\ 45 \\ \hline \end{array} \qquad \begin{array}{r} 71 \\ -\ 36 \\ \hline \end{array}$$

$$\begin{array}{r} 45 \\ -\ 18 \\ \hline \end{array} \qquad \begin{array}{r} 65 \\ -\ 34 \\ \hline \end{array} \qquad \begin{array}{r} 75 \\ -\ 69 \\ \hline \end{array} \qquad \begin{array}{r} 95 \\ -\ 49 \\ \hline \end{array} \qquad \begin{array}{r} 85 \\ -\ 38 \\ \hline \end{array}$$

$$\begin{array}{r} 73 \\ -\ 27 \\ \hline \end{array} \qquad \begin{array}{r} 82 \\ -\ 38 \\ \hline \end{array} \qquad \begin{array}{r} 74 \\ -\ 47 \\ \hline \end{array} \qquad \begin{array}{r} 81 \\ -\ 39 \\ \hline \end{array} \qquad \begin{array}{r} 64 \\ -\ 47 \\ \hline \end{array}$$

$$\begin{array}{r} 61 \\ -\ 14 \\ \hline \end{array} \qquad \begin{array}{r} 52 \\ -\ 17 \\ \hline \end{array} \qquad \begin{array}{r} 61 \\ -\ 19 \\ \hline \end{array} \qquad \begin{array}{r} 53 \\ -\ 23 \\ \hline \end{array} \qquad \begin{array}{r} 73 \\ -\ 44 \\ \hline \end{array}$$

$$\begin{array}{r} 70 \\ -\ 26 \\ \hline \end{array} \qquad \begin{array}{r} 63 \\ -\ 7 \\ \hline \end{array} \qquad \begin{array}{r} 83 \\ -\ 56 \\ \hline \end{array} \qquad \begin{array}{r} 53 \\ -\ 36 \\ \hline \end{array} \qquad \begin{array}{r} 47 \\ -\ 43 \\ \hline \end{array}$$

Subtracting

Write the answer between the lines.

```
    4 16          2 17          4 18
    5̸6̸ ft         3̸7̸ mi         5̸8̸ lb
  −  18 ft       −  19 mi       −  19 lb
     38 ft          18 mi          39 lb
```

Write the answer between the lines.

```
   45 ft        63 ft        74 ft        82 ft        40 ft
 − 23 ft      − 44 ft      − 38 ft      − 29 ft      − 17 ft
```

```
   61 ft        81 ft        62 ft        83 ft        43 ft
 − 27 ft      − 36 ft      − 27 ft      − 36 ft      − 17 ft
```

```
   45 ft        60 ft        73 ft        74 ft        85 ft
 − 26 ft      − 47 ft      − 48 ft      − 39 ft      − 47 ft
```

Write the answer between the lines.

```
   50 mi        37 mi        75 mi        84 mi        90 mi
 − 28 mi      − 18 mi      − 39 mi      − 29 mi      − 37 mi
```

Write the answer between the lines.

```
   68 lb        47 lb        64 lb        79 lb        56 lb
 − 39 lb      − 38 lb      − 27 lb      − 27 lb      − 45 lb
```

Real-life problems

Solve the problem and then write the answer.

Tuhil is reading a book that
has 72 pages. He has read 38 pages.
How many more pages does
Tuhil have to read?

34 pages

$$\begin{array}{r} {\scriptstyle 6\ 12} \\ \not{7}\not{2} \\ -\ 38 \\ \hline 34 \end{array}$$

Solve the problem and then write the answer in the box.

Eric has 37 marbles and plays two
games. He wins another 24 marbles
in the first game but then loses 18 in
the second game. How many marbles
does Eric have now?

Angie has 70 felt-tip pens and gives
26 of them to Abir. She buys 12 new
pens to replace the ones she has
given away. How many pens does
Angie have now?

Edwin empties his trouser pockets
and finds 26¢ in one pocket, 13¢ in
another pocket, and 37¢ in another
one. How much money has Edwin
found altogether?

Isabelle has 64 french fries with her
burger. She eats 16 fries and gives 6
to her baby brother. How many fries
does Isabelle have left?

Multiplying

Write the answer between the lines.

3	1	1	3
27	53	36	19
x 5	x 4	x 3	x 4
135	212	108	76

Write the answer between the lines.

26	43	67	18	74
x 4	x 4	x 4	x 4	x 4

19	41	58	32	94
x 3	x 3	x 3	x 3	x 3

33	49	67	28	63
x 5	x 5	x 5	x 5	x 5

64	85	94	57	78
x 2	x 2	x 2	x 2	x 2

15	53	64	85	72
x 6	x 6	x 6	x 6	x 6

37	85	51	84	47
x 8	x 8	x 8	x 8	x 8

Multiplying

Write the answer between the lines.

1	3	3	3
24	75	58	17
x 4	x 6	x 4	x 5
96	450	232	85

Write the answer between the lines.

43	50	37	29	16
x 7	x 7	x 7	x 7	x 7

27	58	36	14	61
x 9	x 9	x 9	x 9	x 9

53	37	49	58	67
x 10	x 10	x 10	x 10	x 10

37	47	87	17	97
x 4	x 5	x 6	x 7	x 8

58	38	78	28	18
x 6	x 7	x 8	x 9	x 10

49	29	59	89	69
x 5	x 6	x 7	x 8	x 9

Dividing

Write the answer in the box.

$24 \div 7 =$ `3 r 3`

$$5 \overline{)\,2\,1}$$
$$\underline{-2\,0}$$
$$1$$
`4 r 1`

$43 \div 8 =$ `5 r 3`

$$8 \overline{)\,4\,3}$$
$$\underline{-4\,0}$$
$$3$$

Write the answer in the box.

$27 \div 3 =$

$14 \div 3 =$

$23 \div 3 =$

$7 \div 3 =$

$31 \div 4 =$

$14 \div 4 =$

$38 \div 4 =$

$4 \div 4 =$

$42 \div 5 =$

$23 \div 5 =$

$15 \div 5 =$

$27 \div 5 =$

$47 \div 6 =$

$35 \div 5 =$

$46 \div 5 =$

Write the answer in the box.

$$8 \overline{)\,3\,4}$$
$$8 \overline{)\,4\,6}$$
$$8 \overline{)\,2\,1}$$
$$8 \overline{)\,5\,6}$$
$$9 \overline{)\,2\,7}$$

$$2 \overline{)\,3}$$
$$2 \overline{)\,1\,6}$$
$$3 \overline{)\,1\,7}$$
$$3 \overline{)\,2\,3}$$
$$3 \overline{)\,3\,0}$$

Write the answer in the box.

$45 \div 8 =$

$73 \div 8 =$

$56 \div 8 =$

$73 \div 9 =$

$41 \div 9 =$

$50 \div 9 =$

$54 \div 10 =$

$89 \div 10 =$

$42 \div 10 =$

Dividing

Write the answer in the box.

$31 \div 4 =$ `7 r 3`

```
      2 r 5
  6) 1 7
    -1 2
       5
```

$31 \div 9 =$ `3 r 4`

```
      3 r 4
  9) 3 1
    -2 7
       4
```

Write the answer in the box.

$46 \div 9 =$	$28 \div 7 =$	$45 \div 9 =$
$74 \div 8 =$	$32 \div 3 =$	$45 \div 7 =$
$61 \div 7 =$	$65 \div 9 =$	$12 \div 9 =$
$17 \div 4 =$	$24 \div 6 =$	$36 \div 6 =$
$37 \div 8 =$	$37 \div 9 =$	$37 \div 10 =$

Write the answer in the box.

```
7) 4 5        8) 5 6        9) 4 3        9) 3 0        9) 3 5
```

```
9) 5 3        9) 7 6        9) 5 4        9) 4 3        9) 2 7
```

Write the answer in the box.

$8 \div 6 =$	$12 \div 10 =$	$11 \div 9 =$
$13 \div 10 =$	$17 \div 7 =$	$23 \div 8 =$
$70 \div 10 =$	$70 \div 7 =$	$54 \div 6 =$

Choosing the operation

Write either x or ÷ in the box to make the number sentence true.

6 $\times$ 7 = 42   24 ÷ 6 = 4   10 ÷ 2 = 5

Write either x or ÷ in the box to make the number sentence true.

35 ☐ 7 = 5	35 ☐ 5 = 7	7 ☐ 5 = 35
5 ☐ 7 = 35	6 ☐ 9 = 54	54 ☐ 6 = 9
9 ☐ 6 = 54	54 ☐ 9 = 6	32 ☐ 4 = 8
4 ☐ 8 = 32	8 ☐ 4 = 32	32 ☐ 8 = 4
4 ☐ 9 = 36	36 ☐ 4 = 9	9 ☐ 4 = 36
36 ☐ 9 = 4	80 ☐ 8 = 10	8 ☐ 10 = 80
7 ☐ 9 = 63	63 ☐ 7 = 9	63 ☐ 9 = 7
9 ☐ 7 = 63	9 ☐ 9 = 81	81 ☐ 9 = 9
64 ☐ 8 = 8	8 ☐ 8 = 64	25 ☐ 5 = 5
5 ☐ 5 = 25	16 ☐ 4 = 4	4 ☐ 4 = 16
7 ☐ 7 = 49	49 ☐ 7 = 7	3 ☐ 3 = 9
9 ☐ 3 = 3	100 ☐ 10 = 10	10 ☐ 10 = 100
50 ☐ 10 = 5	5 ☐ 8 = 40	40 ☐ 4 = 10
20 ☐ 5 = 4	4 ☐ 10 = 40	36 ☐ 6 = 6
3 ☐ 7 = 21	21 ☐ 3 = 7	7 ☐ 4 = 28
14 ☐ 10 = 140	140 ☐ 2 = 70	70 ☐ 10 = 7
42 ☐ 6 = 7	7 ☐ 10 = 70	72 ☐ 8 = 9
50 ☐ 5 = 10	20 ☐ 4 = 5	3 ☐ 8 = 24

Real-life problems

Write the answer in the box.

There are 8 ink cartridges in each pack.
How many cartridges will there
be in 6 packs?

48 cartridges

$8 \times 6 = 48$

Write the answer in the box.

Ian shares 50 oranges equally
among 6 elephants and gives the
remainder to the giraffes. How many
oranges do the giraffes receive?

There are 9 children at a birthday
party and each child has 4 chocolate
cupcakes. How many cupcakes
do the children have altogether?

Ben has 60 building blocks and puts
them in stacks of 7. How many stacks
of 7 can Ben make?

Katie has seven dimes, four
nickels, and four pennies.
How much does she have altogether?

The dog wants to bury four bones in
each hole. The dog has 36 bones.
How many holes must the dog dig?

Perimeter

Write the perimeter of this shape in the answer box.

2 cm

8 cm

8 cm
2 cm
8 cm
+ 2 cm
20 cm

Write the perimeter of each shape in the answer box.

5 cm
1 cm

4 cm
3 cm

8 cm
4 cm

6 cm
6 cm

2 cm
7 cm

8 cm
5 cm

4 cm
10 cm

9 cm
9 cm

12 cm
5 cm

20 cm
5 cm

Area

Write the area of the shape in the answer box.

1 cm

7 cm

$1 \times 7 = 7$

7 cm²

Write the area of each shape in the answer box.

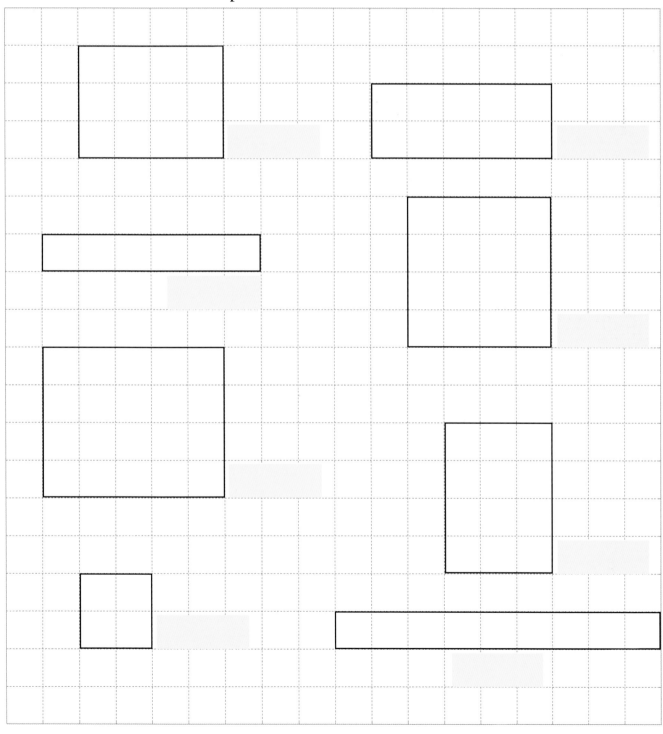

Area

Write the area of this shape in the answer box.

3 ft

8 ft

$3 \times 8 = 24$

24 ft²

Write the area of each shape in the answer box.

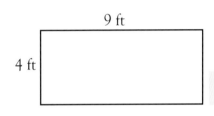
9 ft

4 ft

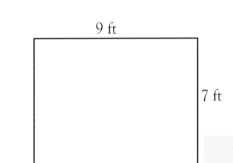
10 ft

3 ft

3 ft

12 ft

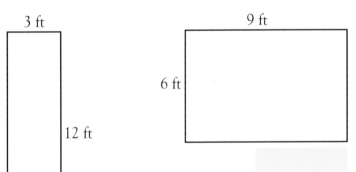
9 ft

6 ft

9 ft

7 ft

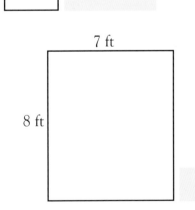
7 ft

8 ft

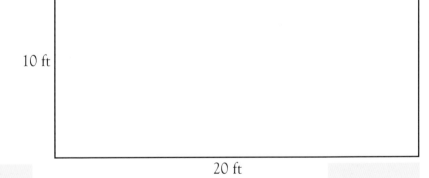
10 ft

20 ft

25 ft

4 ft

Problems using time

Write the answer in the box.

How many minutes until 12 o'clock?

90 minutes

Write the answer in the box.

What time will it be in half an hour?

What time was it ten minutes ago?

How many minutes until 10 o'clock?

The clock is 20 minutes fast. What is the real time?

Write the answer in the box.

What was the time half an hour ago?

How many minutes until 4 o'clock?

How long until a quarter to 4?

How many minutes since 2 o'clock?

Write the answer in the box.

How many minutes since 2:30?

How many minutes until 4 o'clock?

What time did the clock show half an hour ago?

How many hours until 8:15?

Reading timetables

	Frostburg	Elmhusrt	Badger Farm	Winchester
Redline Bus	8:00	8:05	8:15	8:25
Blueline tram	8:05	No stop	8:12	8:20
City taxi	8:30	8:35	8:45	8:55
Greenline Trolley	8:07	No stop	No stop	8:15

The timetable shows the times it takes to travel using different transport companies between Frostburg and Winchester.

Write the answer in the box.

How long does Redline take between Frostburg and Winchester?

When does the tram arrive at Badger Farm?

Where does the trolley not stop?

Where is City taxi at 8:35?

Does the tram stop at Elmhurst?

How long does the bus take to travel between Badger Farm and Winchester?

Which is the fastest trip between Frostburg and Winchester?

Which service arrives at five minutes to nine?

How long does City taxi take between Frostburg and Badger Farm?

Where is the tram at twelve minutes past eight?

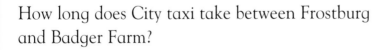

Averages

Write the average of this row in the box.

| 4 | 2 | 2 | 2 | 6 | 3 | 2 |

The average is   3

Write the average of each row in the box.

2	3	7	4	2	7	2	5	
7	4	5	4	8	5	3	4	
5	3	5	3	5	2	4	5	
7	5	9	7	2	4	8	6	
4	3	4	3	4	3	4	7	
1	4	2	7	3	8	2	5	
3	2	1	2	2	3	2	1	
8	3	6	3	8	2	8	2	

Write the average of each row in the box.

4	8	6	3	9	6	6	
5	9	2	6	9	1	3	
6	3	8	6	1	5	6	
3	8	6	7	5	9	4	
1	8	3	4	2	6	4	
9	5	8	7	4	7	9	
1	3	2	3	1	2	2	
6	3	7	4	5	4	6	

Estimating

Estimate to find the answer.

One crate of apples sells for between $8 and $12. If Sam sold 10 crates of apples, about how much did he earn?

Sam earned about $100   .

Estimate to find the answer.

The river ferry makes 5 trips a day. There are between 40 and 60 people on each trip. About how many people ride the ferry every day?

About

Peter has 25 bean plants in his garden. Each plant produces 3 to 5 quarts of beans. About how many quarts of beans will Peter have?

About

Movie tickets cost between $6 and $10. If the theater holds 200 people, about how much money is made in ticket sales when the theater is full?

About

Luz can fit between 300 and 500 beads in a storage bag. If she has 12 bags, about how many beads will she be able to store?

About

Ahmed rides his bike 10 to 20 miles a day. About how many miles does he ride in ten days?

About

Calculating change

Circle the correct change.

Carlo bought a ball.  He paid

How much change did he get?

Circle the correct change.

Snack Menu	
Banana	25¢
Pear	75¢
Apple	60¢

Kate bought an apple. She paid

How much change did she get?

Ali bought a banana. He paid

How much change did he get?

Dan bought a pear. He paid

How much change did he get?

Counting money

Count the coins. Write the total amount.

25¢   +   25¢   +   25¢   +   5¢   +   5¢   +   10¢   =   95¢

Count the coins. Write the total amount.

Number pairs

Look at the grid and then answer the questions below.

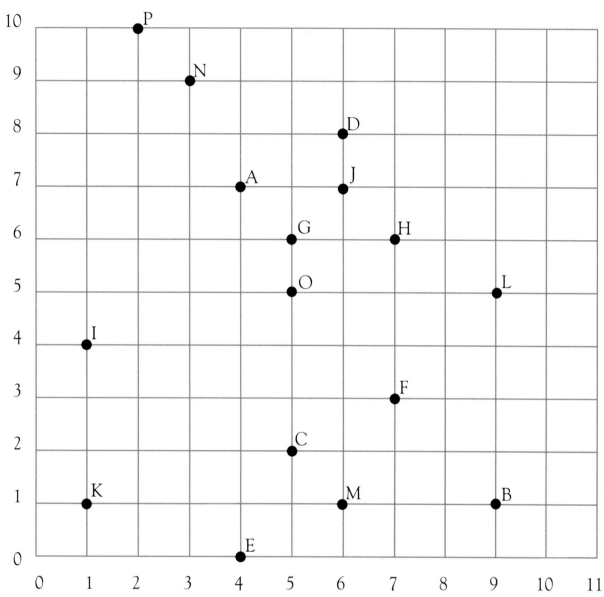

Give the number pair of each letter.

A =   B =   C =   D =

E =   F =   G =   H =

I =   J =   K =   L =

M =   N =   O =   P =

Multiply or divide?

Write x or ÷ in the box.

7 ☐ 5 = 35   10 ☐ 2 = 5   12 ☐ 2 = 6

30 ☐ 5 = 6   30 ☐ 10 = 3   9 ☐ 2 = 18

14 ☐ 2 = 7   35 ☐ 5 = 7   6 ☐ 10 = 60

40 ☐ 10 = 4   20 ☐ 4 = 5   5 ☐ 3 = 15

5 ☐ 6 = 30   3 ☐ 10 = 30   90 ☐ 10 = 9

50 ☐ 5 = 10   18 ☐ 2 = 9   15 ☐ 3 = 5

Write the answers in the boxes.

A number divided by 4 is 10. What is the number?

I multiply a number by 6 and the answer is 30. What is the number?

A number multiplied by 10 gives the answer 10. What is the number?

I divide a number by 8 and the answer is 5. What is the number?

A number divided by 7 is 5. What is the number?

I multiply a number by 2 and the answer is 18. What is the number?

A number multiplied by 5 is 45. What is the number?

I divide a number by 2 and the answer is 1. What is the number?

Write x or ÷ in the box.

7 ☐ 10 = 70   5 ☐ 5 = 25   10 ☐ 10 = 1

5 ☐ 5 = 1   9 ☐ 2 = 18   2 ☐ 2 = 4

15 ☐ 5 = 3   10 ☐ 10 = 100   50 ☐ 5 = 10

100 ☐ 10 = 10   2 ☐ 2 = 1   20 ☐ 5 = 4

Lines of symmetry

Draw the line of symmetry
on each shape.

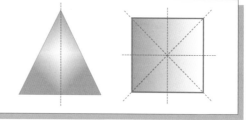

Draw the line of symmetry on each shape.

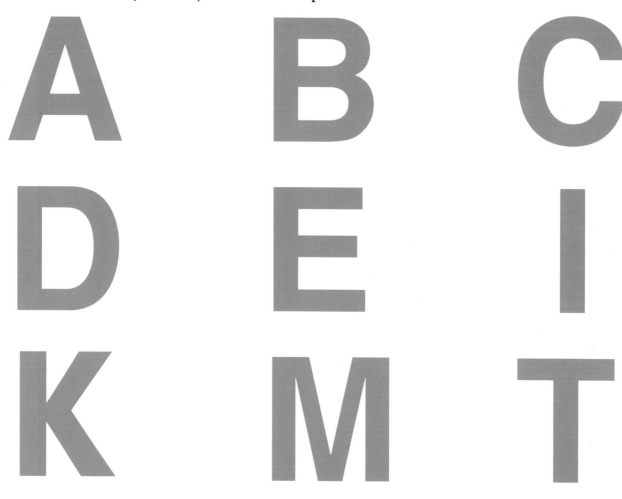

Half of each shape is drawn and the line of symmetry. Draw the other half.

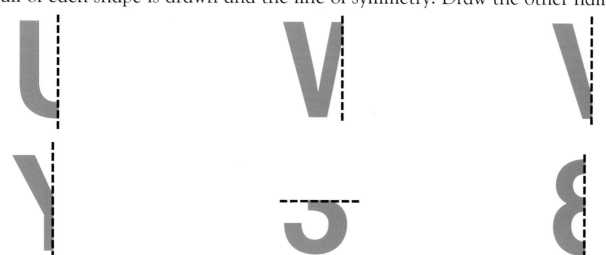

Counting by 3s, 4s, and 5s

Find the pattern. Continue each row.

Count by 3s.	9	12	15	18	21	24	27
Count by 4s.	8	12	16	20	24	28	32
Count by 5s.	55	50	45	40	35	30	25

Find the pattern. Continue each row.

0	3	6					
8	12	16					
38	41	44					
40	45	50					
63	67	71					
85	90	95					
6	10	14					
21	18	15					
68	65	62					
85	80	75					50
43	40	37					
49	45	41					
71	67	63					
83	78	73					48
39	34						4

Multiples

Circle the numbers in the
2 times table.

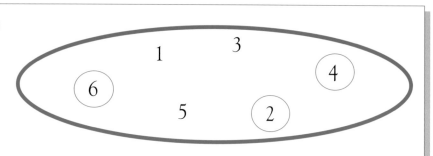

Circle the numbers in the
2 times table.

17 18 23 21 20
22 19 24

Circle the numbers in the
2 times table.

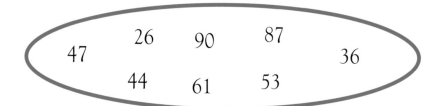

47 26 90 87 36
44 61 53

Circle the numbers in the
5 times table.

10 15 40 47 3
24 18 50

Circle the numbers in the
5 times table.

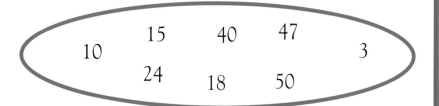

47 76 85 91 48
90 65 60

Circle the numbers in the
10 times table.

20 24 40 44 58
15 1 60

Circle the numbers in the
10 times table.

70 110 260 605 400
99

Comparing and ordering

Write these numbers in order, starting with the smallest.

431   678   273   586 | 273 | 431 | 586 | 678 |

Write these numbers in order, starting with the smallest.

267	931	374	740				
734	218	625	389				
836	590	374	669				
572	197	469	533				
948	385	846	289				
406	560	460	650				
738	837	378	783				
582	285	528	852				
206	620	602	260				
634	436	364	463				
47	740	74	704				
501	150	51	105				
290	92	209	29				
803	380	83	38				
504	450	54	45				

Rounding

What is 327 rounded to the nearest 100?

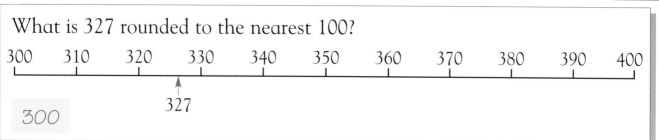

300

What is each number rounded to the nearest 100?

478		231		147		687
342		812		973		439
639		108		374		752
418		639		523		446
857		560		299		809

What is 250 rounded to the nearest 100?

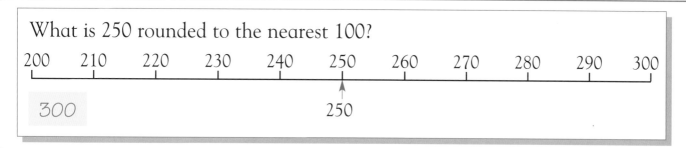

300

What is each number rounded to the nearest 100?

450		850		650		87
21		405		150		950
655		540		980		50
750		250		90		59
550		105		955		350

Fractions

What is $\frac{1}{2}$ of each number?

4	8	10	2
6	12	20	16
14	50	100	60

What is $\frac{1}{3}$ of each number?

6	12	18	9
3	15	21	30
24	60	27	33

What is $\frac{1}{4}$ of each number?

8	16	4	12
20	40	80	1

What is $\frac{1}{8}$ of each number?

16	8	24	40
32	48	80	56

What is $\frac{1}{10}$ of each number?

20	40	80	100
10	30	50	90

Multiplying

Write the answer in the box.

7 x 3 = 21   9 x 5 = 45   6 x 10 = 60

Write the answer in the box.

2 x 3 =   7 x 4 =   4 x 3 =   6 x 4 =

9 x 5 =   8 x 3 =   6 x 3 =   10 x 9 =

3 x 2 =   9 x 4 =   7 x 5 =   5 x 4 =

0 x 3 =   8 x 4 =   4 x 10 =   0 x 4 =

5 x 3 =   4 x 4 =   9 x 3 =   8 x 5 =

Write the answer in the box.

Three times a number is 18.
What is the number?

A child draws 8 squares.
How many sides
have to be drawn?

A box contains 4 cans of beans.
A man buys 9 boxes. How many
cans does he have?

A girl is given 3 stickers for
every point she gains in a
spelling test. How many will
she receive if she gets 10 points?

A number multiplied by 4 is 36.
What is the number?

Light bulbs come in packs of 3.
Erin buys 6 packs. How many
bulbs will she have?

Mari is given eight 5¢ coins.
How much money
is she given?

Four times a number is 24.
What is the number?

A bottle holds 4 liters of
soda. How much will
7 bottles hold?

Six times a number is 30.
What is the number?

Dividing

Work out each division problem.
Some will have remainders, some will not.

$15 \div 3 = \boxed{5}$

$17 \div 4 = \boxed{4\,r\,1}$

$$\begin{array}{r} 5\,r\,1 \\ 2\overline{)11} \\ -\underline{10} \\ 1 \end{array}$$

$$\begin{array}{r} 2\,r\,2 \\ 3\overline{)8} \\ -\underline{6} \\ 2 \end{array}$$

Work out each division problem.

$24 \div 3 =$ $32 \div 4 =$ $18 \div 9 =$ $24 \div 6 =$

$16 \div 4 =$ $24 \div 4 =$ $40 \div 10 =$ $28 \div 4 =$

$40 \div 10 =$ $20 \div 4 =$ $40 \div 4 =$ $12 \div 6 =$

$9 \div 3 =$ $24 \div 3 =$ $35 \div 7 =$ $60 \div 10 =$

$3 \div 1 =$ $25 \div 5 =$ $36 \div 4 =$ $44 \div 4 =$

Work out each division problem. Some will have remainders, some will not.

$4\overline{)16}$ $5\overline{)32}$ $3\overline{)10}$ $5\overline{)13}$

$4\overline{)14}$ $3\overline{)21}$ $10\overline{)70}$ $3\overline{)19}$

Work out the answer to each problem.

23 carrots are shared equally by 4 rabbits. How many carrots does each rabbit receive and how many are left over?

36 apples are shared equally between 5 horses. How many apples does each horse receive and how many are left over?

Bar graphs

Look at the bar graph. Then answer the question.

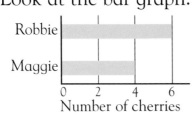

How many cherries does Robbie have?

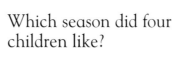

6

Look at the bar graph. Then answer the questions.

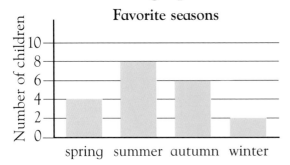

This graph shows the favorite seasons of a group of children.

How many children were asked which season they liked best?

How many children liked autumn best?

Which season did four children like?

Which was the favorite season?

How many more children liked autumn than liked winter?

Look at the bar graph. Then answer the questions.

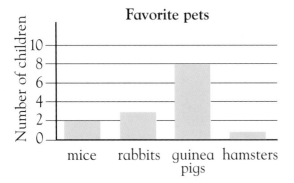

This graph shows the favorite pets of a group of children.

How many children were asked about which pets they liked?

Which pet did eight children like?

How many children liked rabbits?

How many children liked hamsters?

How many more children liked rabbits than liked hamsters?

Symmetry

Draw the lines of symmetry on each shape.

Draw the lines of symmetry on each shape. Some shapes may have no line of symmetry, and some shapes may have more than one line.

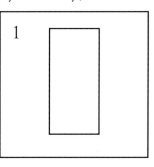 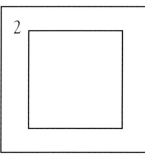 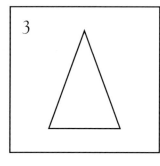 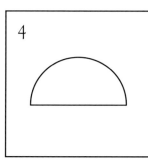

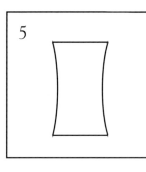 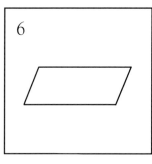 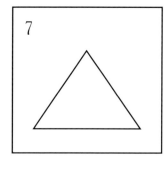 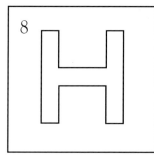

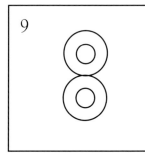 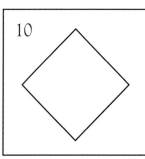 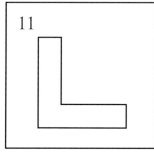 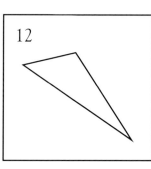

Half of each shape has been drawn as well as the line of symmetry (dotted line). Draw the other half of each shape.

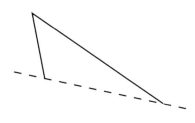  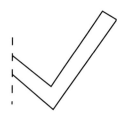

Ordering

Write these numbers in order starting with the smallest.

670　　760　　607　　706

607　　670　　706　　760

Write these numbers in order starting with the smallest.

270	720	207	702

870	780	807	708

906	690	960	609

106	610	601	160

560	506	650	605

849	489	948	984

890	980	809	908

486	684	864	648

405	450	540	504

746	647	764	674

570	586	490	92

76	104	200	92

440	66	781	177

632	236	77	407

842	587	99	88

74	101	12	800

500	468	395	288

600	304	403	89

78	9	302	470

345	543	53	34

Fractions of shapes

Shade half of each shape.

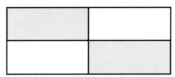

Shade half of each shape.

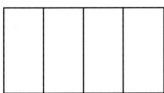 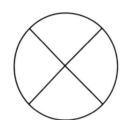 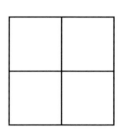

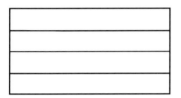 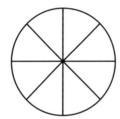 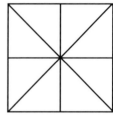

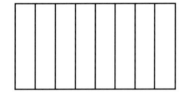 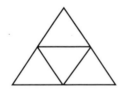 

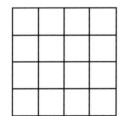 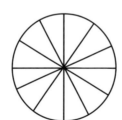 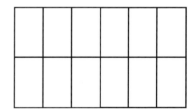

Shade $\frac{1}{3}$ of each shape.

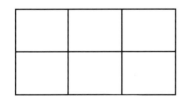 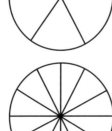 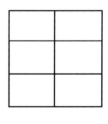

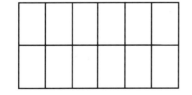 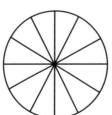 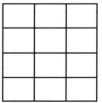

Choosing the operation

Write the answer in the box.

I add 25 to a number and the sum is 40. What number did I start with?   15

I subtract 13 and have 24 left. What number did I start with?   37

Write the answer in the box.

22 is added to a number and the sum is 30. What number did I begin with?

I subtract 14 from a number and end up with 17. What number did I start with?

I add 16 to a number and the total of the two numbers is 30. What number did I begin with?

When 26 is subtracted from a number, the difference is 14. What is the number?

After adding 22 to a number the total is 45. What is the number?

What number must you subtract from 19 to find a difference of 7?

I start with 29 and take away a number. The difference is 14. What number did I subtract?

35 is added to a number and the total is 60. What is the number?

I increase a number by 14 and the total is 30. What number did I start with?

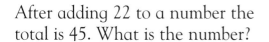

After taking 17 away from a number I am left with 3. What number did I start with?

Paul starts with 50¢ but spends some money in a shop. He goes home with 18¢. How much did Paul spend?

Sue starts out with 23¢ but is given some money by her aunt. Sue then has 50¢. How much was she given?

Alice gives 20¢ to charity. If she started with 95¢, how much has she have left?

Jane has a 32-ounce bottle of orange soda. She drinks 12 ounces. How many ounces does she have left?

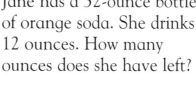

A box contains 60 pins and then some are added so that the new total is 85. How many pins have been added?

A tower is made up of 30 blocks. 45 more are put on the top. How many blocks are in the tower now?

Choosing the operation

Write the answer in the box.

A number is multiplied by 8 and the result is 24. What is the number? **3**

I divide a number by 4 and the answer is 9. What number did I begin with? **36**

Write the answer in the box.

A number is multiplied by 6 and the result is 30. What is the number?

When a number is divided by 7 the result is 4. What is the number?

I multiply a number by 10, and the final number is 70. What number did I multiply?

After dividing a number by 8, I am left with 4. What number did I divide?

When 20 is multiplied by a number the result is 100. What number is used to multiply?

I divide a number by 3 and the result is 9. What is the number?

After multiplying a number by 5, I have 40. What was the number I started with?

When a number is divided by 10 the result is 3. What number was divided?

2 6 4 7 8 3 5 9 1

I multiply a number by 4 and the result is 40. What number was multiplied?

After dividing a number by 2, I am left with 30. What number was divided?

45¢ is shared equally by some children. Each child receives 9¢. How many children are there?

Each box contains 7 markers. I have 28 markers altogether. How many boxes do I have?

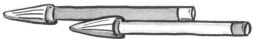

I share 80¢ equally among some children. Each child is given 20¢. How many children have shared the money?

A bag contains 10 chocolate bars. In all I have 100 chocolate bars. How many bags do I have?

50 peanuts are shared equally between 2 squirrels. How many peanuts does each squirrel receive?

I give $25 to each charity. I give away $200. How many charities did I give money to?

Bar graphs and pictographs

Look at the bar graph and answer the question.

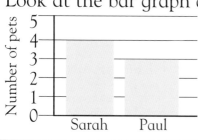

Which child has three pets?   Paul

Look at the bar graph and answer the questions.

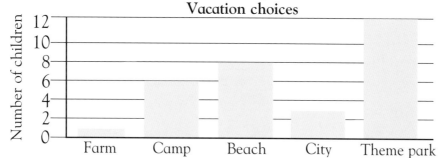

How many children went to camp on vacation?

Which place did three children go to?

Which place did fewer children go to than to the city?

Which was the most popular place for vacations?

How many children altogether went on vacation?

Look at the pictograph and answer the questions.

Children's favorite hobbies

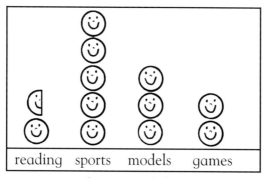

☺ each face stands for 2 children

How many children enjoy making models?

Which hobby is enjoyed by four children?

How many more children like games than like reading?

Which is the most popular hobby?

Adding two numbers

Find each sum.

```
    2 7 1          ¹
  + 5 2 4        4 8 3
  ───────      + 5 7 1
    7 9 5      ───────
               1,0 5 4
```

Remember to regroup if you need to.

Find each sum.

```
    3 3 4          3 5 2          7 2 3          8 4 3
  + 2 6 5        + 1 2 7        + 3 4 5        + 2 9 1
  ───────        ───────        ───────        ───────


    3 8 5          3 6 3          5 3 5          3 9 2
  + 6 0 6        + 1 4 7        + 1 8 7        + 4 8 8
  ───────        ───────        ───────        ───────
```

Write the answer in the box.

213 + 137 = [ ]   535 + 167 = [ ]

Write the missing number in the box.

```
    3 6 2          2 [ ] 6        7 [ ] 1        7 3 9
  + 4 1 9        + 5 8 1        + 2 6 4        + 2 4 [ ]
  ───────        ───────        ───────        ───────
    7 [ ] 1        8 3 7          9 8            [ ] 7 9
```

Find each sum.

One jar contains 204 candies, and another contains 148 candies. How many candies are there altogether?

A boy has 136 baseball cards, and his sister has 159. How many cards do they have altogether?

Adding two numbers

Find each sum.

```
        1  1
 4, 3 2 1      3, 7 9 4
+ 2, 4 6 5    + 5, 3 2 5
 ───────      ───────
 6, 786       9, 1 19
```

Remember to carry if you need to.

Find each sum.

```
   2, 6 4 2        4, 3 2 5         2, 4 7 1
 + 3, 2 4 1      + 2, 6 5 3       + 4, 2 3 8
 ─────────       ─────────        ─────────



   3, 7 4 9        5, 7 6 4         8, 4 8 2
 + 2, 4 7 1      + 3, 9 1 5       + 1, 3 4 9
 ─────────       ─────────        ─────────

```

Write the answer in the box.

1,342 + 1,264   =   2,531 + 4,236   =

2,013 + 3,642   =   1,738 + 4,261   =

Write the missing number in the box.

```
      7 4 1           6 5 2          3, 6 4 2
 + 2, 9 4         + 3, 2   4       +      8 3
 ─────────        ─────────        ─────────
   6, 6 8 4         4, 9 2 6         8, 4 7 3
```

Find each sum.

5,621 people saw the local soccer team play on Saturday, and 3,246 people watched the midweek match. How many people saw the soccer team play that week?

6,214 people went to the rock concert on Saturday night, and 3,471 people went on Sunday night. How many people saw rock concerts that weekend?

⭐ Subtracting three-digit numbers

Write the difference between the lines.

$$
\begin{array}{r}
364 \\
-223 \\
\hline
141
\end{array}
\qquad
\begin{array}{r}
{}^{6\ 11} \\
47\cancel{1}\ \text{cm} \\
-252\ \text{cm} \\
\hline
219\ cm
\end{array}
$$

Write the difference between the lines.

$$
\begin{array}{r}
263 \\
-\ 151 \\
\hline
\end{array}
\qquad
\begin{array}{r}
478 \\
-\ 234 \\
\hline
\end{array}
\qquad
\begin{array}{r}
845 \\
-\ 624 \\
\hline
\end{array}
\qquad
\begin{array}{r}
793 \\
-\ 581 \\
\hline
\end{array}
$$

$$
\begin{array}{r}
580\ \text{ft} \\
-\ 230\ \text{ft} \\
\hline
\end{array}
\qquad
\begin{array}{r}
659\ \text{m} \\
-\ 318\ \text{m} \\
\hline
\end{array}
\qquad
\begin{array}{r}
850\ \text{yd} \\
-740\ \text{yd} \\
\hline
\end{array}
\qquad
\begin{array}{r}
372\ \text{m} \\
-262\ \text{m} \\
\hline
\end{array}
$$

Write the difference in the box.

$365 \ - \ 123 \ =$ ☐ $799 \ - \ 354 \ =$ ☐

$\$876 \ - \ \$515 \ =$ ☐ $\$940 \ - \ \$730 \ =$ ☐

$\$684 \ - \ \$574 \ =$ ☐ $\$220 \ - \ \$120 \ =$ ☐

Write the difference between the lines.

$$
\begin{array}{r}
363 \\
-\ 145 \\
\hline
\end{array}
\qquad
\begin{array}{r}
484 \\
-\ 237 \\
\hline
\end{array}
\qquad
\begin{array}{r}
561 \\
-\ 342 \\
\hline
\end{array}
\qquad
\begin{array}{r}
394 \\
-\ 185 \\
\hline
\end{array}
$$

$$
\begin{array}{r}
937 \\
-\ 719 \\
\hline
\end{array}
\qquad
\begin{array}{r}
568 \\
-\ 209 \\
\hline
\end{array}
\qquad
\begin{array}{r}
225 \\
-\ 116 \\
\hline
\end{array}
\qquad
\begin{array}{r}
752 \\
-\ 329 \\
\hline
\end{array}
$$

Find the answer to each problem.

A grocer has 234 apples. He sells 127. How many apples does he have left?

A store has 860 movie videos to rent. 420 are rented. How many are left in the store?

There are 572 children in a school. 335 are girls. How many are boys?

Subtracting three-digit numbers

Write the difference between the lines.

$$\begin{array}{r} \scriptstyle 3 \ 11 \\ 4\!\!\!/1\!\!\!/5 \\ -\ 152 \\ \hline 263 \end{array}$$

$$\begin{array}{r} \scriptstyle 6\ 10\ 11 \\ 7\!\!\!/1\!\!\!/1\!\!\!/ \text{ m} \\ -392 \text{ m} \\ \hline 319 \text{ m} \end{array}$$

Write the difference between the lines.

524 m	319 m	647 ft	915 yd
− 263 m	− 137 m	− 456 ft	− 193 yd

714	926	421	815
− 407	− 827	− 355	− 786

Write the difference in the box.

512 − 304 =   648 − 239 =

831 − 642 =   377 − 198 =

Write the difference between the lines.

423	615	312	924
− 136	− 418	− 113	− 528

Write the missing number in the box.

$$\begin{array}{r} 7\ 2\ 3 \\ -\ 1\ 2\ \ \ \\ \hline 5\ 9\ 5 \end{array}$$

$$\begin{array}{r} 5\ \ \ 2 \\ -\ 3\ 1\ 7 \\ \hline 2\ 4\ 5 \end{array}$$

$$\begin{array}{r} 8\ 3\ \ \ \\ -\ 2\ 5\ 7 \\ \hline 5\ 7\ 7 \end{array}$$

$$\begin{array}{r} 5\ 3\ 2 \\ -\ \ \ \ 5 \\ \hline 3\ 4\ 7 \end{array}$$

Find the answer to each problem.

A theater holds 645 people. 257 people buy tickets. How many seats are empty?

There are 564 people in a park. 276 are boating on the lake. How many are taking part in other activities?

Multiplying by one-digit numbers

Find each product.

$$
\begin{array}{r} 32 \\ \times\ 2 \\ \hline 64 \end{array}
\qquad
\begin{array}{r} {\scriptstyle 1} \\ 26 \\ \times\ 3 \\ \hline 78 \end{array}
\qquad
\begin{array}{r} {\scriptstyle 1} \\ 34 \\ \times\ 4 \\ \hline 136 \end{array}
$$

Find each product.

$$
\begin{array}{r} 27 \\ \times\quad 2 \\ \hline \end{array}
\qquad
\begin{array}{r} 32 \\ \times\quad 3 \\ \hline \end{array}
\qquad
\begin{array}{r} 16 \\ \times\quad 4 \\ \hline \end{array}
\qquad
\begin{array}{r} 19 \\ \times\quad 2 \\ \hline \end{array}
$$

$$
\begin{array}{r} 22 \\ \times\quad 3 \\ \hline \end{array}
\qquad
\begin{array}{r} 25 \\ \times\quad 4 \\ \hline \end{array}
\qquad
\begin{array}{r} 18 \\ \times\quad 6 \\ \hline \end{array}
\qquad
\begin{array}{r} 33 \\ \times\quad 5 \\ \hline \end{array}
$$

$$
\begin{array}{r} 39 \\ \times\quad 2 \\ \hline \end{array}
\qquad
\begin{array}{r} 26 \\ \times\quad 2 \\ \hline \end{array}
\qquad
\begin{array}{r} 41 \\ \times\quad 2 \\ \hline \end{array}
\qquad
\begin{array}{r} 38 \\ \times\ 3 \\ \hline \end{array}
$$

$$
\begin{array}{r} 29 \\ \times\quad 3 \\ \hline \end{array}
\qquad
\begin{array}{r} 45 \\ \times\quad 2 \\ \hline \end{array}
\qquad
\begin{array}{r} 28 \\ \times\quad 3 \\ \hline \end{array}
\qquad
\begin{array}{r} 16 \\ \times\quad 6 \\ \hline \end{array}
$$

$$
\begin{array}{r} 10 \\ \times\quad 5 \\ \hline \end{array}
\qquad
\begin{array}{r} 40 \\ \times\quad 2 \\ \hline \end{array}
\qquad
\begin{array}{r} 20 \\ \times\quad 4 \\ \hline \end{array}
\qquad
\begin{array}{r} 50 \\ \times\quad 3 \\ \hline \end{array}
$$

Find the answer to each problem.

 Laura has 36 marbles, and Sarah has twice as many. How many marbles does Sarah have?

A ruler is 30 cm long.
How long will 4 rulers be altogether?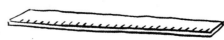

Multiplying by one-digit numbers

Find each product.

```
        53          76          25
    x    3      x    6      x    7
       159         456         175
```

Find each product.

```
     56          46          32          36          45
   x  8        x  7        x  6        x  9        x  4
   ____        ____        ____        ____        ____


     73          96          58          33          48
   x  5        x  3        x  7        x  6        x  5
   ____        ____        ____        ____        ____


     24          19          64          52          81
   x  9        x  8        x  4        x  6        x  3
   ____        ____        ____        ____        ____


     37          40          50          30          20
   x  7        x  8        x  3        x  7        x  9
   ____        ____        ____        ____        ____
```

Find the answer to each problem.

A school bus holds 36 children.
How many children can travel in
6 busloads?

Each of 28 children brings
7 drawings to school. How
many drawings do they
have altogether?

Division with remainders

Find each quotient.

$$5\,r\,1$$
$$3\,\overline{)\,16}$$
$$\underline{15}$$
$$1$$

$$6\,r\,2$$
$$4\,\overline{)\,26}$$
$$\underline{24}$$
$$2$$

Find each quotient.

$$2\,\overline{)\,35}$$ $$4\,\overline{)\,46}$$ $$3\,\overline{)\,22}$$ $$5\,\overline{)\,49}$$

$$4\,\overline{)\,58}$$ $$5\,\overline{)\,63}$$ $$5\,\overline{)\,37}$$ $$4\,\overline{)\,50}$$

$$3\,\overline{)\,76}$$ $$4\,\overline{)\,59}$$ $$5\,\overline{)\,94}$$ $$5\,\overline{)\,83}$$

$$2\,\overline{)\,99}$$ $$4\,\overline{)\,75}$$ $$5\,\overline{)\,77}$$ $$2\,\overline{)\,37}$$

Write the answer in the box.

What is 27 divided by 4?   Divide 78 by 5.

What is 46 divided by 3?   Divide 63 by 2.

148

Division with remainders

Find each quotient.

$$5 \text{ r } 4$$
$$6 \overline{)34}$$
$$\underline{30}$$
$$4$$

$$7 \text{ r } 1$$
$$7 \overline{)50}$$
$$\underline{49}$$
$$1$$

Find each quotient.

$6 \overline{)99}$ $6 \overline{)43}$ $9 \overline{)30}$ $8 \overline{)76}$

$7 \overline{)52}$ $7 \overline{)83}$ $9 \overline{)52}$ $6 \overline{)91}$

$7 \overline{)66}$ $8 \overline{)63}$ $6 \overline{)27}$ $8 \overline{)46}$

$9 \overline{)93}$ $7 \overline{)85}$ $8 \overline{)67}$ $7 \overline{)26}$

Write the answer in the box.

What is 87 divided by 7?   Divide 84 by 8.

What is 75 divided by 6?   Divide 73 by 9.

Appropriate units of measure

Choose the best units to measure the length of each item.

inches	feet	yards

notebook	car	swimming pool
inches	feet	yards

Choose the best units to measure the length of each item.

inches	feet	yards

bed	bicycle	toothbrush	football field

shoe	driveway	canoe	fence

The height of a door is about 7 _____ .

The length of a pencil is about 7 _____ .

The height of a flagpole is about 7 _____ .

Choose the best units to measure the weight of each item.

ounces	pounds	tons

train	kitten	watermelon	tennis ball

shoe	bag of potatoes	elephant	washing machine

The weight of a hamburger is about 6 _____ .

The weight of a bag of apples is about 5 _____ .

The weight of a truck is about 4 _____ .

Real-life problems

Find the answer to each problem.

Jacob spent $4.68 at the store and had $4.77 left.
How much did he have to start with?

$9.45

```
  1 1
  4.77
+ 4.68
  9.45
```

Tracy receives a weekly allowance of $3.00 a week.
How much will she have if she saves all of it for 8 weeks?

$24.00

```
  3.00
×    8
 24.00
```

Find the answer to each problem.

A theater charges $4 for each matinee
ticket. If it sells 360 tickets for a matinee
performance, how much does it take in?

David has saved $9.59. His sister
has $3.24 less. How much does
she have?

The cost for 9 children to go to a
theme park is $72. How much does
each child pay? If only 6 children
go, what will the cost be?

Paul has $3.69. His sister gives him
another $5.25, and he goes out and
buys a CD single for $3.99. How
much does he have left?

Ian has $20 in savings. He
decides to spend $\frac{1}{4}$ of it. How
much will he have left?

Perimeters of squares and rectangles

Find the perimeter of this rectangle.

To find the perimeter of a rectangle
or a square, add the lengths of the
four sides.
6 in. + 6 in. + 4 in. + 4 in. = 20 in.
You can also do this with multiplication.
(2 x 6) in. + (2 x 4) in.
= 12 in. + 8 in. = 20 in.

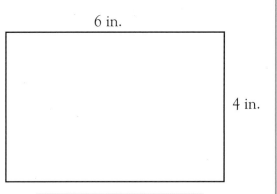

6 in.

4 in.

20 in.

Find the perimeters of these rectangles and squares.

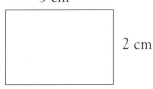

4 in.

1 in.

in.

3 yd

3 yd

yd

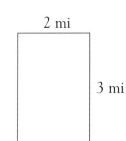

2 mi

3 mi

mi

3 cm

2 cm

1 m

1 m

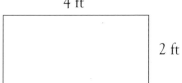

4 ft

2 ft

4 in.

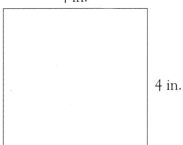

4 in.

4 cm

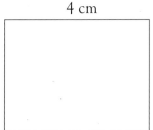

3 cm

2 km

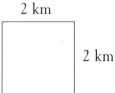

2 km

Comparing areas

Write how many units are in each figure.

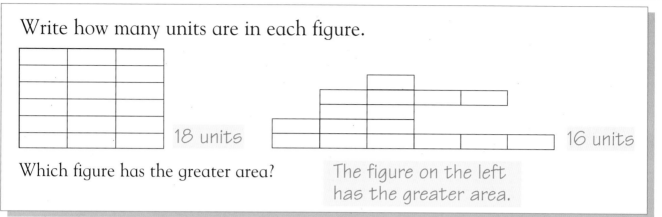

18 units

16 units

Which figure has the greater area?

The figure on the left has the greater area.

Write how many units are in each figure. Then circle the figure with the greatest area in each group.

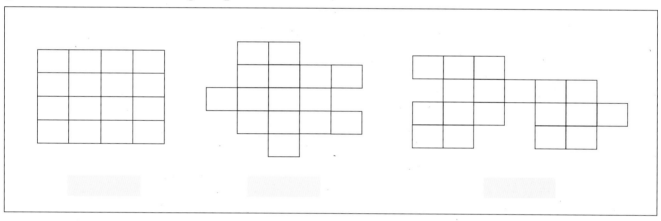

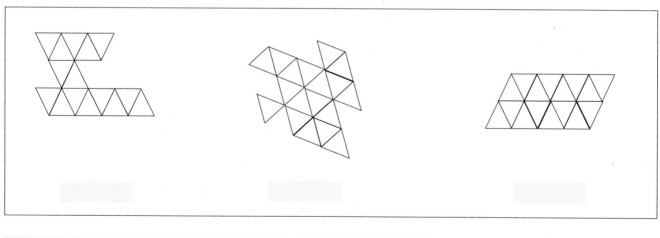

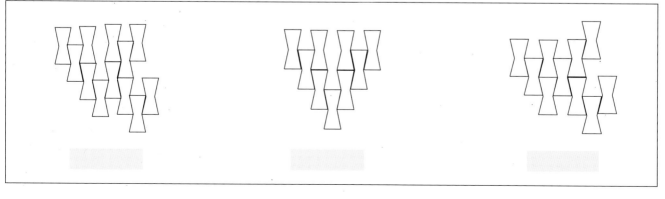

Adding fractions

Write the sum in the simplest form.

$$\frac{1}{8} + \frac{3}{8} = \frac{4}{8} = \frac{1}{2} \qquad\qquad \frac{3}{5} + \frac{3}{5} = \frac{6}{5} = 1\frac{1}{5}$$

Write the sum in the simplest form.

$$\frac{1}{3} + \frac{1}{3} = \underline{}$$

$$\frac{2}{9} + \frac{4}{9} = \underline{} = \underline{}$$

$$\frac{1}{4} + \frac{1}{4} = \underline{} = \underline{}$$

$$\frac{5}{7} + \frac{1}{7} = \underline{}$$

$$\frac{2}{3} + \frac{2}{3} = \underline{} = \underline{}$$

$$\frac{1}{12} + \frac{3}{12} = \underline{} = \underline{}$$

$$\frac{3}{7} + \frac{5}{7} = \underline{} = \underline{}$$

$$\frac{5}{11} + \frac{9}{11} = \underline{} = \underline{}$$

$$\frac{2}{5} + \frac{4}{5} = \underline{} = \underline{}$$

$$\frac{5}{18} + \frac{4}{18} = \underline{} = \underline{}$$

$$\frac{5}{16} + \frac{7}{16} = \underline{} = \underline{}$$

$$\frac{5}{9} + \frac{5}{9} = \underline{} = \underline{}$$

$$\frac{3}{8} + \frac{5}{8} = \underline{} =$$

$$\frac{4}{15} + \frac{7}{15} = \underline{}$$

$$\frac{7}{13} + \frac{8}{13} = \underline{} = \underline{}$$

$$\frac{2}{5} + \frac{1}{5} = \underline{}$$

$$\frac{5}{16} + \frac{7}{16} = \underline{} = \underline{}$$

$$\frac{1}{6} + \frac{5}{6} = \underline{} =$$

$$\frac{9}{10} + \frac{7}{10} = \underline{} = \underline{} = \underline{}$$

$$\frac{3}{4} + \frac{3}{4} = \underline{} = \underline{} = \underline{}$$

$$\frac{4}{5} + \frac{3}{5} = \underline{} = \underline{}$$

$$\frac{1}{8} + \frac{5}{8} = \underline{} = \underline{}$$

$$\frac{7}{12} + \frac{5}{12} = \underline{} =$$

$$\frac{3}{10} + \frac{9}{10} = \underline{} = \underline{} = \underline{}$$

$$\frac{3}{11} + \frac{5}{11} = \underline{}$$

$$\frac{9}{15} + \frac{11}{15} = \underline{} = \underline{} = \underline{}$$

$$\frac{8}{14} + \frac{5}{14} = \underline{}$$

$$\frac{1}{20} + \frac{6}{20} = \underline{}$$

Subtracting fractions

Write the sum in the simplest form.

$$\frac{5}{6} - \frac{4}{6} = \frac{1}{6}$$

$$\frac{5}{8} - \frac{3}{8} = \frac{2}{8} = \frac{1}{4}$$

Write the answer in the simplest form.

$$\frac{2}{3} - \frac{1}{3} = \underline{}$$

$$\frac{7}{9} - \frac{4}{9} = \underline{} = \underline{}$$

$$\frac{1}{4} - \frac{1}{4} = \underline{}$$

$$\frac{5}{7} - \frac{1}{7} = \underline{}$$

$$\frac{7}{12} - \frac{5}{12} = \underline{} = \underline{}$$

$$\frac{5}{11} - \frac{3}{11} = \underline{}$$

$$\frac{6}{7} - \frac{5}{7} = \underline{}$$

$$\frac{9}{12} - \frac{5}{12} = \underline{} = \underline{}$$

$$\frac{18}{30} - \frac{15}{30} = \underline{} = \underline{}$$

$$\frac{4}{5} - \frac{2}{5} = \underline{}$$

$$\frac{3}{6} - \frac{1}{6} = \underline{} = \underline{}$$

$$\frac{7}{8} - \frac{1}{8} = \underline{} = \underline{}$$

$$\frac{11}{16} - \frac{7}{16} = \underline{} = \underline{}$$

$$\frac{5}{9} - \frac{2}{9} = \underline{} = \underline{}$$

$$\frac{7}{13} - \frac{5}{13} = \underline{}$$

$$\frac{14}{15} - \frac{4}{15} = \underline{} = \underline{}$$

$$\frac{12}{13} - \frac{8}{13} = \underline{}$$

$$\frac{4}{5} - \frac{1}{5} = \underline{}$$

$$\frac{9}{10} - \frac{7}{10} = \underline{} = \underline{}$$

$$\frac{5}{6} - \frac{1}{6} = \underline{} = \underline{}$$

$$\frac{8}{17} - \frac{4}{17} = \underline{}$$

$$\frac{11}{18} - \frac{8}{18} = \underline{} = \underline{}$$

$$\frac{4}{5} - \frac{3}{5} = \underline{}$$

$$\frac{9}{11} - \frac{5}{11} = \underline{}$$

$$\frac{7}{8} - \frac{5}{8} = \underline{} = \underline{}$$

$$\frac{3}{16} - \frac{2}{16} = \underline{}$$

$$\frac{7}{12} - \frac{5}{12} = \underline{} = \underline{}$$

$$\frac{8}{14} - \frac{5}{14} = \underline{}$$

$$\frac{9}{10} - \frac{3}{10} = \underline{} = \underline{}$$

$$\frac{17}{20} - \frac{6}{20} = \underline{}$$

Volumes of cubes

This cube is 1 cm long, 1 cm high, and 1 cm wide. We say it has a volume of 1 cubic centimeter (1 cm³).

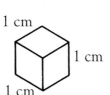

If we put 4 of these cubes together the new shape has a volume of 4 cm³.

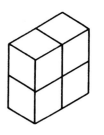

These shapes are made of 1 cm³ cubes. What are their volumes?

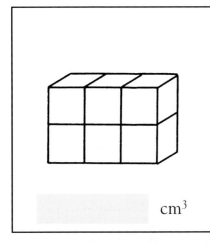

____ cm³

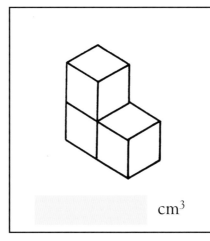

____ cm³

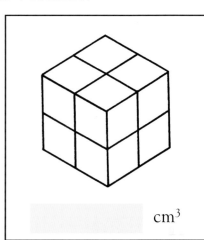

____ cm³

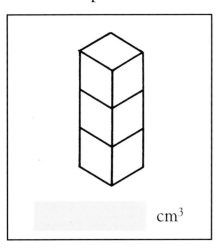

____ cm³

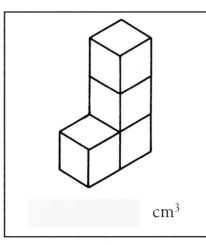

____ cm³

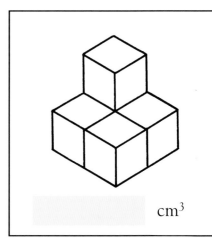

____ cm³

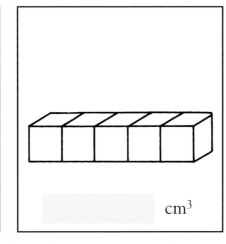

____ cm³

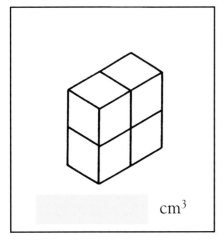

____ cm³

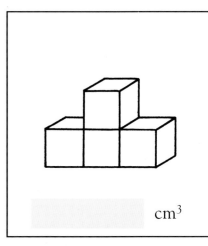

____ cm³

Answer Section with Parents' Notes

Grade 3
ages 8–9
Workbook

This section provides answers to all the activities in the book. These pages will enable you to mark your children's work, or they can be used by your children if they prefer to do their own marking.

The notes for each page help to explain common errors and problems and, where appropriate, indicate the kind of practice needed to ensure that your children understand where and how they have made errors.

Numbers

Write the number in words.
4,567   Four thousand, five hundred sixty-seven

Write the number in standard form.
Two thousand, four hundred eighty-six.   2,486

Write each number in words.

7,285	Seven thousand, two hundred eighty-five
3,926	Three thousand, nine hundred twenty-six
8,143	Eight thousand, one hundred forty-three
4,538	Four thousand, five hundred thirty-eight

Write the numbers in standard form.

Two thousand, six hundred forty-seven.	2,647	Six thousand, one hundred fifty-eight.	6,158
Five thousand, two hundred seventy-three.	5,273	Seven thousand, three hundred eighty-two.	7,382
Nine thousand, five hundred sixty-one.	9,561	Eight thousand, seven hundred twenty-four.	8,724

Write each number in words.

7,207	Seven thousand, two hundred seven
4,046	Four thousand forty-six
5,008	Five thousand eight
8,309	Eight thousand, three hundred nine

Write the numbers in standard form.

Three thousand twenty-one.	3,021	Five thousand, two hundred seven.	5,207
Eight thousand two.	8,002		

Children may use zeros incorrectly in numbers. In word form, zeros are omitted, but children should take care to include them when writing numbers in standard form.

Place value

12,645 is the same as:
1 ten thousand, 2 thousands, 6 hundreds, 4 tens, 5 ones
or
12,645 is the same as 10,000 + 2,000 + 600 + 40 + 5

Write the correct number in the space.

7,945 = 7,000 + 900 + 40 + 5   6,312 = 6,000 + 300 + 10 + 2

4,749 = 4,000 + 700 + 40 + 9   5,263 = 5,000 + 200 + 60 + 3

8,294 = 8,000 + 200 + 90 + 4   13,742 = 10,000 + 3,000 + 700 + 40 + 2

2,176 = 2,000 + 100 + 70 + 6   17,375 = 10,000 + 7,000 + 300 + 70 + 5

7,264 = 7,000 + 200 + 60 + 4   14,286 = 10,000 + 4,000 + 200 + 80 + 6

Write the number that is the same as:

Six thousand, two hundred eighty-four	6,284
Twelve thousand, one hundred sixty-nine	12,169
Fifteen thousand, eight hundred seventy-two	15,872
Two thousand sixty-six	2,066
Seventeen thousand, four hundred twenty-seven	17,427
Nine thousand forty-three	9,043
Sixteen thousand, two hundred ten	16,210
Twenty-one thousand three	21,003
Eleven thousand eleven	11,011
Thirteen thousand thirty-eight	13,038

Look at these numbers: 6 8 3 0 7

Arrange these digits to make the largest number you can.	87,630
Arrange these digits to make the smallest number you can.	30,678

Again, make sure that children understand the use of zeros in numbers. For example, children should understand that they should not write 03,678 or 36,780 as the answer to the final question of the page.

Multiplying by 10

Multiply each number by 10.

7	70	12	120	3	30	13	130

Multiply each of these numbers by 10.

6	60	14	140	12	120	17	170	20	200
9	90	15	150	13	130	2	20	23	230
1	10	19	190	24	240	28	280	22	220
5	50	3	30	26	260	11	110	25	250

Multiply each of these numbers by 10.

20	200	17	170	12	120	14	140	6	60
23	230	2	20	13	130	15	150	9	90
22	220	28	280	24	240	19	190	1	10
25	250	11	110	26	260	3	30	5	50

Multiply each of these numbers by 10.

56	560	48	480	67	670	39	390	82	820
69	690	32	320	74	740	57	570	43	430
95	950	63	630	55	550	77	770	40	400

Multiply each of these numbers by 10.

38	380	67	670	48	480	56	560	74	740
32	320	69	690	82	820	63	630	95	950
43	430	57	570	99	990	40	400	77	770

Children should realize that multiplying by 10 means adding a zero to a number. The ones become tens and the tens become hundreds, leaving a blank space—the zero—in the ones column.

Ordering

Write these numbers in order, from smallest to largest.

4,675	3,830	8,390	2,617
2,617	3,830	4,675	8,390

Write these numbers in order, from smallest to largest.

1,574	4,683	7,847	2,563	1,574	2,563	4,683	7,847
7,473	2,670	5,371	8,421	2,670	5,371	7,473	8,421
8,389	3,726	7,995	1,843	1,843	3,726	7,995	8,389
3,562	7,264	8,923	5,674	3,562	5,674	7,264	8,923
6,853	4,567	5,684	2,557	2,557	4,567	5,684	6,853
3,241	3,785	9,538	7,647	3,241	3,785	7,647	9,538

Write these numbers in order, from smallest to largest.

5,705	6,390	4,903	2,704	2,704	4,903	5,705	6,390
3,067	2,809	6,330	5,035	2,809	3,067	5,035	6,330
4,207	7,380	5,005	3,027	3,027	4,207	5,005	7,380
8,045	3,028	7,036	1,006	1,006	3,028	7,036	8,045
9,004	3,075	6,003	3,800	3,075	3,800	6,003	9,004

Write these numbers in order, from smallest to largest.

5,780	365	968	1,089	365	968	1,089	5,780
7,890	4,078	678	999	678	999	4,078	7,890
4,950	1,230	845	1,002	845	1,002	1,230	4,950
8,004	4,800	840	3,980	840	3,980	4,800	8,004
679	375	5,078	3,001	375	679	3,001	5,078

Children who do not understand the place value of digits may make errors in thinking that a 'hundreds' number is bigger than a 'thousands' number because the first digit is higher.

Rounding

What is 132 rounded to the nearest ten?

100 110 120 130 140 150 160 170 180

132 rounded to the nearest 10 is 130.

Round each number to the nearest ten.

247	250	306	310	493	490	733	730
834	830	651	650	379	380	215	220

Round each number to the nearest ten.

Scale	Answer
120 130 140 150 160 170 180 190 200	160
320 330 340 350 360 370 380 390 400	350
220 230 240 250 260 270 280 290 300	270
480 490 500 510 520 530 540 550 560	550
700 710 720 730 740 750 760 770 780	720
60 70 80 90 100 110 120 130 140	110
450 460 470 480 490 500 510 520 530	500
170 180 190 200 210 220 230 240 250	250
640 650 660 670 680 690 700 710 720	700
500 510 520 530 540 550 560 570 580	530

Children should remember that numbers ending in 5 or greater are rounded up.

Polygons

Match the polygon with a solid figure.

Circle the octagon.

Circle the rectangle.

Match the polygon to the solid object in which it appears.

hexagon   octagon   rectangle   pentagon   triangle

Children can count the sides of the polygons to match them with other polygons or with the names that identify them.

Identifying patterns

Continue each pattern.

0	6	12	18	24	30
0	7	14	21	28	35
60	52	44	36	28	20

Continue each pattern.

3	9	15	21	27	33	39	45
2	9	16	23	30	37	44	51
1	9	17	25	33	41	49	57
7	15	23	31	39	47	55	63
7	13	19	25	31	37	43	49
7	12	17	22	27	32	37	42

Continue each pattern.

71	65	59	53	47	41	35	29
90	82	74	66	58	50	42	34
56	49	42	35	28	21	14	7
72	66	60	54	48	42	36	30
96	88	80	72	64	56	48	40
48	42	36	30	24	18	12	6

Continue each pattern.

36	43	50	57	64	71	78	85
61	55	49	43	37	31	25	19
0	7	14	21	28	35	42	49
7	14	21	28	35	42	49	56
4	12	20	28	36	44	52	60

It may help to point out that some patterns show an increase and some a decrease. Children should double-check that the operation that turns the first number into the second also turns the second number into the third. They can then continue the pattern.

Odds and evens

Multiply the odd number by the odd number. $7 \times 5 = 35$

Multiply the even number by the even number. $6 \times 8 = 48$

Multiply the odd number by the odd number.

$5 \times 7 = 35$	$3 \times 9 = 27$	$1 \times 5 = 5$	$3 \times 5 = 15$
$7 \times 3 = 21$	$9 \times 7 = 63$	$7 \times 1 = 7$	$7 \times 7 = 49$
$3 \times 3 = 9$	$3 \times 1 = 3$	$5 \times 9 = 45$	$1 \times 1 = 1$
$5 \times 3 = 15$	$9 \times 9 = 81$	$5 \times 5 = 25$	$7 \times 9 = 63$

What do you notice about the numbers in your answer boxes?
They are all odd numbers.

Multiply the even number by the even number.

$2 \times 8 = 16$	$6 \times 4 = 24$	$6 \times 10 = 60$	$2 \times 6 = 12$
$4 \times 4 = 16$	$8 \times 2 = 16$	$6 \times 8 = 48$	$6 \times 6 = 36$
$4 \times 6 = 24$	$10 \times 4 = 40$	$4 \times 8 = 32$	$12 \times 12 = 144$
$2 \times 2 = 4$	$8 \times 6 = 48$	$6 \times 2 = 12$	$10 \times 10 = 100$

What do you notice about the numbers in your answer boxes?
They are all even numbers.

Multiply the odd number by the even number.

$3 \times 6 = 18$	$10 \times 5 = 50$	$7 \times 8 = 56$	$2 \times 9 = 18$
$4 \times 7 = 28$	$3 \times 10 = 30$	$4 \times 9 = 36$	$10 \times 7 = 70$
$5 \times 8 = 40$	$6 \times 9 = 54$	$8 \times 5 = 40$	$8 \times 7 = 56$
$9 \times 6 = 54$	$6 \times 3 = 18$	$9 \times 4 = 36$	$10 \times 3 = 30$

What do you notice about the numbers in your answer boxes?
They are all even numbers.

If children fail to notice any similarity in the products, suggest that they check to see if all of the products are even or if all are odd.

Addition fact families

Circle the number sentence that is in the same fact family.

$12 - 5 = 7$ $5 + 7 = 12$	$12 - 4 = 8$	$(7 + 5 = 12)$	$12 + 12 = 24$
$10 - 8 = 2$ $8 + 2 = 10$	$8 - 6 = 2$	$(2 + 8 = 10)$	$8 - 2 = 6$

Circle the number sentence that is in the same fact family.

$7 + 8 = 15$ $8 + 7 = 15$	$7 + 5 = 12$	$15 - 8 = 7$	$8 - 7 = 1$
$17 - 6 = 11$ $11 + 6 = 17$	$17 - 11 = 6$	$17 + 6 = 23$	$5 + 6 = 11$
$14 - 5 = 9$ $14 - 9 = 5$	$9 - 3 = 6$	$14 + 9 = 23$	$5 + 9 = 14$
$9 + 7 = 16$ $7 + 9 = 16$	$16 - 9 = 7$	$16 + 7 = 23$	$9 - 7 = 2$
$19 - 9 = 10$ $19 - 10 = 9$	$9 + 3 = 12$	$9 + 10 = 19$	$18 - 8 = 10$
$4 + 7 = 11$ $11 - 4 = 7$	$11 + 4 = 15$	$7 + 4 = 11$	$7 + 7 = 14$

Write the fact family for each group of numbers.

5, 6, 11	6, 10, 4	5, 13, 8
$5 + 6 = 11$	$6 + 4 = 10$	$5 + 8 = 13$
$6 + 5 = 11$	$4 + 6 = 10$	$8 + 5 = 13$
$11 - 6 = 5$	$10 - 6 = 4$	$13 - 8 = 5$
$11 - 5 = 6$	$10 - 4 = 6$	$13 - 5 = 8$

Children should understand that subtraction "undoes" addition. You may want to use counters to show the addition fact families.

Fractions

Write the fraction for the part that is shaded.

How many shaded circles? 3

How many circles? 8

So, the fraction of circles shaded $= \frac{3}{8}$ numerator / denominator

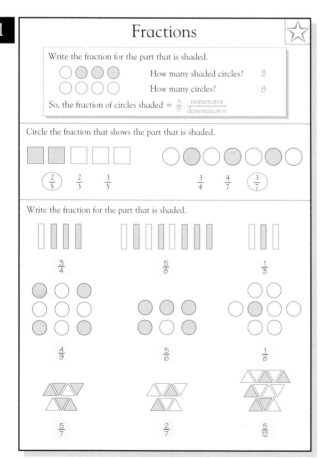

If children have difficulty, point out that the denominator (the bottom number of the fraction) is the total number of parts, and the numerator (the top number of the fraction) is the number of shaded parts.

Fractions

Color $\frac{3}{4}$ of each shape.

Color $\frac{2}{3}$ of each shape.

Color $\frac{3}{4}$ of each shape.

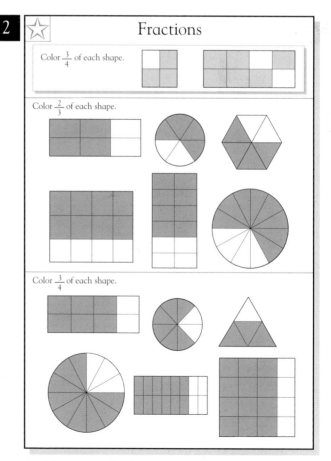

Children may shade in any combination of the sections as long as the total shaded area represents the fraction.

Ordering decimals

Put these decimals in order from smallest to largest.

| 0.6 | 0.3 | 0.7 | 0.5 | 0.9 | 0.3 | 0.5 | 0.6 | 0.7 | 0.9 |

Put these decimals in order from smallest to largest.

0.2	0.8	0.5	0.1	0.9	0.1	0.2	0.5	0.8	0.9
0.4	0.2	0.1	0.7	0.6	0.1	0.2	0.4	0.6	0.7
0.6	0.3	0.2	0.9	0.1	0.1	0.2	0.3	0.6	0.9
0.5	0.6	0.1	0.4	0.2	0.1	0.2	0.4	0.5	0.6
0.3	0.5	0.7	0.9	0.6	0.3	0.5	0.6	0.7	0.9

Put these decimals in order from smallest to largest.

1.6	1.2	1.9	1.5	1.8	1.2	1.5	1.6	1.8	1.9
1.3	1.1	1.7	1.9	1.5	1.1	1.3	1.5	1.7	1.9
1.7	1.8	1.1	1.3	1.9	1.1	1.3	1.7	1.8	1.9
1.5	1.6	1.9	1.2	1.4	1.2	1.4	1.5	1.6	1.9
1.8	1.4	1.2	1.0	1.9	1.0	1.2	1.4	1.8	1.9

Put these decimals in order from smallest to largest.

2.8	2.0	2.3	2.5	2.7	2.0	2.3	2.5	2.7	2.8
3.7	3.4	3.9	3.6	3.2	3.2	3.4	3.6	3.7	3.9
4.2	7.5	2.6	1.4	3.5	1.4	2.6	3.5	4.2	7.5
2.8	3.4	4.6	1.8	2.3	1.8	2.3	2.8	3.4	4.6
5.3	4.8	2.9	1.9	3.5	1.9	2.9	3.5	4.8	5.3

In the final section, children must compare not only the decimal parts of the numbers but also the whole number parts. For example, they should realize that 3.4 is greater than 1.8.

Adding

Write the answer between the lines.

34	28	75
+ 42	+ 11	+ 14
76	39	89

Write the answer between the lines.

24	36	45	61
+ 14	+ 23	+ 13	+ 17
38	59	58	78

63	71	48	53
+ 14	+ 16	+ 10	+ 16
77	87	58	69

60	46	54	83
+ 36	+ 21	+ 33	+ 6
96	67	87	89

28	53	74	38
+ 31	+ 36	+ 25	+ 21
59	89	99	59

57	65	79	47
+ 22	+ 14	+ 10	+ 12
79	79	89	59

35	46	57	68
+ 13	+ 22	+ 31	+ 40
48	68	88	108

44	53	26	62
+ 25	+ 34	+ 33	+ 17
69	87	59	79

50	47	66	45
+ 37	+ 11	+ 22	+ 32
87	58	88	77

These are straightforward addition problems with no regrouping needed. This page prepares children for the next page, which involves regrouping.

Adding

Write the answer between the lines.

15	25	55
+ 20	+ 40	+ 5
35	65	60

Write the answer between the lines.

50	70	90	20
+ 25	+ 15	+ 5	+ 45
75	85	95	65

65	25	35	85
+ 30	+ 40	+ 50	+ 10
95	65	85	95

30	60	55	75
+ 25	+ 35	+ 30	+ 20
55	95	85	95

25	45	65	15
+ 15	+ 5	+ 25	+ 15
40	50	90	30

75	15	35	45
+ 10	+ 25	+ 25	+ 15
85	40	60	60

65	45	5	55
+ 35	+ 25	+ 65	+ 35
100	70	70	90

35	45	15	75
+ 45	+ 35	+ 30	+ 5
80	80	45	80

5	50	45	80
+ 95	+ 35	+ 45	+ 15
100	85	90	95

Children must remember that when they regroup, they must add 1 to the tens column.

Subtracting

Write the answer between the lines.

36	25	57
− 14	− 13	− 26
22	12	31

Write the answer between the lines.

27	35	47	63
− 14	− 12	− 32	− 20
13	23	15	43

54	38	47	56
− 23	− 16	− 12	− 21
31	22	35	35

44	57	65	78
− 32	− 24	− 32	− 35
12	33	33	43

66	75	84	93
− 26	− 35	− 64	− 33
40	40	20	60

87	76	67	49
− 34	− 45	− 33	− 28
53	31	34	21

56	73	47	54
− 35	− 40	− 25	− 32
21	33	22	22

79	45	76	75
− 38	− 21	− 43	− 12
41	24	33	63

43	55	67	53
− 30	− 12	− 33	− 12
13	43	34	41

Children will not need to regroup to subtract the numbers on this page. Discuss any mistakes with them to determine whether they are due to lapses of concentration or a basic misunderstanding of subtraction.

Subtracting

Write the answer between the lines.

23 − 16 **7**	34 − 17 **17**	43 − 18 **25**

Write the answer between the lines.

36 − 28 **8**	41 − 35 **6**	53 − 46 **7**	65 − 47 **18**
44 − 27 **17**	35 − 18 **17**	62 − 24 **38**	73 − 44 **29**
56 − 46 **10**	37 − 18 **19**	43 − 26 **17**	68 − 49 **19**
34 − 12 **22**	45 − 18 **27**	63 − 46 **17**	37 − 15 **22**
60 − 43 **17**	47 − 24 **23**	63 − 40 **23**	86 − 29 **57**
73 − 34 **39**	56 − 47 **9**	48 − 36 **12**	80 − 45 **35**
54 − 38 **16**	70 − 45 **25**	37 − 18 **19**	53 − 26 **27**
34 − 18 **16**	71 − 44 **27**	25 − 17 **8**	83 − 29 **54**

Most of the problems on this page require regrouping. Make sure that children do not neglect to regroup when it is necessary.

Choosing the operation

Write either + or − in the box to make each problem correct.

15 **+** 25 = 40   30 **−** 8 = 22   50 **−** 25 = 25

Write either + or − in the box to make each problem correct.

45 **−** 12 = 33   48 **−** 14 = 34   31 **+** 15 = 46

17 **+** 13 = 30   60 **−** 35 = 25   70 **−** 35 = 35

27 **−** 15 = 12   26 **+** 18 = 44   50 **+** 12 = 62

65 **−** 25 = 40   80 **−** 35 = 45   63 **−** 23 = 40

Write either + or − in the box to make each problem correct.

12 yd **+** 5 yd = 27 yd   34 ft **−** 18 ft = 16 ft

29 cm **−** 17 cm = 12 cm   42 in. **+** 20 in. = 62 in.

28 in. **+** 28 in. = 56 in.   60 cm **−** 15 cm = 45 cm

40 ft **−** 8 ft = 32 ft   90 cm **−** 35 cm = 55 cm

28 cm **+** 15 cm = 43 cm   70 yd **−** 29 yd = 41 yd

90 in. **−** 12 in. = 78 in.   28 m **+** 21 m = 49 m

Write the answer in the box.

I start with 12 apples and end up with 18 apples. How many have I added or subtracted?	**added 6**	A number is added to 14 and the result is 20. What number has been added?	**6**
I start with 14 pens. I finish up with 9 pens. How many pens have I lost or gained?	**lost 5**	I take a number away from 30 and have 12 left. What number did I take away?	**18**

Children should realize that if the answer is greater than the first number, they should add, and if the answer is smaller than the first number, they should subtract. They should check some of their answers to make sure that they are correct.

Multiplying

Solve the problems.

12 × 2 **24**	51 × 3 **153**	30 × 4 **120**	35 × 2 **70**

Solve the problems.

11 × 4 **44**	13 × 3 **39**	14 × 2 **28**	12 × 4 **48**
32 × 4 **128**	23 × 3 **69**	41 × 4 **164**	33 × 2 **66**
30 × 3 **90**	40 × 2 **80**	12 × 3 **36**	24 × 2 **48**

Solve the problems.

23 × 2 **46**	32 × 3 **96**	41 × 3 **123**	44 × 2 **88**
21 × 4 **84**	22 × 4 **88**	30 × 2 **60**	50 × 2 **100**
14 × 1 **14**	25 × 2 **50**	42 × 2 **84**	34 × 2 **68**
16 × 1 **16**	13 × 2 **26**	24 × 3 **72**	31 × 3 **93**
14 × 3 **42**	15 × 3 **45**	22 × 3 **66**	32 × 2 **64**

Make sure that children multiply the ones first, and then the tens. None of the problems on this page require regrouping.

Multiplying

Solve each problem.

16 × 4 = (10 × 4) + (6 × 4)
= 40 + 24
= 64

10   6
× 4   × 4
40   **24**

40 + 24 = 64

Solve each problem.

18 × 4 **72**	15 × 6 **90**
17 × 5 **85**	14 × 7 **98**
19 × 3 **57**	16 × 6 **96**
23 × 4 **92**	26 × 5 **130**
24 × 6 **144**	27 × 4 **108**
32 × 7 **224**	34 × 4 **136**

Some children may use the distributive property, as shown in the example, to multiply. Others may set up the problems in vertical format, and multiply with regrouping. Both methods are acceptable.

Dividing

Write the answer to each division problem.

$27 \div 4 =$ 6 r 3 $36 \div 10 =$ 3 r 6   5)38 = 7 r 3
$\underline{-35}$
3

Write the answer to each division problem.

$43 \div 10 =$ 4 r 3 $31 \div 4 =$ 7 r 3 $19 \div 2 =$ 9 r 1 $42 \div 5 =$ 8 r 2

$27 \div 10 =$ 2 r 7 $42 \div 4 =$ 10 r 2 $21 \div 2 =$ 10 r 1 $35 \div 5 =$ 7

$61 \div 10 =$ 6 r 1 $26 \div 4 =$ 6 r 2 $17 \div 2 =$ 8 r 1 $46 \div 5 =$ 9 r 1

$90 \div 10 =$ 9 $47 \div 4 =$ 11 r 3 $13 \div 2 =$ 6 r 1 $29 \div 5 =$ 5 r 4

Write the answer in the box.

5 r 2   5   5 r 3   8 r 1   7
5)27   3)15   4)23   2)17   3)21
-25   -15   -20   -16   -21
  2   0   3   1   0

4   7 r 7   6 r 1   11   5 r 1
2)8   10)77   5)31   3)33   2)11
-8   -70   -30   -33   -10
 0   7   1   0   1

Write the answer in the box.

What is the remainder when 15 is divided by 2?   1

How many groups of 5 are there in 45?   9

How many groups of 3 are there in 21 and what is the remainder?   7, none

What is the remainder when 63 is divided by 10?   3

Divide 27 by 3.   9

How many groups of 4 are there in 26?   6

Solving division problems tests children's knowledge of times tables. If they have difficulty with long division, "walk" them through a few examples.

Dividing

Write the answer to each division problem.

$14 \div 3 =$ 4 r 2 $18 \div 5 =$ 3 r 3   2)9 = 4 r 1
$\underline{-8}$
1

Write the answer in the box.

$17 \div 3 =$ 5 r 2 $24 \div 5 =$ 4 r 4 $17 \div 10 =$ 1 r 7 $29 \div 4 =$ 7 r 1

$13 \div 3 =$ 4 r 1 $19 \div 5 =$ 3 r 4 $58 \div 10 =$ 5 r 8 $36 \div 4 =$ 9

$24 \div 3 =$ 8 $37 \div 5 =$ 7 r 2 $44 \div 10 =$ 4 r 4 $18 \div 4 =$ 4 r 2

$31 \div 3 =$ 10 r 1 $29 \div 5 =$ 5 r 4 $80 \div 10 =$ 8 $24 \div 4 =$ 6

Write the answer in the box.

5 r 1   3 r 2   4 r 1   3   8 r 1
3)16   5)17   10)41   4)12   3)25
-15   -15   -40   -12   -24
  1   2   1   0   1

3   2 r 4   6 r 4   5   6 r 9
3)9   5)14   10)64   4)20   10)69
-9   -10   -60   -20   -60
 0   4   4   0   9

Write the answer in the box.

What is the remainder when 36 is divided by 10?   6

How many whole sets of 3 are there in 16?   5

How many sets of 4 are there in 30 and what is the remainder?   7 r 2

What is the remainder when 44 is divided by 40?   4

Divide 26 by 3.   8 r 2

Divide 40 by 6.   6 r 4

As with the previous page, most of the questions involve remainders. Make sure children do not feel they have to include a remainder if there is none. In the final section, the question that asks how many whole sets there are does not require a remainder.

Choosing the operation

Write either x or ÷ in the box to make the product correct.

$12 \div 2 = 6$ $12 \times 2 = 24$ $10 \div 2 = 5$

Write either x or ÷ in the box to make the product correct.

$18 \div 3 = 6$ $20 \div 10 = 2$ $6 \times 3 = 18$

$2 \times 9 = 18$ $20 \div 2 = 10$ $12 \div 4 = 3$

$12 \times 10 = 120$ $24 \div 3 = 8$ $30 \div 10 = 3$

$27 \div 3 = 9$ $18 \div 3 = 6$ $14 \times 2 = 28$

$16 \div 4 = 4$ $24 \div 4 = 6$ $30 \div 3 = 10$

$3 \times 8 = 24$ $5 \times 10 = 50$ $6 \div 2 = 3$

Write either x or ÷ in the box to make the product correct.

$27 \text{ cm} \div 3 = 9 \text{ cm}$ $40 \text{ in.} \div 10 = 4 \text{ in.}$ $15 \text{ cm} \div 3 = 5 \text{ cm}$

$18 \text{ in.} \div 2 = 9 \text{ in.}$ $4 \text{ m} \times 5 = 20 \text{ m}$ $10 \text{ cm} \times 4 = 40 \text{ cm}$

$30 \text{ in.} \div 10 = 3 \text{ in.}$ $50 \text{ ft} \div 5 = 10 \text{ ft}$ $60 \text{ in.} \div 2 = 30 \text{ in.}$

$5 \text{ yd} \times 8 = 40 \text{ yd}$ $4 \text{ cm} \div 2 = 2 \text{ cm}$ $4 \text{ m} \times 2 = 8 \text{ m}$

$20 \text{ cm} \div 10 = 2 \text{ cm}$ $20 \text{ in.} \div 4 = 5 \text{ in.}$ $20 \text{ cm} \times 2 = 40 \text{ cm}$

$12 \text{ m} \div 2 = 6 \text{ m}$ $1 \text{ ft} \times 10 = 10 \text{ ft}$ $4 \text{ yd} \times 3 = 12 \text{ yd}$

Write the answer in the box.

Which number multiplied by 3 equals 24?   8

Which number divided by 10 equals 7?   70

Which number divided by 8 equals 5?   40

Which number multiplied by 6 equals 6?   1

Which number multiplied by 9 equals 36?   4

Which number multiplied by 5 equals 30?   6

Children will probably realize that if the answer is greater than the first number, they should multiply, and if the answer is smaller than the first number, they should divide. They should check some of the answers to make sure they are correct.

Word problems

Write the answer in the box.
I multiply a number by 6 and the answer is 24.
What number did I begin with?   4

Write the answer in the box.

A number multiplied by 7 equals 35. What is the number?   5

I divide a number by 10 and the answer is 3. What number did I divide?   30

I multiply a number by 4 and the answer is 20. What is the number I multiplied?   5

After dividing a piece of wood into four equal sections, each section is 4 in. long. How long was the piece of wood I started with?   16 in.

A number multiplied by 6 gives the answer 24. What is the number?   4

Some money is divided into five equal amounts. Each amount is 10 cents. How much money was there before it was divided?   50¢

I multiply a number by 9 and the result is 45. What number was multiplied?   5

A number divided by 6 is 3. What number was divided?   18

Three children share 18 peanuts equally among themselves. How many peanuts does each child receive?   6

A number divided by 4 is 8. What is the number?   32

I multiply a number by 6 and the answer is 30. What is the number?   5

Four sets of a number equal 16. What is the number?   4

A number divided by 5 is 5. What is the number?   25

A child divides a number by 8 and gets 2. What number was divided?   16

Three groups of a number equal 27. What is the number?   9

I multiply a number by 10 and the result is 100. What is the number?   10

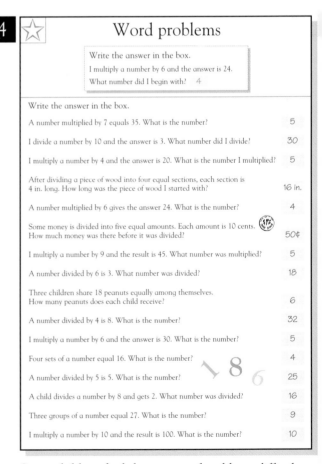

Some children find these sorts of problems difficult even if they are good with times tables and division. Many of the problems require children to perform the inverse operation to the one named. Ask them to check their answers to make sure they are correct.

Word problems

Write the answer in the box.

A child is given four dimes. How much money does she have altogether? 40¢

Write the answer in the box.

A box contains 6 eggs. How many boxes would I need to buy to have 18 eggs? **3**

When Peter multiplies his apartment number by 3, the result is 75. What is his apartment number? **25**

A boy is given three bags of candy. There are 20 pieces in each bag. How many pieces of candy does the boy have in total? **60**

One photograph costs $1.80. How much will two photographs cost? **$3.60**

Four lifeboats carry a total of 100 people. How many people are in each boat? **25**

A dog buries 20 bones on Monday, 30 bones on Tuesday, and 40 bones on Wednesday. How many bones has the dog buried altogether? **90**

A shepherd had 200 sheep but 70 were lost in a snowstorm. How many sheep does the shepherd have left? **130**

Three women win the lottery and share $900 equally among themselves. How much does each woman receive? **$300**

A truck contains 50 barrels of oil. It delivers 27 barrels to one garage. How many barrels are left on the truck? **23**

A car trip is supposed to be 70 miles long but the car breaks down half-way. How far has the car gone when it breaks down? **35 miles**

Andrej has a collection of 150 baseball cards. He sells 30 of them to a friend. How many cards does he have left? **120**

A teacher has 32 children in her class. 13 children are out with the flu. How many children are left in class? **19**

Children will need to think carefully about how they will solve each question. If they have difficulty, talk each problem through with them.

Problems with measures

Which would be the best unit to use for the length of a worm? inch

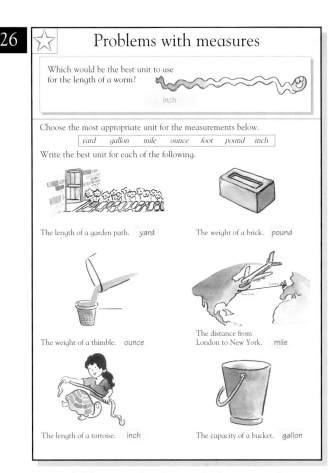

Choose the most appropriate unit for the measurements below.

| yard | gallon | mile | ounce | foot | pound | inch |

Write the best unit for each of the following.

The length of a garden path. **yard**

The weight of a brick. **pound**

The weight of a thimble. **ounce**

The distance from London to New York. **mile**

The length of a tortoise. **inch**

The capacity of a bucket. **gallon**

Most children are familiar with the units of measurement given. If necessary, give other examples of items that would be measured using these units.

Telling time

What time is shown by these clocks?

28 minutes to 7   3:14   14 minutes past 3

What time is shown by these clocks?

13 minutes to 8

10 past 4

5:52

8 minutes to 6

twenty-six minutes past 6

12 minutes to 10

10:54

6 minutes to 11

24 minutes to 2

12:08

8 minutes past 12

Because of the popularity of digital watches, children could write 7:47 for the first answer and be correct, although the convention is to say the minutes to an hour or past an hour. Children should know both ways of saying the time.

Telling time

Draw the time on each clock face.
Twenty-six minutes past four.   4:26

Draw the time on each clock face.

Twelve minutes to eight   7:48

Twenty to nine   8:40

Seventeen minutes past four   4:17

Eleven minutes to six   5:49

Twenty-seven minutes past twelve   12:27

Make sure that children can position the hands or numbers on the clocks. Show them that the space between numbers on an analog clock is divided into five minutes. The hour hand can be drawn in an approximate position between the correct numbers.

Tables and graphs

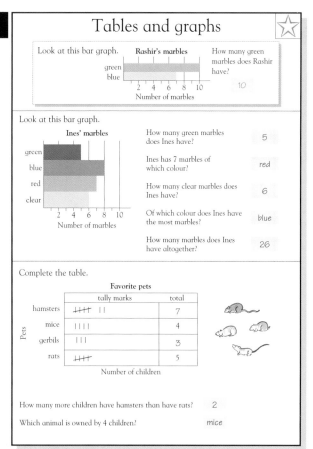

Look at this bar graph.

Rashir's marbles

green

blue

2 4 6 8 10
Number of marbles

How many green marbles does Rashir have?

10

Look at this bar graph.

Ines' marbles

green

blue

red

clear

2 4 6 8 10
Number of marbles

How many green marbles does Ines have? — 5

Ines has 7 marbles of which colour? — red

How many clear marbles does Ines have? — 6

Of which colour does Ines have the most marbles? — blue

How many marbles does Ines have altogether? — 26

Complete the table.

Favorite pets

Pets	tally marks	total
hamsters	⊥⊥⊥⊥ ‖	7
mice	‖‖‖‖	4
gerbils	‖‖‖	3
rats	⊥⊥⊥⊥	5

Number of children

How many more children have hamsters than have rats? — 2

Which animal is owned by 4 children? — mice

The first section requires children to notice that the divisions on the scale are in twos rather than ones. To answer some of the questions about the bar graph, children will have to add and compare data.

Necessary information

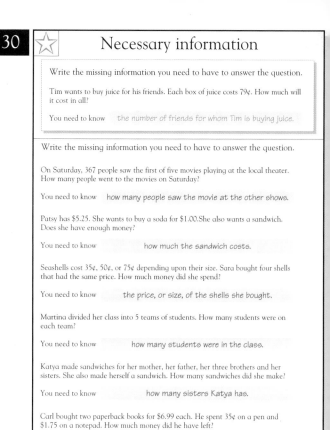

Write the missing information you need to have to answer the question.

Tim wants to buy juice for his friends. Each box of juice costs 79¢. How much will it cost in all?

You need to know — *the number of friends for whom Tim is buying juice.*

Write the missing information you need to have to answer the question.

On Saturday, 367 people saw the first of five movies playing at the local theater. How many people went to the movies on Saturday?

You need to know — how many people saw the movie at the other shows.

Patsy has $5.25. She wants to buy a soda for $1.00. She also wants a sandwich. Does she have enough money?

You need to know — how much the sandwich costs.

Seashells cost 35¢, 50¢, or 75¢ depending upon their size. Sara bought four shells that had the same price. How much money did she spend?

You need to know — the price, or size, of the shells she bought.

Martina divided her class into 5 teams of students. How many students were on each team?

You need to know — how many students were in the class.

Katya made sandwiches for her mother, her father, her three brothers and her sisters. She also made herself a sandwich. How many sandwiches did she make?

You need to know — how many sisters Katya has.

Carl bought two paperback books for $6.99 each. He spent 35¢ on a pen and $1.75 on a notepad. How much money did he have left?

You need to know — how much money he started with.

Some children may read a problem and not know how to proceed. Suggest several pieces of information, one of which needs to be found to solve the problem. Help them understand how to identify the missing information.

Number pairs

Write the number pairs of the letter A.

A = (2,1)

Look at this grid and write the number pairs of each letter.

A = (4,6)   G = (0,6)

B = (3,1)   H = (4,2)

C = (2,5)   I = (3,3)

D = (0,3)   J = (2,3)

E = (1,4)   K = (5,1)

F = (5,4)   L = (1,6)

Use the grid to write the number pairs.

Write the number pairs of each corner of the square.

(1,3)   (1,7)   (5,7)   (5,3)

Write the number pairs of each corner of the triangle.

(4,0)   (8,0)   (8,4)

Make sure that children understand that the order of the number pairs is important. The first number is from the horizontal or *x*-axis, and the second number is from the vertical or *y*-axis.

2 times table

Count in 2s, color, and find a pattern.

1	2	3	4	5
6	7	8	9	10
11	12	13	14	15
16	17	18	19	20
21	22	23	24	25

Write the answers.

$1 \times 2 = 2$ $2 \times 2 = 4$ $3 \times 2 = 6$ $4 \times 2 = 8$

$5 \times 2 = 10$ $6 \times 2 = 12$ $7 \times 2 = 14$ $8 \times 2 = 16$

$9 \times 2 = 18$ $10 \times 2 = 20$

How many ears?

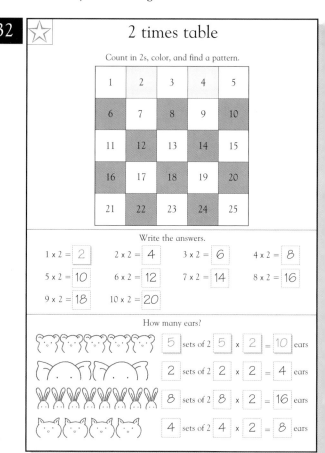

5 sets of 2 $5 \times 2 = 10$ ears

2 sets of 2 $2 \times 2 = 4$ ears

8 sets of 2 $8 \times 2 = 16$ ears

4 sets of 2 $4 \times 2 = 8$ ears

Multiplying by 2

Write the problems.

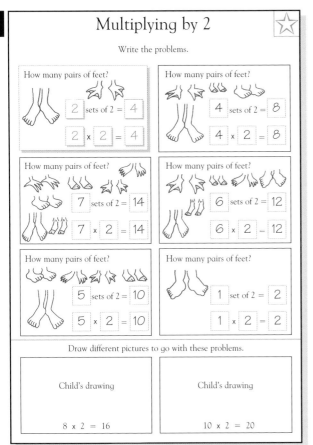

How many pairs of feet?

2 sets of 2 = 4

2 x 2 = 4

How many pairs of feet?

4 sets of 2 = 8

4 x 2 = 8

How many pairs of feet?

7 sets of 2 = 14

7 x 2 = 14

How many pairs of feet?

6 sets of 2 = 12

6 x 2 = 12

How many pairs of feet?

5 sets of 2 = 10

5 x 2 = 10

How many pairs of feet?

1 set of 2 = 2

1 x 2 = 2

Draw different pictures to go with these problems.

Child's drawing

8 x 2 = 16

Child's drawing

10 x 2 = 20

Dividing by 2

Share the eggs equally between the nests.

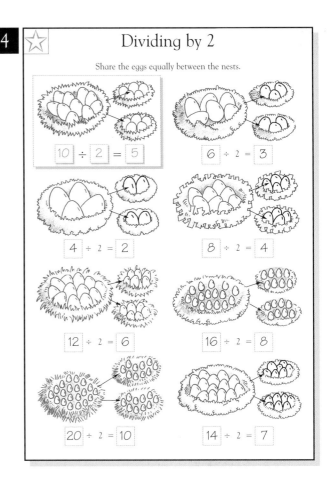

10 ÷ 2 = 5

6 ÷ 2 = 3

4 ÷ 2 = 2

8 ÷ 2 = 4

12 ÷ 2 = 6

16 ÷ 2 = 8

20 ÷ 2 = 10

14 ÷ 2 = 7

Using the 2 times table

Write the problems to match the stamps.

6 rows of 2

6 x 2 = 12

8 rows of 2

8 x 2 = 16

3 rows of 2

3 x 2 = 6

5 rows of 2

5 x 2 = 10

9 rows of 2

9 x 2 = 18

1 row of 2

1 x 2 = 2

Draw the stamps to match these problems.

3 x 2

4 x 2

2 x 2

7 x 2

Using the 2 times table

Each face stands for 2. Join each set of faces to the correct number.

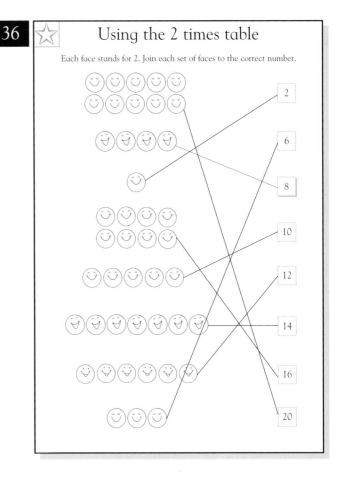

2

6

8

10

12

14

16

20

Using the 2 times table

How many eyes?

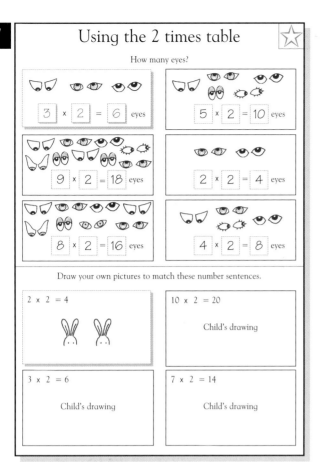

3 x 2 = 6 eyes

5 x 2 = 10 eyes

9 x 2 = 18 eyes

2 x 2 = 4 eyes

8 x 2 = 16 eyes

4 x 2 = 8 eyes

Draw your own pictures to match these number sentences.

2 x 2 = 4

10 x 2 = 20

Child's drawing

3 x 2 = 6

Child's drawing

7 x 2 = 14

Child's drawing

---

5 times table

Count in 5s, color, and find a pattern.

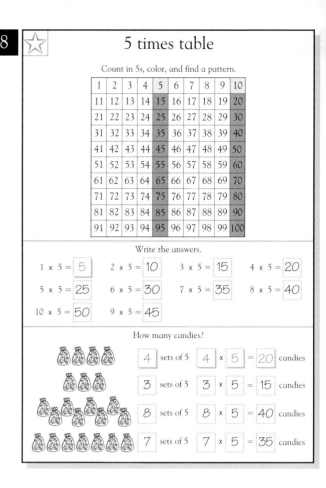

1	2	3	4	5	6	7	8	9	10
11	12	13	14	15	16	17	18	19	20
21	22	23	24	25	26	27	28	29	30
31	32	33	34	35	36	37	38	39	40
41	42	43	44	45	46	47	48	49	50
51	52	53	54	55	56	57	58	59	60
61	62	63	64	65	66	67	68	69	70
71	72	73	74	75	76	77	78	79	80
81	82	83	84	85	86	87	88	89	90
91	92	93	94	95	96	97	98	99	100

Write the answers.

1 x 5 = 5 2 x 5 = 10 3 x 5 = 15 4 x 5 = 20

5 x 5 = 25 6 x 5 = 30 7 x 5 = 35 8 x 5 = 40

10 x 5 = 50 9 x 5 = 45

How many candies?

4 sets of 5 4 x 5 = 20 candies

3 sets of 5 3 x 5 = 15 candies

8 sets of 5 8 x 5 = 40 candies

7 sets of 5 7 x 5 = 35 candies

Multiplying by 5

Draw a ring around rows of 5. Complete the problem.

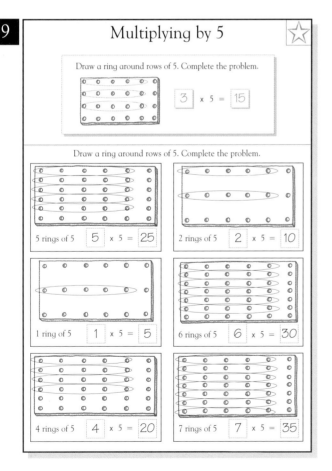

3 x 5 = 15

Draw a ring around rows of 5. Complete the problem.

5 rings of 5 5 x 5 = 25

2 rings of 5 2 x 5 = 10

1 ring of 5 1 x 5 = 5

6 rings of 5 6 x 5 = 30

4 rings of 5 4 x 5 = 20

7 rings of 5 7 x 5 = 35

Dividing by 5

Write a number sentence to show how many cubes are in each stack.

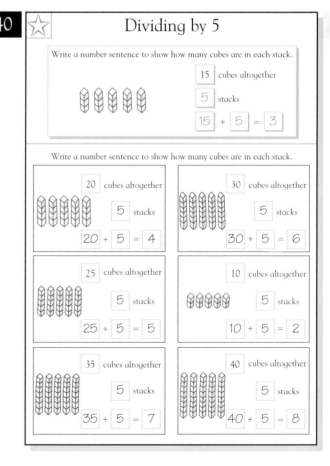

15 cubes altogether

5 stacks

15 ÷ 5 = 3

Write a number sentence to show how many cubes are in each stack.

20 cubes altogether

5 stacks

20 ÷ 5 = 4

30 cubes altogether

5 stacks

30 ÷ 5 = 6

25 cubes altogether

5 stacks

25 ÷ 5 = 5

10 cubes altogether

5 stacks

10 ÷ 5 = 2

35 cubes altogether

5 stacks

35 ÷ 5 = 7

40 cubes altogether

5 stacks

40 ÷ 5 = 8

Using the 5 times table

Write the number that is hiding under the star.

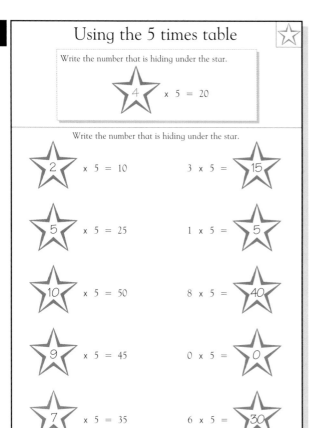

★ 4 x 5 = 20

Write the number that is hiding under the star.

★ 2 x 5 = 10   3 x 5 = ★ 15

★ 5 x 5 = 25   1 x 5 = ★ 5

★ 10 x 5 = 50   8 x 5 = ★ 40

★ 9 x 5 = 45   0 x 5 = ★ 0

★ 7 x 5 = 35   6 x 5 = ★ 30

Using the 5 times table

Each frog stands for 5. Join each set of frogs to the correct number.

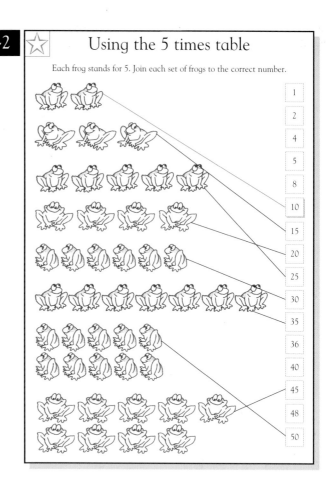

| 1 |
| 2 |
| 4 |
| 5 |
| 8 |
| 10 |
| 15 |
| 20 |
| 25 |
| 30 |
| 35 |
| 36 |
| 40 |
| 45 |
| 48 |
| 50 |

Using the 5 times table

How many altogether?

Georgia had 7 cats. Each cat had 5 kittens.
How many kittens were there altogether?   7 x 5 = 35 kittens

How many altogether?

Charlie had 6 boxes. He had 5 trains
in each box. How many trains did
he have altogether?   6 x 5 = 30 trains

Zoe had 3 jackets. Each jacket
had 5 buttons. How many
buttons were there altogether?   3 x 5 = 15 buttons

Yan had 8 fish tanks. Each tank had
5 fish in it. How many fish were
there altogether?   8 x 5 = 40 fish

How many in each?

Joe had 45 pencils and 5 pencil cases.
How many pencils were in each case?   45 ÷ 5 = 9 pencils

How many in each?

Heather had 10 mice and 5 cages.
How many mice were in each cage?   10 ÷ 5 = 2 mice

Shannon had 35 candies in 5 bags.
How many candies were in each bag?   35 ÷ 5 = 7 candies

Mark put 25 seeds into 5 pots.
How many seeds were in each pot?   25 ÷ 5 = 5 seeds

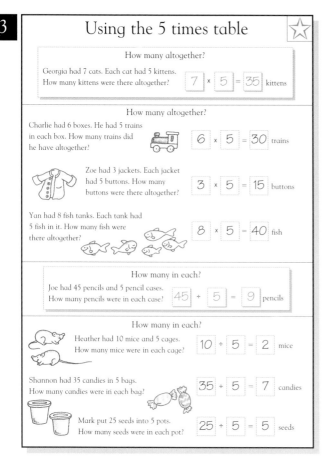

---

10 times table

Count in 10s, color, and find a pattern.

1	2	3	4	5	6	7	8	9	10
11	12	13	14	15	16	17	18	19	20
21	22	23	24	25	26	27	28	29	30
31	32	33	34	35	36	37	38	39	40
41	42	43	44	45	46	47	48	49	50
51	52	53	54	55	56	57	58	59	60
61	62	63	64	65	66	67	68	69	70
71	72	73	74	75	76	77	78	79	80
81	82	83	84	85	86	87	88	89	90
91	92	93	94	95	96	97	98	99	100

Write the answers.

1 x 10 = 10   2 x 10 = 20   3 x 10 = 30   4 x 10 = 40

5 x 10 = 50   6 x 10 = 60   7 x 10 = 70   8 x 10 = 80

10 x 10 = 100   9 x 10 = 90

Each box contains 10 crayons. How many crayons are there altogether?

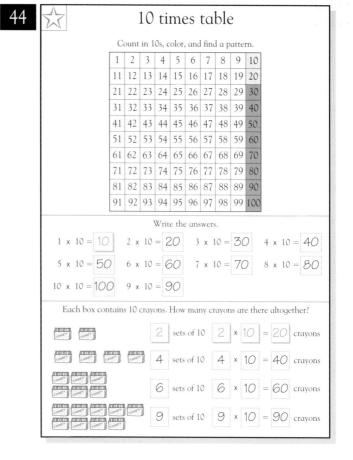

2 sets of 10   2 x 10 = 20 crayons

4 sets of 10   4 x 10 = 40 crayons

6 sets of 10   6 x 10 = 60 crayons

9 sets of 10   9 x 10 = 90 crayons

Multiplying and dividing

Each pod contains 10 peas. How many peas are there altogether?

How many pods? `2`

`2` x 10 = `20` peas

Write how many peas.

How many pods? `4`

`4` x 10 = `40` peas

How many pods? `3`

`3` x 10 = `30` peas

How many pods? `6`

`6` x 10 = `60` peas

How many pods? `5`

`5` x 10 = `50` peas

How many pods did the peas come from?

30

`30` ÷ 10 = `3` pods

Write how many pods.

`10` ÷ 10 = `1` pod

`100` ÷ 10 = `10` pods

`20` ÷ 10 = `2` pods

`70` ÷ 10 = `7` pods

Dividing by 10

One dollar is worth the same as ten dimes.

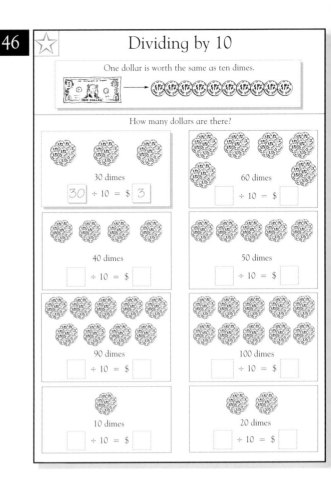

How many dollars are there?

30 dimes
`30` ÷ 10 = $ `3`

60 dimes
☐ ÷ 10 = $ ☐

40 dimes
☐ ÷ 10 = $ ☐

50 dimes
☐ ÷ 10 = $ ☐

90 dimes
☐ ÷ 10 = $ ☐

100 dimes
☐ ÷ 10 = $ ☐

10 dimes
☐ ÷ 10 = $ ☐

20 dimes
☐ ÷ 10 = $ ☐

Using the 10 times table

How many altogether?

The squirrels had 4 food dens. Each den had 10 acorns. How many acorns were there altogether?

`4` x `10` = `40` acorns

How many altogether?

The monkeys had 6 trees. There were 10 bananas in each tree. How many bananas did they have altogether?

☐ x ☐ = ☐ bananas

The frogs had 2 ponds. Each pond had 10 lily pads. How many lily pads were there altogether?

☐ x ☐ = ☐ lily pads

The snakes had 5 nests. Each nest had 10 eggs in it. How many eggs were there altogether?

☐ x ☐ = ☐ eggs

The lions had 7 cubs. Each cub already had 10 teeth. How many teeth did the cubs have altogether?

☐ x ☐ = ☐ teeth

How many in each?

The crows had 40 eggs and 10 nests. How many eggs were in each nest?

`40` ÷ `10` = `4` eggs

How many in each?

There were 90 mice living in 10 nests. How many mice were in each nest?

☐ ÷ ☐ = ☐ mice

There were 60 foxes hiding in 10 dens. How many foxes were in each den?

☐ ÷ ☐ = ☐ foxes

Using the 10 times table

Match each dog to the right bone.

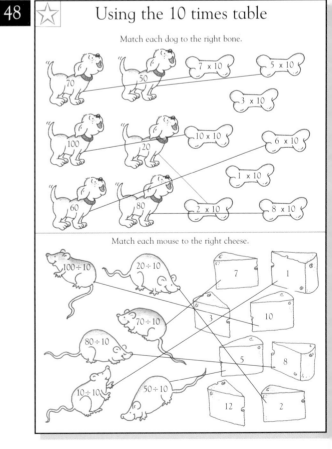

Match each mouse to the right cheese.

Using the 10 times table

Write in the missing numbers.

3	x	10	=	30
10	x	3	=	30
30	÷	3	=	10
30	÷	10	=	3

5	x	10	=	50
10	x	5	=	50
50	÷	10	=	5
50	÷	5	=	10

7	x	10	=	70
10	x	7	=	70
70	÷	10	=	7
70	÷	7	=	10

9	x	10	=	90
10	x	9	=	90
90	÷	10	=	9
90	÷	9	=	10

2	x	10	=	20
10	x	2	=	20
20	÷	10	=	2
20	÷	2	=	10

4	x	10	=	40
10	x	4	=	40
40	÷	10	=	4
40	÷	4	=	10

8	x	10	=	80
10	x	8	=	80
80	÷	10	=	8
80	÷	8	=	10

6	x	10	=	60
10	x	6	=	60
60	÷	10	=	6
60	÷	6	=	10

---

3 times table

Count in 3s, color, and find a pattern.

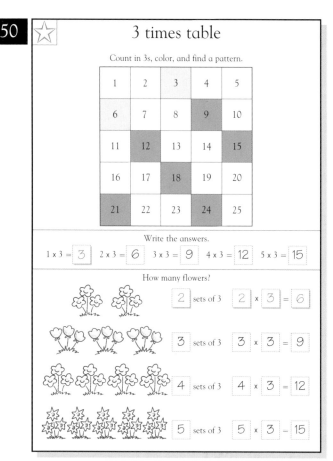

1	2	3	4	5
6	7	8	9	10
11	12	13	14	15
16	17	18	19	20
21	22	23	24	25

Write the answers.

$1 \times 3 = 3$ $2 \times 3 = 6$ $3 \times 3 = 9$ $4 \times 3 = 12$ $5 \times 3 = 15$

How many flowers?

2 sets of 3 $2 \times 3 = 6$

3 sets of 3 $3 \times 3 = 9$

4 sets of 3 $4 \times 3 = 12$

5 sets of 3 $5 \times 3 = 15$

Multiplying by 3

Write the number sentences to match the pictures.

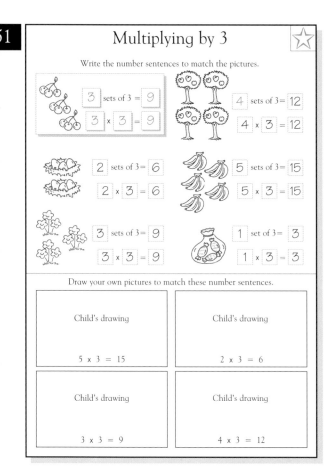

3 sets of 3 = 9 $3 \times 3 = 9$

4 sets of 3 = 12 $4 \times 3 = 12$

2 sets of 3 = 6 $2 \times 3 = 6$

5 sets of 3 = 15 $5 \times 3 = 15$

3 sets of 3 = 9 $3 \times 3 = 9$

1 set of 3 = 3 $1 \times 3 = 3$

Draw your own pictures to match these number sentences.

Child's drawing	Child's drawing
$5 \times 3 = 15$	$2 \times 3 = 6$
Child's drawing	Child's drawing
$3 \times 3 = 9$	$4 \times 3 = 12$

Dividing by 3

Divide the money equally among the purses.
Write a problem to show what you have done.
You might find it easier to change all the money into 1¢ coins.

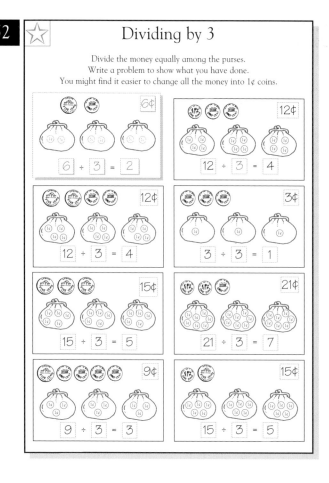

6¢ $6 \div 3 = 2$

12¢ $12 \div 3 = 4$

12¢ $12 \div 3 = 4$

3¢ $3 \div 3 = 1$

15¢ $15 \div 3 = 5$

21¢ $21 \div 3 = 7$

9¢ $9 \div 3 = 3$

15¢ $15 \div 3 = 5$

4 times table

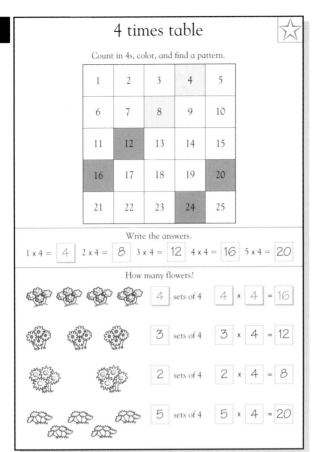

Count in 4s, color, and find a pattern.

1	2	3	4	5
6	7	8	9	10
11	12	13	14	15
16	17	18	19	20
21	22	23	24	25

Write the answers.

1 x 4 = 4   2 x 4 = 8   3 x 4 = 12   4 x 4 = 16   5 x 4 = 20

How many flowers?

4 sets of 4   4 x 4 = 16

3 sets of 4   3 x 4 = 12

2 sets of 4   2 x 4 = 8

5 sets of 4   5 x 4 = 20

Multiplying by 4

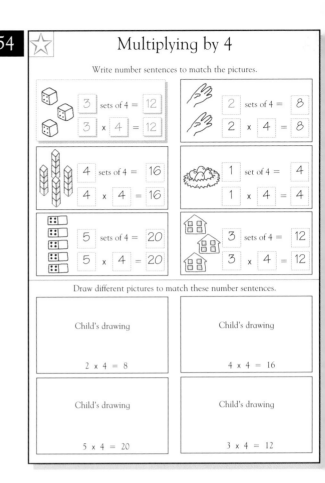

Write number sentences to match the pictures.

3 sets of 4 = 12
3 x 4 = 12

2 sets of 4 = 8
2 x 4 = 8

4 sets of 4 = 16
4 x 4 = 16

1 set of 4 = 4
1 x 4 = 4

5 sets of 4 = 20
5 x 4 = 20

3 sets of 4 = 12
3 x 4 = 12

Draw different pictures to match these number sentences.

Child's drawing	Child's drawing
2 x 4 = 8	4 x 4 = 16
Child's drawing	Child's drawing
5 x 4 = 20	3 x 4 = 12

Dividing by 4

How many on each plate?

There are 4 children. How many things will each child have?
Draw the objects in the circles.

8 sandwiches
8 ÷ 4 = 2 each

12 cookies
12 ÷ 4 = 3 each

4 drinks
4 ÷ 4 = 1 each

20 cherries
20 ÷ 4 = 5 each

16 cupcakes
16 ÷ 4 = 4 each

8 cheese triangles
8 ÷ 4 = 2 each

Mixed tables

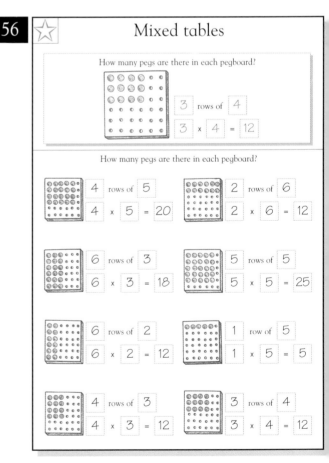

How many pegs are there in each pegboard?

3 rows of 4
3 x 4 = 12

How many pegs are there in each pegboard?

4 rows of 5
4 x 5 = 20

2 rows of 6
2 x 6 = 12

6 rows of 3
6 x 3 = 18

5 rows of 5
5 x 5 = 25

6 rows of 2
6 x 2 = 12

1 row of 5
1 x 5 = 5

4 rows of 3
4 x 3 = 12

3 rows of 4
3 x 4 = 12

Mixed tables

Divide the 12 pennies equally. Draw the coins
and write the problem to show how many each person gets.

$12 \div 3 = 4$

4 ¢ each

$12 \div 2 = 6$

6 ¢ each

$12 \div 6 = 2$

2 ¢ each

$12 \div 1 = 12$

12 ¢ each

$12 \div 12 = 1$

1 ¢ each

Mixed tables

How much will they get paid?

Price List for Jobs
Dust bedroom   3¢
Feed rabbit   2¢
Put toys away   6¢
Fetch newspaper   5¢
Walk dog   10¢

Write a problem to show how much money
Joe and Jasmine will get for these jobs.

Feed 4 rabbits — $4 \times 2¢ = 8¢$

Dust 2 bedrooms — $2 \times 3¢ = 6¢$

Walk the dog 4 times — $4 \times 10¢ = 40¢$

Put the toys away 3 times — $3 \times 6¢ = 18¢$

Fetch the newspaper 5 times — $5 \times 5¢ = 25¢$

How much will they get for these jobs?
Use the space to work out the problems.

Dust 3 bedrooms and walk
the dog twice

$3 \times 3 = 9$
$2 \times 10 = 20$

$9¢ + 20¢ = 29¢$

Feed the rabbit 10 times and
put the toys away twice

$10 \times 2 = 20$
$2 \times 6 = 12$

$20¢ + 12¢ = 32¢$

Mixed tables

Write the numbers that the raindrops are hiding.

$4 \times 5 = 20$

$2 \times 4 = 8$

$8 \div 2 = 4$

$20 \div 4 = 5$

$1 \times 3 = 3$

$2 \times 3 = 6$

$6 \div 3 = 2$

$3 \times 1 = 3$

$45 \div 5 = 9$

$5 \times 9 = 45$

$8 \times 2 = 16$

$16 \div 2 = 8$

$60 \div 10 = 6$

$10 \times 6 = 60$

$3 \times 4 = 12$

$12 \div 4 = 3$

$7 \times 5 = 35$

$35 \div 5 = 7$

$5 \times 10 = 50$

$50 \div 10 = 5$

Mixed tables

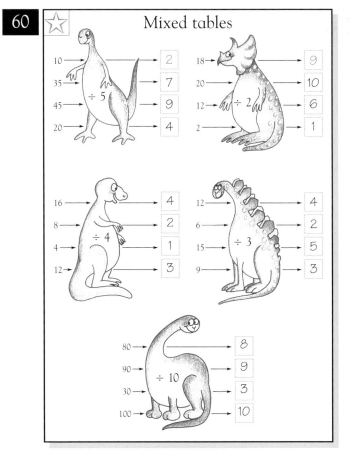

$10 \to 2$
$35 \to 7$ ÷ 5
$45 \to 9$
$20 \to 4$

$18 \to 9$
$20 \to 10$ ÷ 2
$12 \to 6$
$2 \to 1$

$16 \to 4$
$8 \to 2$ ÷ 4
$4 \to 1$
$12 \to 3$

$12 \to 4$
$6 \to 2$ ÷ 3
$15 \to 5$
$9 \to 3$

$80 \to 8$
$90 \to 9$ ÷ 10
$30 \to 3$
$100 \to 10$

Mixed tables

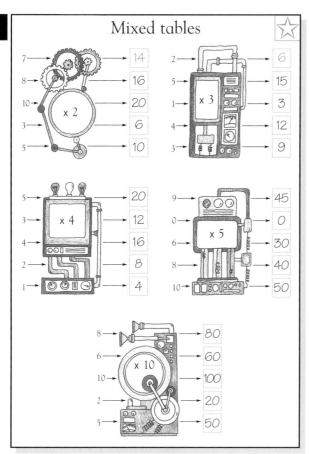

x 2	7 → 14
	8 → 16
	10 → 20
	3 → 6
	5 → 10

x 3	2 → 6
	5 → 15
	1 → 3
	4 → 12
	3 → 9

x 4	5 → 20
	3 → 12
	4 → 16
	2 → 8
	1 → 4

x 5	9 → 45
	0 → 0
	6 → 30
	8 → 40
	10 → 50

x 10	8 → 80
	6 → 60
	10 → 100
	2 → 20
	5 → 50

Mixed tables

Work out how many.

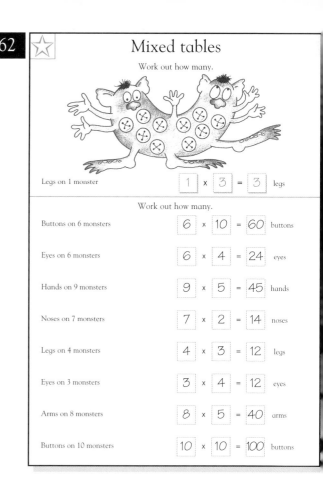

Legs on 1 monster	1	x	3	=	3	legs

Work out how many.

Buttons on 6 monsters	6	x	10	=	60	buttons
Eyes on 6 monsters	6	x	4	=	24	eyes
Hands on 9 monsters	9	x	5	=	45	hands
Noses on 7 monsters	7	x	2	=	14	noses
Legs on 4 monsters	4	x	3	=	12	legs
Eyes on 3 monsters	3	x	4	=	12	eyes
Arms on 8 monsters	8	x	5	=	40	arms
Buttons on 10 monsters	10	x	10	=	100	buttons

Number pairs

Put an X at (3,2).

Put an X on this grid at each of these number pairs:
(1,1) (1,9) (3,9) (3,6) (7,6) (7,9) (9,9) (9,1) (7,1) (7,4) (3,4) (3,1) (1,1)

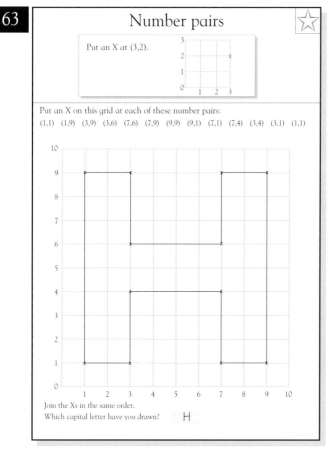

Join the Xs in the same order.
Which capital letter have you drawn?   H

If children complete the number pairs so that they form a capital letter H, they understand the concept. If not, find any errors that they have made and help them see what they did incorrectly.

Logic problems

Read the clues to find the secret number.

3 4 5 6 7 8   (2 5 4 7)   (triangle: 1 3 5 6)

It is in both the rectangle and the circle.
It is not in the triangle. It is greater than 5.
What number is it?   7

Read the clues to find the secret number.

(triangle: 13 15 17 16 19)   (square: 12 15 11 14 13)   (rectangle: 21 20 16 12 14 18)

It is not in the square. It is an even number.
It is greater than any number in the triangle.
What number is it?   20

(square: 10 11 16 18 12 13)   (circle: 13 14 15 19 20)   (rectangle: 16 18 19 20 21)

It is in the square and the circle.
It is greater than 10 and less than 16. It is an odd number.
What number is it?   13

It is in the triangle.
It is not an even number.
It is in the rectangle and the square.
What number is it?   9

Children can solve these problems by guess-and-check, or they can use a systematic approach by eliminating numbers that do not meet the conditions given.

Dividing ☆

Write the answer in the box.

$60 \div 10 = \quad 6$ 　　　　 $\frac{8}{10 \overline{)80}}$ 　　 $20 \div 10 = \quad 2$

Write the answer in the box.

$50 \div 10 = 5$	$80 \div 10 = 8$	$10 \div 10 = 1$
$120 \div 10 = 12$	$60 \div 10 = 6$	$190 \div 10 = 19$
$230 \div 10 = 23$	$40 \div 10 = 4$	$160 \div 10 = 16$
$30 \div 10 = 3$	$300 \div 10 = 30$	$330 \div 10 = 33$
$70 \div 10 = 7$	$390 \div 10 = 39$	$560 \div 10 = 56$
$90 \div 10 = 9$	$420 \div 10 = 42$	$850 \div 10 = 85$

Write the answer in the box.

$\frac{6}{10 \overline{)60}}$	$\frac{9}{10 \overline{)90}}$	$\frac{12}{10 \overline{)120}}$	$\frac{7}{10 \overline{)70}}$
$\frac{1}{10 \overline{)10}}$	$\frac{20}{10 \overline{)200}}$	$\frac{4}{10 \overline{)40}}$	$\frac{26}{10 \overline{)260}}$
$\frac{37}{10 \overline{)370}}$	$\frac{41}{10 \overline{)410}}$	$\frac{56}{10 \overline{)560}}$	$\frac{63}{10 \overline{)630}}$
$\frac{69}{10 \overline{)690}}$	$\frac{80}{10 \overline{)800}}$	$\frac{85}{10 \overline{)850}}$	$\frac{90}{10 \overline{)900}}$

Write the answer in the box.

$1,630 \div 10 = 163$	$2,480 \div 10 = 248$	$2,700 \div 10 = 270$
$3,040 \div 10 = 304$	$6,000 \div 10 = 600$	$3,980 \div 10 = 398$
$4,500 \div 10 = 450$	$2,000 \div 10 = 200$	$4,020 \div 10 = 402$
$5,320 \div 10 = 532$	$6,800 \div 10 = 680$	$8,000 \div 10 = 800$

Children should understand quickly that dividing multiples of 10 by 10 results in the removal of the final zero. Make sure that they remove the commas in any thousands when they divide by 10.

☆ Rounding

Round each amount to the nearest whole unit.

$1.70	$2.80	1.30 m	1.50 m
$2.00	$3.00	1.00 m	2.00 m

Round each amount to the nearest dollar.

$1.45 $1.00	$4.10 $4.00	$7.25 $7.00	$2.65 $3.00
$4.15 $4.00	$6.35 $6.00	$8.90 $9.00	$4.70 $5.00
$5.60 $6.00	$8.25 $8.00	$7.40 $7.00	$2.90 $3.00
$12.75 $13.00	$6.20 $6.00	$13.80 $14.00	$12.65 $13.00
$11.65 $12.00	$0.80 $1.00	$17.75 $18.00	$18.25 $18.00

Round each amount to the nearest meter.

1.45 m 1.00 m	2.60 m 3.00 m	1.15 m 1.00 m	5.65 m 6.00 m
3.35 m 3.00 m	7.70 m 8.00 m	8.35 m 8.00 m	2.25 m 2.00 m
4.70 m 5.00 m	2.90 m 3.00 m	6.05 m 6.00 m	2.45 m 2.00 m
7.30 m 7.00 m	4.05 m 4.00 m	6.55 m 7.00 m	3.80 m 4.00 m
2.95 m 3.00 m	1.60 m 2.00 m	9.25 m 9.00 m	6.45 m 6.00 m

Round each amount to the nearest whole unit.

$3.50 $4.00	4.50 m 5.00 m	1.50 m 2.00 m	$6.50 $7.00
6.50 m 7.00 m	$0.50 $1.00	$10.50 $11.00	12.50 m 13.00 m
20.50 m 21.00 m	$3.50 $4.00	5.50 m 6.00 m	$7.50 $8.00

Children should recognize that amounts of 50¢ or 50 cm and above are rounded up, and amounts below 50¢ and 50 cm are rounded down. Make sure that children increase the whole number by 1 when they round up.

Congruency ☆

Figures that are the same size and shape are congruent. Are these figures congruent?

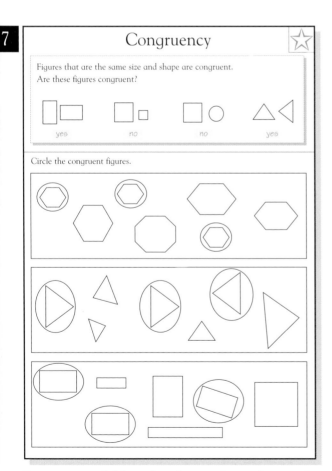

yes 　　　 no 　　　 no 　　　 yes

Circle the congruent figures.

Point out to children that figures do not have to be oriented in the same way to be congruent; it is the size and shape that is important. Make sure they know that there may be more than two congruent figures to identify.

☆ Identifying patterns

Complete each pattern.

48	42	36	30	24	18	12	6
44	41	38	35	32	29	26	23

Complete each pattern.

21	19	17	15	13	11	9	7
38	34	30	26	22	18	14	10
36	31	26	21	16	11	6	1
55	50	45	40	35	30	25	20
42	37	32	27	22	17	12	7
52	48	44	40	36	32	28	24
62	57	52	47	42	37	32	27
35	31	27	23	19	15	11	7
41	39	37	35	33	31	29	27
38	33	28	23	18	13	8	3
42	36	30	24	18	12	6	0
50	44	38	32	26	20	14	8
63	57	51	45	39	33	27	21
37	34	31	28	25	22	19	16
58	53	48	43	38	33	28	23
78	70	62	54	46	38	30	22
67	60	53	46	39	32	25	18

Point out that some of the patterns show an increase and some a decrease. Children should check that the operation that turns the first number into the second also turns the second number into the third. They can then continue the pattern.

Odds and evens

Write the answer in the box.

3 + 3 = 6	4 + 6 = 10	7 + 3 = 10	2 + 6 = 8

Add the even numbers to the even numbers.

4 + 8 = 12	12 + 6 = 18	10 + 6 = 16	8 + 14 = 22
20 + 14 = 34	14 + 12 = 26	16 + 10 = 26	30 + 20 = 50
14 + 16 = 30	18 + 6 = 24	22 + 8 = 30	20 + 40 = 60

What do you notice about each answer?   _All the answers are even numbers._

Add the odd numbers to the odd numbers.

7 + 9 = 16	5 + 7 = 12	11 + 5 = 16	9 + 5 = 14
7 + 7 = 14	9 + 3 = 12	15 + 5 = 20	13 + 7 = 20
11 + 3 = 14	17 + 9 = 26	15 + 9 = 24	13 + 15 = 28

What do you notice about each answer?   _All the answers are even numbers._

Add the odd numbers to the even numbers.

3 + 8 = 11	9 + 12 = 21	5 + 18 = 23	7 + 14 = 21
11 + 4 = 15	13 + 10 = 23	15 + 6 = 21	21 + 4 = 25
7 + 20 = 27	13 + 30 = 43	11 + 12 = 23	17 + 6 = 23

What do you notice about each answer?   _All the answers are odd numbers._

Add the even numbers to the odd numbers.

6 + 7 = 13	8 + 5 = 13	10 + 9 = 19	2 + 17 = 19
10 + 29 = 39	14 + 3 = 17	8 + 13 = 21	12 + 5 = 17
14 + 7 = 21	8 + 51 = 59	16 + 9 = 25	30 + 17 = 47

What do you notice about each answer?   _All the answers are odd numbers._

Children should note that adding two even numbers results in an even number, adding two odd numbers results in an odd number, and adding an odd and an even number results in an odd number. The order in which numbers are added does not matter.

Probability

Look at the marbles in the bag.

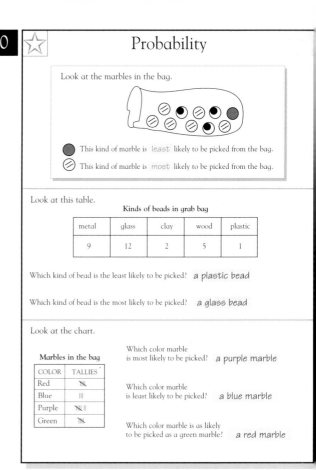

This kind of marble is *least* likely to be picked from the bag.

This kind of marble is *most* likely to be picked from the bag.

Look at this table.

Kinds of beads in grab bag

metal	glass	clay	wood	plastic
9	12	2	5	1

Which kind of bead is the least likely to be picked?   *a plastic bead*

Which kind of bead is the most likely to be picked?   *a glass bead*

Look at the chart.

Marbles in the bag

COLOR	TALLIES
Red	卌
Blue	|||
Purple	卌 ||
Green	卌

Which color marble is most likely to be picked?   *a purple marble*

Which color marble is least likely to be picked?   *a blue marble*

Which color marble is as likely to be picked as a green marble?   *a red marble*

Children should realize that the more of a particular item there is in a set, the more likely it is to be picked.

Place value

What is the value of each of the numbers in 573?

The value of 5 in 573 is   500   or   five hundred

The value of 7 in 573 is   70   or   seventy

The value of 3 in 573 is   3   or   three

What is the value of 4 in these numbers? Write using number and words.

34	142	4,906	12,412
4	40	4,000	400
four	forty	four thousand	four hundred

547,902	7,462	13,034	6,140
40,000	400	4	40
forty thousand	four hundred	four	forty

Circle each number with a 5 having the value of fifty.

457,682   （67,954）   870,534   （575,555）

Circle each number with a 4 having the value of four hundred.

（457,482）   67,954   （870,434）   544,985

Write increases or decreases and by how much.

Change the 2 in 24 to 3. The value of the number   increases   by   10

Change the 6 in 86 to 3. The value of the number   decreases   by   3

Change the 1 in 17 to 9. The value of the number   increases   by   80

Change the 9 in 921 to 8. The value of the number   decreases   by   100

Change the 7 in 276 to 9. The value of the number   increases   by   20

Change the 5 in 5,247 to 1. The value of the number   decreases   by   4,000

If children have difficulty, suggest that they read the numbers aloud, so that they can more easily identify the place value of each digit.

Fractions

Write the answer in the box.

$1\frac{1}{2} + \frac{1}{4} = 1\frac{3}{4}$ $2\frac{1}{2} + 3\frac{1}{2} = 6$ $1\frac{1}{4} + 2\frac{1}{2} = 3\frac{3}{4}$

Write the answer in the box.

$2\frac{1}{4} + 1\frac{1}{4} = 3\frac{1}{2}$	$1\frac{1}{2} + 1\frac{1}{2} = 3$	$1\frac{1}{4} + \frac{1}{4} = 1\frac{1}{2}$
$3\frac{1}{2} + 1 = 4\frac{1}{2}$	$3\frac{1}{2} + 1\frac{1}{4} = 4\frac{3}{4}$	$2\frac{1}{4} + 4 = 6\frac{1}{4}$
$4\frac{1}{2} + 1\frac{1}{4} = 5\frac{3}{4}$	$2\frac{1}{2} + 1\frac{1}{2} = 4$	$5 + 1\frac{1}{2} = 6\frac{1}{2}$
$3\frac{1}{4} + 1\frac{1}{2} = 4\frac{3}{4}$	$2 + 3\frac{1}{2} = 5\frac{1}{2}$	$7 + \frac{1}{2} = 7\frac{1}{2}$
$3 + \frac{1}{4} = 3\frac{1}{4}$	$4\frac{1}{4} + \frac{1}{4} = 4\frac{1}{2}$	$5 + 4\frac{1}{2} = 9\frac{1}{2}$

Write the answer in the box.

$1\frac{1}{3} + 2\frac{1}{3} = 3\frac{2}{3}$	$3\frac{1}{3} + 4\frac{2}{3} = 8$	$1\frac{2}{3} + 5 = 6\frac{2}{3}$
$3\frac{2}{3} + 2 = 5\frac{2}{3}$	$4\frac{1}{3} + 1\frac{2}{3} = 6$	$2\frac{2}{3} + 1\frac{2}{3} = 4\frac{1}{3}$
$1\frac{1}{3} + 1\frac{2}{3} = 3\frac{1}{3}$	$4\frac{1}{3} + 2\frac{1}{3} = 6\frac{2}{3}$	$3 + 2\frac{1}{3} = 5\frac{1}{3}$
$6 + 2\frac{2}{3} = 8\frac{2}{3}$	$2\frac{1}{3} + 3\frac{2}{3} = 6$	$3\frac{1}{3} + 1\frac{1}{3} = 4\frac{2}{3}$
$5\frac{2}{3} + 2\frac{2}{3} = 8\frac{1}{3}$	$7 + \frac{1}{3} = 7\frac{1}{3}$	$2\frac{2}{3} + 5\frac{2}{3} = 8\frac{1}{3}$

Write the answer in the box.

$2\frac{1}{5} + 2\frac{2}{5} = 4\frac{3}{5}$	$3\frac{1}{5} + 2\frac{3}{5} = 5\frac{4}{5}$	$1\frac{4}{5} + 6 = 7\frac{4}{5}$
$3\frac{1}{5} + 3\frac{2}{5} = 6\frac{3}{5}$	$4 + 2\frac{2}{5} = 6\frac{2}{5}$	$5\frac{3}{5} + 1\frac{1}{5} = 6\frac{4}{5}$
$\frac{3}{5} + \frac{3}{5} = 1\frac{1}{5}$	$3\frac{2}{5} + \frac{4}{5} = 4\frac{1}{5}$	$3\frac{2}{5} + \frac{2}{5} = 3\frac{4}{5}$

It is technically correct if children add $\frac{1}{4}$ and $\frac{1}{4}$ to get $\frac{2}{4}$, but they should be encouraged to simplify this as $\frac{1}{2}$. Some children may not simplify improper fractions that are part of a mixed number (such as $3\frac{6}{5}$). Show them how to do this.

Part of a whole ☆

Write the fraction that shows the shaded part.

How many parts are shaded? **3 parts**

How many parts in all? **4 parts**

The shaded part is **$\frac{3}{4}$**

Circle the fraction that shows the shaded part.

$\left(\frac{1}{2}\right)$ $\frac{1}{3}$ $\frac{1}{4}$ $\frac{2}{5}$ $\frac{3}{4}$ $\left(\frac{3}{5}\right)$ $\left(\frac{7}{8}\right)$ $\frac{1}{6}$ $\frac{4}{5}$

Write the fraction that shows the shaded part.

$\frac{1}{6}$ $\frac{3}{8}$ $\frac{3}{5}$

$\frac{5}{8}$ $\frac{4}{12}$ $\frac{4}{8}$

$\frac{3}{10}$ $\frac{4}{9}$ $\frac{5}{6}$

$\frac{2}{6}$ $\frac{5}{16}$ $\frac{5}{8}$

If children have difficulty, point out that the denominator (the bottom number of the fraction) is the total number of parts. The numerator (the top number of the fraction) is the number of shaded parts.

☆ Decimals

Write these decimals in order, from least to greatest.

0.35 0.4 0.25 0.15 0.2   *0.15 0.2 0.25 0.35 0.4*

Write each row of decimals in order, from least to greatest.

0.41	0.48	0.42	0.45	0.40	*0.40*	*0.41*	*0.42*	*0.45*	*0.48*
1.45	1.75	1.35	1.80	1.40	*1.35*	*1.40*	*1.45*	*1.75*	*1.80*
4.23	4.73	4.83	4.13	4.93	*4.13*	*4.23*	*4.73*	*4.83*	*4.93*
6.28	6.48	6.98	6.08	6.18	*6.08*	*6.18*	*6.28*	*6.48*	*6.98*
4.34	3.34	8.34	2.34	7.34	*2.34*	*3.34*	*4.34*	*7.34*	*8.34*
2.16	3.65	4.64	5.38	1.37	*1.37*	*2.16*	*3.65*	*4.64*	*5.38*
5.31	2.85	4.97	6.35	1.44	*1.44*	*2.85*	*4.97*	*5.31*	*6.35*
8.32	6.17	9.32	7.43	2.38	*2.38*	*6.17*	*7.43*	*8.32*	*9.32*
5.98	4.06	3.07	2.38	6.27	*2.38*	*3.07*	*4.06*	*5.98*	*6.27*

Write each row of decimals in order, from least to greatest.

2.67	5.28	1.73	4.92	2.56	*1.73*	*2.56*	*2.67*	*4.92*	*5.28*
7.27	4.94	2.91	4.38	5.68	*2.91*	*4.38*	*4.94*	*5.68*	*7.27*
8.27	4.56	8.42	9.28	8.44	*4.56*	*8.27*	*8.42*	*8.44*	*9.28*
1.37	1.94	2.36	3.16	4.21	*1.37*	*1.94*	*2.36*	*3.16*	*4.21*
4.36	7.27	5.25	6.28	5.29	*4.36*	*5.25*	*5.29*	*6.28*	*7.27*
3.34	2.63	4.13	3.21	4.28	*2.63*	*3.21*	*3.34*	*4.13*	*4.28*
7.35	6.48	7.21	6.22	4.46	*4.46*	*6.22*	*6.48*	*7.21*	*7.35*
5.45	4.97	5.21	4.89	5.03	*4.89*	*4.97*	*5.03*	*5.21*	*5.45*

Children should understand that place value with decimals is just as important as it is with whole numbers. Make sure they compare the numbers in order—the whole number first, then the first decimal place, and then the second decimal place.

Fractions and decimals ☆

Write each fraction as a decimal.

$1\frac{1}{10}$ = *1.1* $1\frac{2}{10}$ = *1.2* $1\frac{7}{10}$ = *1.7*

Write each decimal as a fraction.

2.5 = *$2\frac{1}{2}$*   1.7 = *$1\frac{7}{10}$*   3.2 = *$3\frac{2}{10}$*

Write each fraction as a decimal.

$2\frac{1}{2}$	*2.5*	$3\frac{1}{10}$	*3.1*	$4\frac{3}{10}$	*4.3*	$1\frac{1}{2}$	*1.5*
$5\frac{1}{10}$	*5.1*	$2\frac{3}{10}$	*2.3*	$8\frac{1}{10}$	*8.1*	$5\frac{1}{2}$	*5.5*
$7\frac{8}{10}$	*7.8*	$2\frac{4}{10}$	*2.4*	$6\frac{1}{2}$	*6.5*	$8\frac{1}{2}$	*8.5*
$7\frac{6}{10}$	*7.6*	$9\frac{1}{2}$	*9.5*	$6\frac{7}{10}$	*6.7*	$10\frac{1}{2}$	*10.5*

Write each decimal as a fraction.

3.2	*$3\frac{2}{10}$*	4.5	*$4\frac{1}{2}$*	1.7	*$1\frac{7}{10}$*	1.2	*$1\frac{2}{10}$*
6.5	*$6\frac{1}{2}$*	2.7	*$2\frac{7}{10}$*	5.2	*$5\frac{2}{10}$*	5.5	*$5\frac{1}{2}$*
7.2	*$7\frac{2}{10}$*	8.5	*$8\frac{1}{2}$*	9.7	*$9\frac{7}{10}$*	10.2	*$10\frac{2}{10}$*
11.5	*$11\frac{1}{2}$*	12.7	*$12\frac{7}{10}$*	13.2	*$13\frac{2}{10}$*	14.5	*$14\frac{1}{2}$*
15.7	*$15\frac{7}{10}$*	16.2	*$16\frac{2}{10}$*	17.5	*$17\frac{1}{2}$*	18.7	*$18\frac{7}{10}$*

Write each fraction as a decimal.

$\frac{1}{2}$ = *0.5* $\frac{2}{10}$ = *0.2* $\frac{3}{10}$ = *0.3*

Write each decimal as a fraction.

0.5 = *$\frac{1}{2}$*   0.2 = *$\frac{2}{10}$*   0.7 = *$\frac{7}{10}$*

If children have difficulty, you may want to use a number line showing tenths and decimals.

☆ Adding

Write the answer between the lines.

```
  46      57      48
+ 25    + 24    + 24
----    ----    ----
  71      81      72
```

Write the answer between the lines.

26 + 15 = *41*	37 + 16 = *53*	48 + 14 = *62*	59 + 12 = *71*	25 + 15 = *40*
38 + 15 = *53*	25 + 16 = *41*	36 + 17 = *53*	43 + 19 = *62*	27 + 15 = *42*
56 + 17 = *73*	18 + 14 = *32*	28 + 14 = *42*	47 + 26 = *73*	58 + 15 = *73*
27 + 14 = *41*	19 + 14 = *33*	23 + 16 = *39*	57 + 15 = *72*	68 + 13 = *81*
26 + 35 = *61*	34 + 48 = *82*	13 + 27 = *40*	18 + 32 = *50*	25 + 45 = *70*
17 + 44 = *61*	33 + 58 = *91*	29 + 53 = *82*	32 + 53 = *85*	23 + 48 = *71*

Children must regroup to answer these addition problems. If they get confused when the lower number is larger than the upper, point out that the order of addition does not change the sum.

Adding

Write the answer between the lines.

45 + 15 60	66 + 23 89	43 + 18 61

Write the answer between the lines.

17 + 13 30	23 + 17 40	45 + 25 70	62 + 18 80	38 + 12 50
25 + 25 50	37 + 23 60	42 + 28 70	50 + 37 87	30 + 48 78
46 + 34 80	74 + 16 90	42 + 38 80	67 + 23 90	37 + 43 80
54 + 46 100	38 + 32 70	47 + 43 90	83 + 17 100	31 + 39 70
76 + 24 100	68 + 32 100	73 + 27 100	55 + 45 100	74 + 26 100
73 + 16 89	48 + 33 81	49 + 42 91	28 + 26 54	65 + 45 110

Many of these questions result in sums with a zero in the ones place. Make sure that children do not neglect to add the additional 10 when they regroup.

Subtracting

Write the answer between the lines.

38 − 23 15	42 − 20 22	64 − 34 30

Write the answer between the lines.

45 − 23 22	27 − 14 13	53 − 20 33	85 − 41 44	47 − 25 22
29 − 16 13	53 − 12 41	82 − 40 42	37 − 26 11	44 − 31 13
63 − 21 42	74 − 32 42	47 − 36 11	63 − 42 21	76 − 35 41
85 − 42 43	83 − 41 42	95 − 35 60	67 − 53 14	86 − 45 41
65 − 35 30	74 − 54 20	86 − 66 20	96 − 86 10	67 − 17 50
59 − 39 20	48 − 27 21	46 − 32 14	78 − 47 31	67 − 56 11

Children do not need to regroup to answer any of the questions on this page. Check any errors and make sure children understand what they did incorrectly.

Subtracting

Write the answer between the lines.

43 − 27 16	54 − 28 26	61 − 43 18

Write the answer between the lines.

45 − 28 17	36 − 18 18	42 − 17 25	50 − 45 5	62 − 17 45
43 − 29 14	74 − 47 27	90 − 37 53	65 − 48 17	63 − 49 14
57 − 39 18	64 − 48 16	62 − 34 28	78 − 69 9	36 − 27 9
54 − 26 28	68 − 39 29	50 − 27 23	38 − 28 10	44 − 36 8
31 − 16 15	43 − 28 15	70 − 36 34	53 − 37 16	46 − 28 18
90 − 46 44	50 − 26 24	54 − 35 19	66 − 48 18	90 − 44 46

Children must regroup to answer these subtraction questions.

Real-life problems

Write the answer in the box.

Sarah has eight wrenches and is given six more. How many wrenches does she have now?

$8 + 6 = 14$

Write the answer in the box.

Karl has 20 marbles but loses 12 in a game of marbles contest. How many marbles does he have left?

$20 − 12 = 8$

After buying some candy for 30¢, Naomi still has 65¢ left. How much did she have to begin with?

$30¢ + 65¢ = 95¢$

Billy takes 20 balls out of a barrel and leaves 15 in the barrel. How many balls are there altogether?

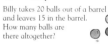

$20 + 15 = 35$

June collected 150 stamps and her father gave her 60 more. How many stamps does June have now?

$150 + 60 = 210$

Angela puts 40 toys in a box that already has 35 toys in it. How many toys are in the box now?

$40 + 35 = 75$

Patrick leaves 45¢ at home and takes 50¢ with him. How much money does Patrick have altogether?

$45 + 50 = 95¢$

Don gives some of his allowance to his sister. He gives his sister 80¢ and has 60¢ left. How much allowance did Don have in the first place?

$80¢ + 60¢ = 140¢$
 $= \$1.40$

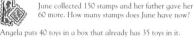

Five letters of the alphabet are vowels. How many letters of the alphabet are not vowels?

$26 − 5 = 21$

These problems test whether children know when to add and when to subtract. Some words such as 'altogether' may need to be explained.

1 — Multiplying

Write the answer between the lines.

| 24 × 3 = 72 | 71 × 6 = 426 | 36 × 3 = 108 |

Write the answer between the lines.

46 × 2 = 92	28 × 2 = 56	72 × 2 = 144	65 × 2 = 130	76 × 2 = 152
43 × 3 = 129	75 × 3 = 225	53 × 3 = 159	39 × 3 = 117	55 × 3 = 165
47 × 4 = 188	28 × 4 = 112	64 × 4 = 256	45 × 4 = 180	62 × 4 = 248
75 × 5 = 375	72 × 5 = 360	94 × 5 = 470	38 × 5 = 190	64 × 5 = 320
46 × 6 = 276	73 × 6 = 438	72 × 6 = 432	78 × 6 = 468	94 × 6 = 564
85 × 7 = 595	48 × 7 = 336	93 × 7 = 651	37 × 7 = 259	55 × 7 = 385

Some of the multiplications will require children to regroup. Go through any incorrect answers with them to find out whether the problem results from incorrect regrouping or poor knowledge of times tables.

82 — Multiplying

Write the answer between the lines.

| 25 × 7 = 175 | 37 × 4 = 148 | 62 × 6 = 372 |

Write the answer between the lines.

28 × 8 = 224	64 × 8 = 512	85 × 8 = 680	28 × 8 = 224	83 × 8 = 664
43 × 9 = 387	94 × 9 = 846	52 × 9 = 468	93 × 9 = 837	46 × 9 = 414
53 × 4 = 212	74 × 4 = 296	84 × 4 = 336	83 × 4 = 332	49 × 4 = 196
39 × 5 = 195	38 × 5 = 190	29 × 5 = 145	47 × 5 = 235	57 × 5 = 285
29 × 4 = 116	59 × 5 = 295	39 × 6 = 234	69 × 7 = 483	79 × 8 = 632
46 × 4 = 184	36 × 5 = 180	96 × 6 = 576	26 × 7 = 182	56 × 8 = 448

See the comments for the previous page.

83 — Dividing

Write the answer in the box.

65 ÷ 8 = 8 r 1   34 ÷ 7 = 4 r 6   37 ÷ 9 = 4 r 1

Write the answer in the box.

26 ÷ 6 = 4 r 2	34 ÷ 6 = 5 r 4	63 ÷ 6 = 10 r 3
42 ÷ 6 = 7	38 ÷ 6 = 6 r 2	54 ÷ 6 = 9
19 ÷ 6 = 3 r 1	25 ÷ 6 = 4 r 1	30 ÷ 6 = 5
21 ÷ 6 = 3 r 3	33 ÷ 6 = 5 r 3	44 ÷ 6 = 7 r 2

57 ÷ 7 = 8 r 1	46 ÷ 7 = 6 r 4	52 ÷ 7 = 7 r 3
38 ÷ 7 = 5 r 3	28 ÷ 7 = 4	64 ÷ 7 = 9 r 1
39 ÷ 7 = 5 r 4	35 ÷ 7 = 5	24 ÷ 7 = 3 r 3
63 ÷ 7 = 9	82 ÷ 7 = 11 r 5	64 ÷ 7 = 9 r 1

43 ÷ 8 = 5 r 3	53 ÷ 8 = 6 r 5	73 ÷ 8 = 9 r 1
52 ÷ 8 = 6 r 4	78 ÷ 8 = 9 r 6	46 ÷ 8 = 5 r 6
54 ÷ 8 = 6 r 6	32 ÷ 8 = 4	51 ÷ 8 = 6 r 3
49 ÷ 8 = 6 r 1	37 ÷ 8 = 4 r 5	44 ÷ 8 = 5 r 4

64 ÷ 9 = 7 r 1	73 ÷ 9 = 8 r 1	38 ÷ 9 = 4 r 2
63 ÷ 9 = 7	37 ÷ 9 = 4 r 1	40 ÷ 9 = 4 r 4
45 ÷ 9 = 5	22 ÷ 9 = 2 r 4	43 ÷ 9 = 4 r 7
51 ÷ 9 = 5 r 6	48 ÷ 9 = 5 r 3	70 ÷ 9 = 7 r 7

These division problems test children's knowledge of times tables. Children should be able to calculate the remainders easily.

84 — Dividing

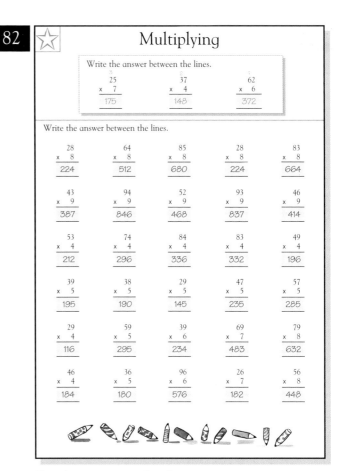

Write the answer above the line.

| 5 r 2 — 6) 32, 30, 2 | 4 r 1 — 7) 29, 28, 1 | 6 r 2 — 9) 56, 54, 2 |

Write the answer in the box above the line.

7 r 3 — 6) 45, 42, 3	6 r 1 — 6) 37, 36, 1	4 r 3 — 6) 27, 24, 3	6 r 5 — 6) 41, 36, 5	6 r 2 — 6) 38, 36, 2
4 r 6 — 7) 34, 28, 6	6 — 7) 42, 42, 0	10 r 4 — 7) 74, 70, 4	5 r 1 — 7) 36, 35, 1	5 r 6 — 7) 41, 35, 6
4 r 5 — 8) 37, 32, 5	3 r 5 — 8) 29, 24, 5	5 r 4 — 8) 44, 40, 4	9 r 1 — 8) 73, 72, 1	4 r 7 — 8) 39, 32, 7
2 r 2 — 9) 20, 18, 2	3 r 7 — 9) 34, 27, 7	4 r 8 — 9) 44, 36, 8	8 r 2 — 9) 74, 72, 2	4 r 2 — 9) 38, 36, 2

These problems are similar to those on the previous page, but are presented using a division housing or box. Look for errors that highlight particular times tables that children need to work on.

Choosing the operation

Write either x or ÷ in the box.

4 x 9 = 36   24 ÷ 4 = 6   80 ÷ 8 = 10

Write either x or ÷ in the box.

9 x 7 = 63	8 x 6 = 48	54 ÷ 9 = 6
5 x 8 = 40	30 ÷ 6 = 5	49 ÷ 7 = 7
36 ÷ 4 = 9	45 ÷ 9 = 5	7 x 8 = 56
48 ÷ 6 = 8	7 x 9 = 63	27 ÷ 3 = 9
4 x 6 = 24	24 ÷ 8 = 3	81 ÷ 9 = 9
8 x 8 = 64	28 ÷ 7 = 4	48 ÷ 8 = 6
63 ÷ 7 = 9	30 ÷ 5 = 6	3 x 8 = 24
6 x 8 = 48	40 ÷ 8 = 5	56 ÷ 7 = 8
54 ÷ 6 = 9	18 ÷ 3 = 6	64 ÷ 8 = 8
16 ÷ 8 = 2	21 ÷ 7 = 3	28 ÷ 4 = 7
27 ÷ 9 = 3	80 ÷ 10 = 8	70 ÷ 7 = 10
8 x 7 = 56	4 x 9 = 36	5 x 9 = 45
20 x 6 = 120	700 ÷ 7 = 100	8 x 8 = 1
100 ÷ 5 = 20	400 ÷ 8 = 50	84 ÷ 7 = 12
42 ÷ 6 = 7	600 ÷ 100 = 6	9 ÷ 9 = 1
5 x 5 = 25	100 ÷ 10 = 10	6 ÷ 6 = 1

Children will probably realize that if the answer is larger than the first number, they should multiply, and if the answer is smaller than the first number they should divide. They can check some of their answers to make sure that they are correct.

Real-life problems

Write the answer in the box.
A number multiplied by 8 is 56.
What is the number?   7

I divide a number by 9 and the result is 6.
What is the number?   54

Write the answer in the box.

A number multiplied by 6 is 42. What is the number?   7

I divide a number by 4 and the result is 7. What is the number?   28

I divide a number by 8 and the result is 6. What number did I begin with?   48

A number multiplied by itself gives the answer 25. What is the number?   5

I divide a number by 7 and the result is 7. What number did I begin with?   49

A number multiplied by itself gives the answer 49. What is the number?   7

I multiply a number by 7 and I end up with 56. What number did I begin with?   8

Seven times a number is 63. What is the number?   9

What do I have to multiply 8 by to get the result 72?   9

Nine times a number is 81. What is the number?   9

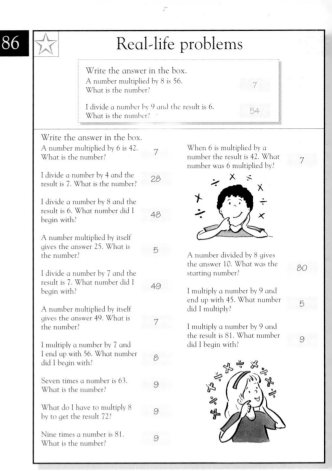

When 6 is multiplied by a number the result is 42. What number was 6 multiplied by?   7

A number divided by 8 gives the answer 10. What was the starting number?   80

I multiply a number by 9 and end up with 45. What number did I multiply?   5

I multiply a number by 9 and the result is 81. What number did I begin with?   9

Some children find these problems difficult even if they are good with times tables and division. Many of the problems require children to perform the operation inverse to the one named. Have children check their answers to make sure they are correct.

Real-life problems

Solve the problem. Write the answer in the box.
A jump rope is supposed to be 1.30 m long but 35 cm has been cut off. How much of the skipping rope is left?

0.95 m

```
    12
  1.30  m
- 0.35  m
  0.95  m
```

Solve the problem. Write the answer in the box.

Mario is given three cans of juice. Each can contains 425 ml. How much does Mario have altogether?

1275 ml or 1.275 liters

```
   1
   425
 x   3
  1275
```

Trang sees these toys on sale in a store window. She buys two of the toys and pays $10.10. Which toys does Trang buy?

$4.30 $6.40
$7.50 $3.70

Kite and ball

```
   1
   6.40
 + 3.70
  10.10
```

A school playground is 145 m long. 68 m are used by the 3rd grade children and the rest by the 4th grade children. How much space is used by the 4th grade children?

77 m

```
   3 15
  1 4 5
 -  68
    77
```

Mary buys a box of chocolates that costs $7.85. She pays for the chocolates with a ten dollar bill. How much change should she receive?

$2.15

```
  9 9 10
 10.00
 - 7.85
   2.15
```

A box of tea contains 350 grams. Half of the tea has been used. How much of the tea is left?

175 g

```
      175
  2) 350
     2
     15
     14
      10
      10
       0
```

These problems involve fairly large or awkward numbers and may be a challenge. Answers in metric units can be given as whole numbers (for example, 1,275 milliliters) or as decimals (1.275 liters).

Real-life problems

Solve the problem. Write the answer in the box.

A boy weighs 15 lb more than his sister. His sister weighs 72 lb. How much does the brother weigh?

87 lb

```
  72
+ 15
  87
```

Solve the problem. Write the answer in the box.

Two bags of cement weigh a total of 150 kg. One bag weighs 80 kg. How much does the other bag weigh?

70 kg

```
  150
 - 80
   70
```

There are 44 bars of chocolate in each box. How many bars will there be in 7 boxes?

308

```
   2
   44
 x  7
  308
```

One box contains 186 tissues. How many tissues will there be in 4 boxes?

744

```
   32
   186
 x   4
   744
```

Dean's older sister weighs 95 lb, and he is 13 lb lighter than her. How much does Dean weigh?

82 lb

```
  95
 - 13
  82
```

A boy has a bottle of lemonade that contains 2 liters. He drinks 465 ml. How much lemonade is left?

1 liter 535 ml or 1.535 liters

```
  1 9 9 10
  2000
 - 465
  1535
```

Kitchen countertops can be measured in millimeters. How long is 1.50 m in mm?

1500 mm

```
  1.50 x 100
  = 1500
```

The two final problems require children to convert between units. Make sure that children understand how to convert metrical units.

Problems using time

Write the answer in the box.

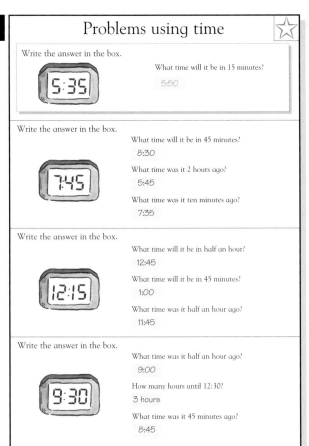

What time will it be in 15 minutes?
5:50

Write the answer in the box.

What time will it be in 45 minutes?
8:30

What time was it 2 hours ago?
5:45

What time was it ten minutes ago?
7:35

Write the answer in the box.

What time will it be in half an hour?
12:45

What time will it be in 45 minutes?
1:00

What time was it half an hour ago?
11:45

Write the answer in the box.

What time was it half an hour ago?
9:00

How many hours until 12:30?
3 hours

What time was it 45 minutes ago?
8:45

When regrouping in addition problems involving time, children should avoid using decimal regrouping and must understand that 60 minutes (not 100 minutes) is added as 1 hour.

Charts

	Period 1	Period 2	Period 3	Period 4
Monday	Math	English	History	Design Technology
Tuesday	Math	English	Spanish	Gym
Wednesday	Math	English	Science	Science
Thursday	Math	English	Art	Art
Friday	English	Gym	Science	Music

A.M.   P.M.

Write the answer in the box.

What subject does the class have last period on Tuesday? Gym

How many periods of Math does the class have? 4

When does the class have an afternoon of Art? Thursday

How many periods of English does the class have? 5

What subject comes before Music? Science

Which day is the Spanish lesson? Tuesday

Which subject is taught third period on Monday? History

What is the last lesson on Friday morning? Gym

When is Science? Wednesday and Friday

What subject is taught second period on Thursday? English

If children have difficulty reading the information in the chart, help them to answer one question, reading across the appropriate row and down the appropriate column, to show them the intersection of the two.

Symmetry

The dotted line is a mirror line. Complete each shape.

Complete each shape.

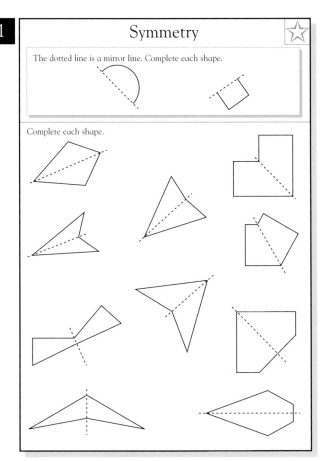

If children have difficulty with these shapes, let them use a mirror. Even if they are confident, let them check the shapes with a mirror when they finish.

3-dimensional shapes

Draw a small circle around each vertex in this shape.

Draw a small circle around each vertex in these shapes.

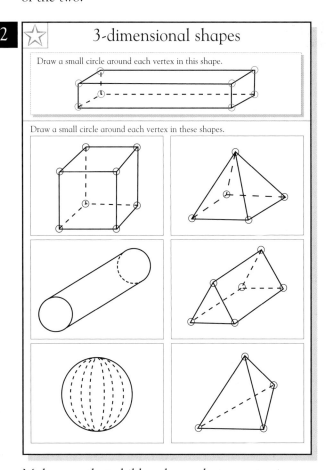

Make sure that children know that a vertex is a single point and that a cylinder and a sphere have no vertices.

Number pairs

Look at this grid.

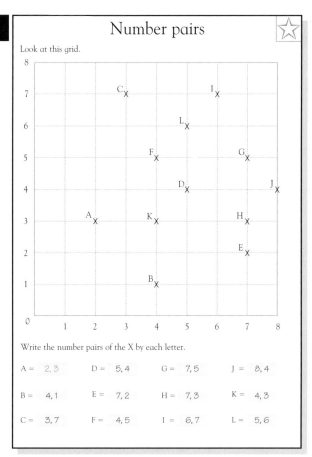

Write the number pairs of the X by each letter.

A = 2, 3   D = 5, 4   G = 7, 5   J = 8, 4

B = 4, 1   E = 7, 2   H = 7, 3   K = 4, 3

C = 3, 7   F = 4, 5   I = 6, 7   L = 5, 6

Make sure that children understand that the order of the number pairs is important. The first number is from the horizontal or *x*-axis, and the second number is from the vertical or *y*-axis.

Adding and subtracting

Add 100 to 356.   Add 100 to 2,376.
456   2,476

Subtract 100 from 5,324.   Subtract 100 from 7,296.
5,224   7,196

Add 100 to each number.

376	476	795	895	646	746	585	685
286	386	57	157	4,312	4,412	5,634	5,734
12	112	4,789	4,889	724	824	3,803	3,903

Add 100 to each number.

485	585	607	707	37	137	843	943
3,587	3,687	7,056	7,156	5,045	5,145	2,707	2,807
5,897	5,997	9,564	9,664	5,499	5,599	9,001	9,101

Subtract 100 from each number.

364	264	729	629	477	377	765	665
103	3	146	46	1,203	1,103	599	499
100	0	5,745	5,645	3,178	3,078	6,107	6,007

Subtract 100 from each number.

4,734	4,634	8,610	8,510	5,307	5,207	9,362	9,262
2,675	2,575	4,907	4,807	8,445	8,345	1,401	1,301
1,400	1,300	5,638	5,538	6,832	6,732	4,256	4,156

There is no regrouping on this page, so children should realize that they need only change the digit in the hundreds place for each number.

Dividing by 10

Divide 90 by 10.   Divide 3,400 by 10.
9   340

Divide each number by 10.

60	6	80	8	10	1	50	5
100	10	150	15	230	23	300	30
210	21	170	17	20	2	260	26
40	4	360	36	590	59	730	73
420	42	380	38	820	82	540	54

Multiply each number by 10.

30	300	70	700	90	900	10	100
60	600	80	800	11	110	140	1,400
170	1,700	190	1,900	230	2,300	280	2,800
380	3,800	410	4,100	840	8,400	940	9,400
600	6,000	100	1,000	750	7,500	560	5,600

Divide each number by 10.

700	70	2,300	230	4,100	410	3,650	365
6,480	648	7,080	708	3,540	354	2,030	203
1,030	103	9,670	967	6,320	632	1,400	140
300	30	900	90	1,020	102	3,660	366
20	2	18,000	1,800	13,600	1,360	17,890	1,789

Children should understand quickly that dividing multiples of 10 by 10 results in the removal of the final zero. Make sure that they remove the commas in any thousands when they divide by 10.

Length

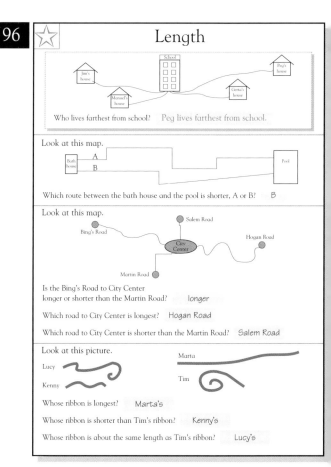

Who lives farthest from school?   Peg lives farthest from school.

Look at this map.

Which route between the bath house and the pool is shorter, A or B?   B

Look at this map.

Is the Bing's Road to City Center longer or shorter than the Martin Road?   longer

Which road to City Center is longest?   Hogan Road

Which road to City Center is shorter than the Martin Road?   Salem Road

Look at this picture.

Whose ribbon is longest?   Marta's

Whose ribbon is shorter than Tim's ribbon?   Kenny's

Whose ribbon is about the same length as Tim's ribbon?   Lucy's

If children have difficulty visualizing lengths, have them use a ruler or a piece of string for making comparisons.

Identifying patterns

Continue each pattern.

| 11 | 22 | 33 | 44 | 55 | 66 | 77 | 88 |
| 12 | 24 | 36 | 48 | 60 | 72 | 84 | 96 |

Continue each pattern.

12	23	34	45	56	67	78	89
9	21	33	45	57	69	81	93
32	43	54	65	76	87	98	109
2	14	26	38	50	62	74	86
2	13	24	35	46	57	68	79
6	18	30	42	54	66	78	90
3	8	13	18	23	28	33	38
12	24	36	48	60	72	84	96

Continue each pattern.

78	67	56	45	34	23	12	1
94	82	70	58	46	34	22	10
88	77	66	55	44	33	22	11
96	84	72	60	48	36	24	12
7	18	29	40	51	62	73	84
14	26	38	50	62	74	86	98
8	19	30	41	52	63	74	85
10	22	34	46	58	70	82	94

Point out that some of the patterns show an increase and some a decrease. Children should check that the operation that turns the first number into the second also turns the second into the third. They can then continue the pattern.

Properties of polygons

Circle the polygon that has 4 sides of the same length.

Circle the polygon described.

The 3 sides are all the same length.

Exactly 2 pairs of sides are parallel.

Exactly 1 pair of sides is parallel.

All the sides are of equal length and each side is parallel to one other side.

Each of the sides is a different length.

Has 6 sides of equal length.

Make sure children understand the term *parallel*.

Square numbers

This square has two rows and two columns. It is 2 x 2.
How many dots are there? 4

Draw a picture like the one above to show each of these numbers.

3 x 3 How many dots are there? 9

4 x 4 How many dots are there? 16

5 x 5 How many dots are there? 25

6 x 6 How many dots are there? 36

7 x 7 How many dots are there? 49

8 x 8 How many dots are there? 64

9 x 9 How many dots are there? 81

10 x 10 How many dots are there? 100

This page introduces the concept of square numbers, and is a precursor to understanding area.

Fractions and decimals

Write each fraction as a decimal.

$\frac{1}{2} = 0.5$ $\frac{1}{10} = 0.1$

Write this decimal as a fraction.

$0.25 = \frac{25}{100} = \frac{1}{4}$

Write each fraction as a decimal.

$\frac{1}{10}$	0.1	$\frac{1}{2}$	0.5	$\frac{3}{10}$	0.3	$\frac{5}{10}$	0.5
$\frac{2}{10}$	0.2	$\frac{9}{10}$	0.9	$\frac{6}{10}$	0.6	$\frac{1}{10}$	0.1
$\frac{8}{10}$	0.8	$\frac{3}{10}$	0.3	$\frac{4}{10}$	0.4	$\frac{5}{10}$	0.5
$\frac{6}{10}$	0.6	$\frac{7}{10}$	0.7	$\frac{8}{10}$	0.8	$\frac{9}{10}$	0.9

Write each decimal as a fraction.

0.8	$\frac{8}{10}$	0.5	$\frac{5}{10}$	0.3	$\frac{3}{10}$	0.4	$\frac{2}{5}$
0.25	$\frac{1}{4}$	0.7	$\frac{7}{10}$	0.2	$\frac{1}{5}$	0.75	$\frac{3}{4}$
0.2	$\frac{2}{10}$	0.6	$\frac{6}{10}$	0.5	$\frac{1}{2}$	0.8	$\frac{4}{5}$
0.1	$\frac{1}{10}$	0.4	$\frac{4}{10}$	0.6	$\frac{3}{5}$	0.9	$\frac{9}{10}$

Write the answer in the box.

Which two of the fractions above are the same as 0.5? $\frac{5}{10}, \frac{1}{2}$

Which two of the fractions above are the same as 0.8? $\frac{8}{10}, \frac{4}{5}$

Which two of the fractions above are the same as 0.6? $\frac{6}{10}, \frac{3}{5}$

Which two of the fractions above are the same as 0.2? $\frac{2}{10}, \frac{1}{5}$

Which two of the fractions above are the same as 0.4? $\frac{4}{10}, \frac{2}{5}$

Children should realize that $\frac{1}{10}$ is equivalent to 0.1. If necessary, help them understand that $\frac{2}{10}$ is equivalent to 0.2, and so on. Children also need to know the decimal equivalents of $\frac{1}{4}$ and $\frac{3}{4}$.

Fractions of shapes

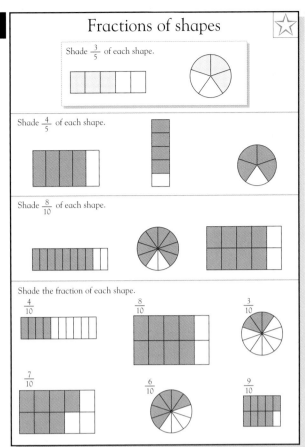

Shade $\frac{3}{5}$ of each shape.

Shade $\frac{4}{5}$ of each shape.

Shade $\frac{8}{10}$ of each shape.

Shade the fraction of each shape.

$\frac{4}{10}$ $\frac{8}{10}$ $\frac{3}{10}$

$\frac{7}{10}$ $\frac{6}{10}$ $\frac{9}{10}$

Children may shade in any combination of the sections as long as the shaded area represents the fraction.

Comparing fractions

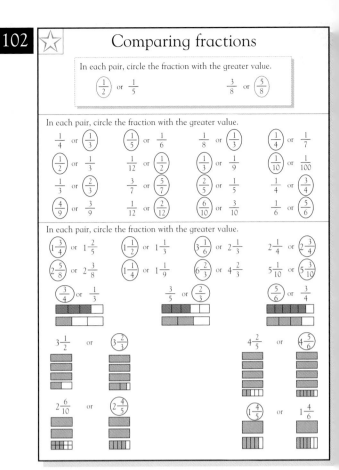

In each pair, circle the fraction with the greater value.

$\left(\frac{1}{2}\right)$ or $\frac{1}{5}$ $\frac{3}{8}$ or $\left(\frac{5}{8}\right)$

In each pair, circle the fraction with the greater value.

$\frac{1}{4}$ or $\left(\frac{1}{3}\right)$ $\left(\frac{1}{5}\right)$ or $\frac{1}{6}$ $\frac{1}{8}$ or $\left(\frac{1}{3}\right)$ $\left(\frac{1}{4}\right)$ or $\frac{1}{7}$

$\left(\frac{1}{2}\right)$ or $\frac{1}{3}$ $\frac{1}{12}$ or $\left(\frac{1}{2}\right)$ $\left(\frac{1}{3}\right)$ or $\frac{1}{9}$ $\left(\frac{1}{10}\right)$ or $\frac{1}{100}$

$\frac{1}{3}$ or $\left(\frac{2}{3}\right)$ $\frac{3}{7}$ or $\left(\frac{5}{7}\right)$ $\left(\frac{2}{5}\right)$ or $\frac{1}{5}$ $\frac{1}{4}$ or $\left(\frac{3}{4}\right)$

$\left(\frac{4}{9}\right)$ or $\frac{3}{9}$ $\frac{1}{12}$ or $\left(\frac{2}{12}\right)$ $\left(\frac{6}{10}\right)$ or $\frac{3}{10}$ $\frac{1}{6}$ or $\left(\frac{5}{6}\right)$

In each pair, circle the fraction with the greater value.

$\left(1\frac{3}{4}\right)$ or $1\frac{2}{5}$ $\left(1\frac{1}{2}\right)$ or $1\frac{1}{3}$ $3\frac{1}{6}$ or $\left(2\frac{1}{3}\right)$ $2\frac{1}{4}$ or $\left(2\frac{3}{4}\right)$

$\left(2\frac{5}{8}\right)$ or $2\frac{3}{8}$ $\left(1\frac{1}{4}\right)$ or $1\frac{1}{9}$ $6\frac{2}{3}$ or $4\frac{2}{3}$ $5\frac{1}{10}$ or $\left(5\frac{3}{10}\right)$

$\left(\frac{3}{4}\right)$ or $\frac{1}{3}$ $\frac{3}{5}$ or $\left(\frac{2}{3}\right)$ $\left(\frac{5}{6}\right)$ or $\frac{3}{4}$

$3\frac{1}{2}$ or $\left(3\frac{2}{3}\right)$ $4\frac{2}{5}$ or $\left(4\frac{5}{6}\right)$

$2\frac{6}{10}$ or $\left(2\frac{4}{5}\right)$ $\left(1\frac{4}{5}\right)$ or $1\frac{4}{6}$

If children have difficulty comparing fractions, you may want to model the fractions with a cut-up paper plate or sheet of paper.

Rounding decimals

Write each amount to the nearest dollar.

$1.67	$2.83	$1.23	$3.28
$2.00	$3.00	$1.00	$3.00

Write each amount to the nearest dollar.

$2.67	$3.00	$3.18	$3.00	$6.75	$7.00	$7.43	$7.00
$8.28	$8.00	$8.67	$9.00	$4.97	$5.00	$2.43	$2.00
$4.66	$5.00	$8.12	$8.00	$6.08	$6.00	$5.40	$5.00
$7.02	$7.00	$6.74	$7.00	$7.83	$8.00	$12.78	$13.00
$11.64	$12.00	$10.64	$11.00	$15.67	$16.00	$21.37	$21.00

Write each length to the nearest meter.

1.76 m	2 m	4.32 m	4 m	6.75 m	7 m	3.84 m	4 m
7.40 m	7 m	3.18 m	3 m	7.31 m	7 m	9.63 m	10 m
5.42 m	5 m	12.82 m	13 m	18.53 m	19 m	16.45 m	16 m
10.53 m	11 m	20.65 m	21 m	17.45 m	17 m	14.32 m	14 m
12.64 m	13 m	19.05 m	19 m	15.51 m	16 m	27.47 m	27 m

Write each amount to the nearest dollar or meter.

3.46 m	3 m	$2.50	$3.00	4.50 m	5 m	$7.50	$8.00
12.50 m	13 m	18.99 m	19 m	$12.50	$13.00	23.50 m	24 m
35.50 m	36 m	$61.67	$62.00	50.50 m	51 m	67.50 m	68 m
$45.67	$46.00	$63.50	$64.00	$89.78	$90.00	34.50 m	35 m
$58.50	$59.00	$21.56	$22.00	$95.50	$96.00	64.50 m	65 m

Children should recognize that amounts of 50¢ or 50 cm and above are rounded up, and amounts below 50¢ and 50 cm are rounded down. Make sure that children increase the whole number by 1 when they round up.

Adding

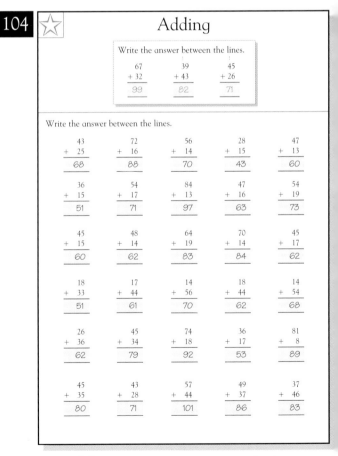

Write the answer between the lines.

67	39	45
+ 32	+ 43	+ 26
99	82	71

Write the answer between the lines.

43	72	56	28	47
+ 25	+ 16	+ 14	+ 15	+ 13
68	88	70	43	60

36	54	84	47	54
+ 15	+ 17	+ 13	+ 16	+ 19
51	71	97	63	73

45	48	64	70	45
+ 15	+ 14	+ 19	+ 14	+ 17
60	62	83	84	62

18	17	14	18	14
+ 33	+ 44	+ 56	+ 44	+ 54
51	61	70	62	68

26	45	74	36	81
+ 36	+ 34	+ 18	+ 17	+ 8
62	79	92	53	89

45	43	57	49	37
+ 35	+ 28	+ 44	+ 37	+ 46
80	71	101	86	83

Most of the sums require regrouping. Make sure that children do not neglect to add 10 to the tens column when they regroup.

Adding

Write the answer between the lines.

35 ft	74 ft	46 ft
+ 25 ft	+ 18 ft	+ 36 ft
60 ft	92 ft	82 ft

Write the answer between the lines.

37 ft	56 ft	68 ft	49 ft	28 ft
+ 46 ft	+ 36 ft	+ 45 ft	+ 27 ft	+ 36 ft
83 ft	92 ft	113 ft	76 ft	64 ft

47 mi	29 mi	56 mi	55 mi	38 mi
+ 44 mi	+ 34 mi	+ 35 mi	+ 37 mi	+ 44 mi
91 mi	63 mi	91 mi	92 mi	82 mi

65 lb	43 lb	52 lb	47 lb	36 lb
+ 27 lb	+ 18 lb	+ 17 lb	+ 27 lb	+ 17 lb
92 lb	61 lb	69 lb	74 lb	53 lb

57 oz	48 oz	44 oz	66 oz	43 oz
+ 42 oz	+ 24 oz	+ 18 oz	+ 27 oz	+ 29 oz
99 oz	72 oz	62 oz	93 oz	72 oz

Write the answer between the lines.

$23.00	$36.00	$75.00	$27.00
+ $18.00	+ $43.00	+ $16.00	+ $38.00
$41.00	$79.00	$91.00	$65.00

This page is similar to the previous page, but includes units of measure. Make sure that children include the units in their answers.

Adding

Write the answer between the lines.

35	18	24
17	14	16
+ 16	+ 17	+ 19
68	49	59

Write the answer between the lines.

12	17	15	12	18
13	10	13	14	10
+ 13	+ 11	+ 11	+ 12	+ 11
38	38	39	38	39

17	19	16	12	19
26	13	21	25	32
+ 12	+ 14	+ 31	+ 33	+ 12
55	46	68	70	63

20	30	40	50	60
32	26	42	21	14
+ 16	+ 25	+ 25	+ 21	+ 8
68	81	107	92	82

25	35	45	55	65
15	25	15	35	15
+ 5	+ 5	+ 5	+ 5	+ 5
45	65	65	95	85

23	34	45	56	67
45	32	16	16	12
+ 32	+ 13	+ 9	+ 7	+ 8
100	79	70	79	87

Children should add the ones column first, regrouping when necessary. In some of the questions, children must add 20 to the tens column, rather than 10.

Subtracting

Write the answer between the lines.

57	42	36
− 15	− 16	− 29
42	26	7

Write the answer between the lines.

40	60	70	50	90
− 18	− 23	− 37	− 18	− 27
22	37	33	32	63

41	62	85	64	71
− 14	− 15	− 37	− 45	− 36
27	47	48	19	35

45	65	75	95	85
− 18	− 34	− 69	− 49	− 38
27	31	6	46	47

73	82	74	81	64
− 27	− 38	− 47	− 39	− 47
46	44	27	42	17

61	52	61	53	73
− 14	− 17	− 19	− 23	− 44
47	35	42	30	29

70	63	83	53	47
− 26	− 7	− 56	− 36	− 43
44	56	27	17	4

Most of the subtraction problems on this page require regrouping.

Subtracting

Write the answer between the lines.

56 ft	37 mi	58 lb
− 18 ft	− 19 mi	− 19 lb
38 ft	18 mi	39 lb

Write the answer between the lines.

45 ft	63 ft	74 ft	82 ft	40 ft
− 23 ft	− 44 ft	− 38 ft	− 29 ft	− 17 ft
22 ft	19 ft	36 ft	53 ft	23 ft

61 ft	81 ft	62 ft	83 ft	43 ft
− 27 ft	− 36 ft	− 27 ft	− 36 ft	− 17 ft
34 ft	45 ft	35 ft	47 ft	26 ft

45 ft	60 ft	73 ft	74 ft	85 ft
− 26 ft	− 47 ft	− 48 ft	− 39 ft	− 47 ft
19 ft	13 ft	25 ft	35 ft	38 ft

Write the answer between the lines.

50 mi	37 mi	75 mi	84 mi	90 mi
− 28 mi	− 18 mi	− 39 mi	− 29 mi	− 37 mi
22 mi	19 mi	36 mi	55 mi	53 mi

Write the answer between the lines.

68 lb	47 lb	64 lb	79 lb	56 lb
− 39 lb	− 38 lb	− 27 lb	− 27 lb	− 45 lb
29 lb	9 lb	37 lb	52 lb	11 lb

This page is similar to the previous page, but includes units of measure. Make sure that children include the units in their answers.

Real-life problems

Solve the problem and then write the answer.

Tuhil is reading a book that
has 72 pages. He has read 38 pages.
How many more pages does
Tuhil have to read?   34 pages

$$\begin{array}{r} 6\ \text{\small 12}\\ 7\,2\\ -3\,8\\ \hline 3\,4 \end{array}$$

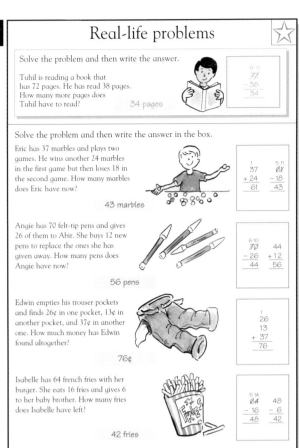

Solve the problem and then write the answer in the box.

Eric has 37 marbles and plays two
games. He wins another 24 marbles
in the first game but then loses 18 in
the second game. How many marbles
does Eric have now?

43 marbles

$$\begin{array}{r} 1\\ 37\\ +24\\ \hline 61 \end{array} \qquad \begin{array}{r} 5\ 11\\ 6\,1\\ -1\,8\\ \hline 4\,3 \end{array}$$

Angie has 70 felt-tip pens and gives
26 of them to Abir. She buys 12 new
pens to replace the ones she has
given away. How many pens does
Angie have now?

56 pens

$$\begin{array}{r} 6\ 10\\ 7\,0\\ -2\,6\\ \hline 4\,4 \end{array} \qquad \begin{array}{r} 44\\ +12\\ \hline 56 \end{array}$$

Edwin empties his trouser pockets
and finds 26¢ in one pocket, 13¢ in
another pocket, and 37¢ in another
one. How much money has Edwin
found altogether?

76¢

$$\begin{array}{r} 1\\ 26\\ 13\\ +37\\ \hline 76 \end{array}$$

Isabelle has 64 french fries with her
burger. She eats 16 fries and gives 6
to her baby brother. How many fries
does Isabelle have left?

42 fries

$$\begin{array}{r} 5\ 14\\ 6\,4\\ -1\,6\\ \hline 4\,8 \end{array} \qquad \begin{array}{r} 48\\ -\ 6\\ \hline 42 \end{array}$$

These problems require children to do multiple
operations. If they have difficulty, discuss the
problems and "walk" them through the steps.

Multiplying

Write the answer between the lines.

27	53	36	19
x 5	x 4	x 3	x 4
135	212	108	76

Write the answer between the lines.

26	43	67	18	74
x 4	x 4	x 4	x 4	x 4
104	172	268	72	296

19	41	58	32	94
x 3	x 3	x 3	x 3	x 3
57	123	174	96	282

33	49	67	28	63
x 5	x 5	x 5	x 5	x 5
165	245	335	140	315

64	85	94	57	78
x 2	x 2	x 2	x 2	x 2
128	170	188	114	156

15	53	64	85	72
x 6	x 6	x 6	x 6	x 6
90	318	384	510	432

37	85	51	84	47
x 8	x 8	x 8	x 8	x 8
296	680	408	672	376

Most of the multiplications require children to
regroup. Go through any incorrect answers with
children to find out whether the problem results
from incorrect regrouping or poor knowledge of
times tables.

Multiplying

Write the answer between the lines.

24	75	58	17
x 4	x 6	x 4	x 5
96	450	232	85

Write the answer between the lines.

43	50	37	29	16
x 7	x 7	x 7	x 7	x 7
301	350	259	203	112

27	58	36	14	61
x 9	x 9	x 9	x 9	x 9
243	522	324	126	549

53	37	49	58	67
x 10	x 10	x 10	x 10	x 10
530	370	490	580	670

37	47	87	17	97
x 4	x 5	x 6	x 7	x 8
148	235	522	119	776

58	38	78	28	18
x 6	x 7	x 8	x 9	x 10
348	266	624	252	180

49	29	59	89	69
x 5	x 6	x 7	x 8	x 9
245	174	413	712	621

See the comments for the previous page.

Dividing

Write the answer in the box.

24 ÷ 7 = 3 r 3   4 r 1   43 ÷ 8 = 5 r 3

$$\begin{array}{r} 4\,r\,1\\ 5\overline{)2\,1}\\ -2\,0\\ \hline 1 \end{array} \qquad \begin{array}{r} 5\,r\,3\\ 8\overline{)4\,3}\\ -4\,0\\ \hline 3 \end{array}$$

Write the answer in the box.

27 ÷ 3 =	9	14 ÷ 3 =	4 r 2	23 ÷ 3 =	7 r 2
7 ÷ 3 =	2 r 1	31 ÷ 4 =	7 r 3	14 ÷ 4 =	3 r 2
38 ÷ 4 =	9 r 2	4 ÷ 4 =	1	42 ÷ 5 =	8 r 2
23 ÷ 5 =	4 r 3	15 ÷ 5 =	3	27 ÷ 5 =	5 r 2
47 ÷ 6 =	7 r 5	35 ÷ 5 =	7	46 ÷ 5 =	9 r 1

Write the answer in the box.

4 r 2	5 r 6	2 r 5	7	3
8)34	8)46	8)21	8)56	9)27
−32	−40	−16	−56	−27
2	6	5	0	0

1 r 1	8	5 r 2	7 r 2	10
2)3	2)16	3)17	3)23	3)30
−2	−16	−15	−21	−30
1	0	2	2	0

Write the answer in the box.

45 ÷ 8 =	5 r 5	73 ÷ 8 =	9 r 1	56 ÷ 8 =	7
73 ÷ 9 =	8 r 1	41 ÷ 9 =	4 r 5	50 ÷ 9 =	5 r 5
54 ÷ 10 =	5 r 4	89 ÷ 10 =	8 r 9	42 ÷ 10 =	4 r 2

These division problems test children's knowledge
of times tables. Children should be able to
calculate the remainders easily.

Dividing

Write the answer in the box.

31 ÷ 4 = 7 r 3

        2 r 5
    6) 1 7
      -1 2
        5

31 ÷ 9 = 3 r 4

    9) 3 1
      -2 7
        4

Write the answer in the box.

46 ÷ 9 = 5 r 1	28 ÷ 7 = 4	45 ÷ 9 = 5
74 ÷ 8 = 9 r 2	32 ÷ 3 = 10 r 2	45 ÷ 7 = 6 r 3
61 ÷ 7 = 8 r 5	65 ÷ 9 = 7 r 2	12 ÷ 9 = 1 r 3
17 ÷ 4 = 4 r 1	24 ÷ 6 = 4	36 ÷ 6 = 6
37 ÷ 8 = 4 r 5	37 ÷ 9 = 4 r 1	37 ÷ 10 = 3 r 7

Write the answer in the box.

      6 r 3   7   4 r 7   3 r 3   3 r 8
   7) 4 5   8) 5 6   9) 4 3   9) 3 0   9) 3 5
    -4 2   -5 6   -3 6   -2 7   -2 7
      3   0   7   3   8

      5 r 8   8 r 4   6   4 r 7   3
   9) 5 3   9) 7 6   9) 5 4   9) 4 3   9) 2 7
    -4 5   -7 2   -5 4   -3 6   -2 7
      8   4   0   7   0

Write the answer in the box.

8 ÷ 6 = 1 r 2	12 ÷ 10 = 1 r 2	11 ÷ 9 = 1 r 2
13 ÷ 10 = 1 r 3	17 ÷ 7 = 2 r 3	23 ÷ 8 = 2 r 7
70 ÷ 10 = 7	70 ÷ 7 = 10	54 ÷ 6 = 9

See the comments for the previous page.

Choosing the operation

Write either x or ÷ in the box to make the number sentence true.

6 × 7 = 42   24 ÷ 6 = 4   10 ÷ 2 = 5

Write either x or ÷ in the box to make the number sentence true.

35 ÷ 7 = 5	35 ÷ 5 = 7	7 x 5 = 35
5 x 7 = 35	6 x 9 = 54	54 ÷ 6 = 9
9 x 6 = 54	54 ÷ 9 = 6	32 ÷ 4 = 8
4 x 8 = 32	8 x 4 = 32	32 ÷ 8 = 4
4 x 9 = 36	36 ÷ 4 = 9	9 x 4 = 36
36 ÷ 9 = 4	80 ÷ 8 = 10	8 x 10 = 80
7 x 9 = 63	63 ÷ 7 = 9	63 ÷ 9 = 7
9 x 7 = 63	9 x 9 = 81	81 ÷ 9 = 9
64 ÷ 8 = 8	8 x 8 = 64	25 ÷ 5 = 5
5 x 5 = 25	16 ÷ 4 = 4	4 x 4 = 16
7 x 7 = 49	49 ÷ 7 = 7	3 x 3 = 9
9 ÷ 3 = 3	100 ÷ 10 = 10	10 x 10 = 100
50 ÷ 10 = 5	5 x 8 = 40	40 ÷ 4 = 10
20 ÷ 5 = 4	4 x 10 = 40	36 ÷ 6 = 6
3 x 7 = 21	21 ÷ 3 = 7	7 x 4 = 28
14 x 10 = 140	140 ÷ 2 = 70	70 ÷ 10 = 7
42 ÷ 6 = 7	7 x 10 = 70	72 ÷ 8 = 9
50 ÷ 5 = 10	20 ÷ 4 = 5	3 x 8 = 24

Children will probably realize that if the answer is
larger than the first number, they should multiply,
and if the answer is smaller than the first number
they should divide. They can check some of their
answers to make sure that they are correct.

Real-life problems

Write the answer in the box.

There are 8 ink cartridges in each pack.
How many cartridges will there
be in 6 packs?   8 x 6 = 48

        48 cartridges

Write the answer in the box.

Ian shares 50 oranges equally
among 6 elephants and gives the
remainder to the giraffes. How many
oranges do the giraffes receive?

        8 r 2
     6) 50
        48
         2

    2 oranges

There are 9 children at a birthday
party and each child has 4 chocolate
cupcakes. How many cupcakes
do the children have altogether?

    9 x 4 = 36

    36 cupcakes

Ben has 60 building blocks and puts
them in stacks of 7. How many stacks
of 7 can Ben make?

        8 r 4
     7) 60
        56
         4

    8 stacks

Katie has seven dimes, four
nickels, and four pennies.
How much does she have altogether?

    10 x 7 = 70
    4 x 5 = 20
    4 x 1 = 4 +
            94

    94¢

The dog wants to bury four bones in
each hole. The dog has 36 bones.
How many holes must the dog dig?

         9
     4) 36
        36
         0

    9 holes

Make sure that children understand which
operation to perform for each problem.

Perimeter

Write the perimeter of this shape in the answer box.

        8 cm
        2 cm
    2 cm   8 cm
          + 2 cm
    8 cm   20 cm

Write the perimeter of each shape in the answer box.

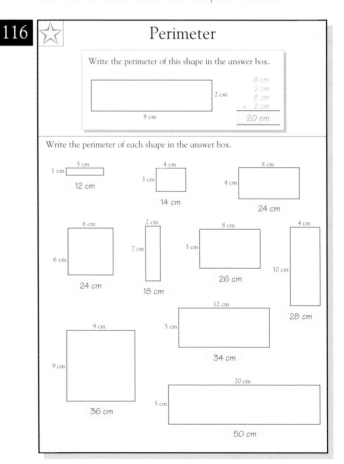

1 cm
    5 cm
    12 cm

3 cm
    4 cm
    14 cm

    8 cm
4 cm
    24 cm

    6 cm
6 cm
    24 cm

2 cm
7 cm
    18 cm

    8 cm
5 cm
    26 cm

4 cm
10 cm
    28 cm

    9 cm
9 cm
    36 cm

    12 cm
5 cm
    34 cm

    20 cm
5 cm
    50 cm

Some children may add all the four sides; others
may double each different length and add the
results; yet others may add the two different
lengths and then double the sum. Each of these
methods is acceptable.

Area

Write the area of the shape in the answer box.

1 cm
7 cm

$1 \times 7 = 7$

7 cm²

Write the area of each shape in the answer box.

12 cm²

10 cm²

6 cm²

16 cm²

20 cm²

12 cm²

4 cm²

9 cm²

Since the area of a shape is the amount of space inside it, the number of squares inside each shape gives the area. Children may realize that multiplying one side of a rectangle by the other will give the same result more quickly.

Area

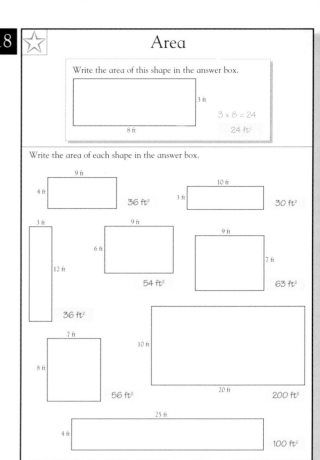

Write the area of this shape in the answer box.

3 ft
8 ft

$3 \times 8 = 24$

24 ft²

Write the area of each shape in the answer box.

9 ft
4 ft
36 ft²

10 ft
3 ft
30 ft²

3 ft
6 ft
12 ft
36 ft²

9 ft
54 ft²

9 ft
7 ft
63 ft²

7 ft
8 ft
56 ft²

10 ft
20 ft
200 ft²

25 ft
4 ft
100 ft²

Following from the last page, this page requires children to find the areas by multiplying the sides together. If they are unsure of the method, sketch in squares on the shapes to help.

Problems using time

Write the answer in the box.

How many minutes until 12 o'clock?

90 minutes

Write the answer in the box.

What time will it be in half an hour?	9:15 or quarter past 9
What time was it ten minutes ago?	8:35 or 25 to 9
How many minutes until 10 o'clock?	75 minutes
The clock is 20 minutes fast. What is the real time?	8:25 or 25 past 8

Write the answer in the box.

What was the time half an hour ago?	2:55 or 5 to 3
How many minutes until 4 o'clock?	35 minutes
How long until a quarter to 4?	20 minutes
How many minutes since 2 o'clock?	85 minutes

Write the answer in the box.

How many minutes since 2:30?	45 minutes
How many minutes until 4 o'clock?	45 minutes
What time did the clock show half an hour ago?	2:45
How many hours until 8:15?	5 hours

Children may use any method that gives the correct answers.

Reading timetables

	Frostburg	Elmhusrt	Badger Farm	Winchester
Redline Bus	8:00	8:05	8:15	8:25
Blueline tram	8:05	No stop	8:12	8:20
City taxi	8:30	8:35	8:45	8:55
Greenline Trolley	8:07	No stop	No stop	8:15

The timetable shows the times it takes to travel using different transport companies between Frostburg and Winchester.

Write the answer in the box.

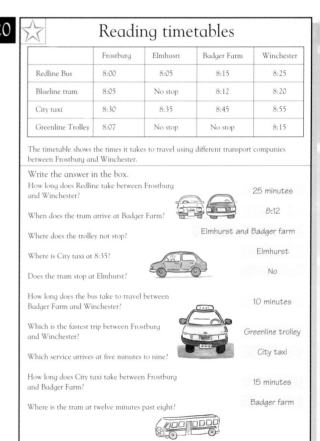

How long does Redline take between Frostburg and Winchester?
25 minutes

When does the tram arrive at Badger Farm?
8:12

Where does the trolley not stop?
Elmhurst and Badger farm

Where is City taxi at 8:35?
Elmhurst

Does the tram stop at Elmhurst?
No

How long does the bus take to travel between Badger Farm and Winchester?
10 minutes

Which is the fastest trip between Frostburg and Winchester?
Greenline trolley

Which service arrives at five minutes to nine?
City taxi

How long does City taxi take between Frostburg and Badger Farm?
15 minutes

Where is the tram at twelve minutes past eight?
Badger farm

Children should find this exercise fairly straightforward. If they have difficulty, help them read across the rows and down the columns to find the information they need.

Averages

Write the average of this row in the box.

4	2	2	2	6	3	2

The average is   3 .

Write the average of each row in the box.

2	3	7	4	2	7	2	5	4
7	4	5	4	8	5	3	4	5
5	3	5	3	5	2	4	5	4
7	5	9	7	2	4	8	6	6
4	3	4	3	4	3	4	7	4
1	4	2	7	3	8	2	5	4
3	2	1	2	2	3	2	1	2
8	3	6	3	8	2	8	2	5

Write the average of each row in the box.

4	8	6	3	9	6	6	6
5	9	2	6	9	1	3	5
6	3	8	6	1	5	6	5
3	8	6	7	5	9	4	6
1	8	3	4	2	6	4	4
9	5	8	7	4	7	9	7
1	3	2	3	1	2	2	2
6	3	7	4	5	4	6	5

If necessary, remind children that the average of a set of quantities is the sum of the quantities divided by the number of quantities.

Estimating

Estimate to find the answer.

One crate of apples sells for between $8 and $12. If Sam sold 10 crates of apples, about how much did he earn?

Sam earned about $100 .

Estimate to find the answer.

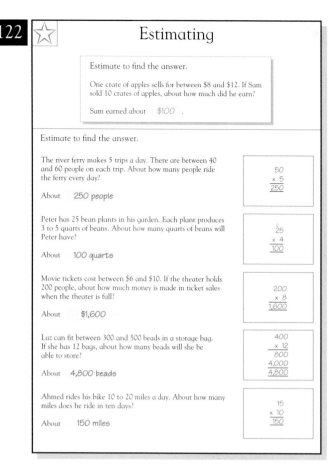

The river ferry makes 5 trips a day. There are between 40 and 60 people on each trip. About how many people ride the ferry every day?

About   250 people

$$\begin{array}{r} 50 \\ \times\ 5 \\ \hline 250 \end{array}$$

Peter has 25 bean plants in his garden. Each plant produces 3 to 5 quarts of beans. About how many quarts of beans will Peter have?

About   100 quarts

$$\begin{array}{r} 25 \\ \times\ 4 \\ \hline 100 \end{array}$$

Movie tickets cost between $6 and $10. If the theater holds 200 people, about how much money is made in ticket sales when the theater is full?

About $1,600

$$\begin{array}{r} 200 \\ \times\ 8 \\ \hline 1,600 \end{array}$$

Luz can fit between 300 and 500 beads in a storage bag. If she has 12 bags, about how many beads will she be able to store?

About   4,800 beads

$$\begin{array}{r} 400 \\ \times\ 12 \\ \hline 800 \\ 4,000 \\ \hline 4,800 \end{array}$$

Ahmed rides his bike 10 to 20 miles a day. About how many miles does he ride in ten days?

About   150 miles

$$\begin{array}{r} 15 \\ \times\ 10 \\ \hline 150 \end{array}$$

Children should use a compatible number—one that is easy to manipulate in the problem—while they estimate.

Calculating change

Circle the correct change.

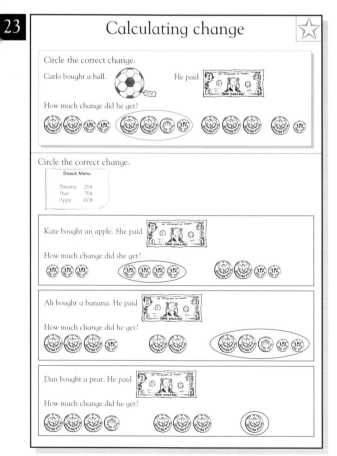

Carlo bought a ball. He paid

How much change did he get?

Circle the correct change.

Snack Menu

Banana   25¢
Pear   75¢
Apple   60¢

Kate bought an apple. She paid

How much change did she get?

Ali bought a banana. He paid

How much change did he get?

Dan bought a pear. He paid

How much change did he get?

Allow children to set up subtraction problems if they cannot complete the calculations mentally.

Counting money

Count the coins. Write the total amount.

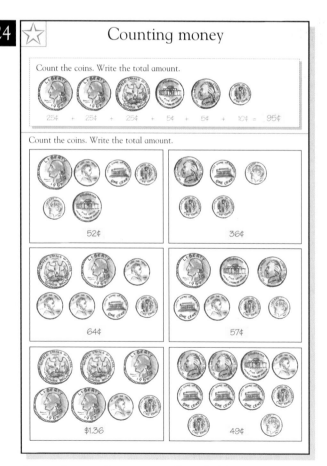

25¢ + 25¢ + 25¢ + 5¢ + 5¢ + 10¢ = 95¢

Count the coins. Write the total amount.

52¢

36¢

64¢

57¢

$1.36

49¢

As on the previous page, allow children to set up addition problems if they need to.

125 Number pairs ☆

Look at the grid and then answer the questions below.

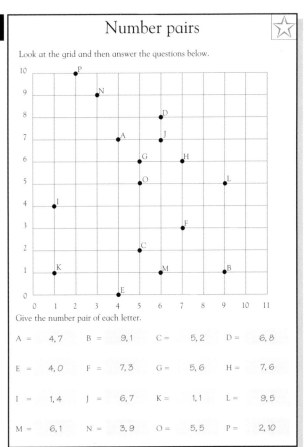

Give the number pair of each letter.

A =	4, 7	B =	9, 1	C =	5, 2	D =	6, 8
E =	4, 0	F =	7, 3	G =	5, 6	H =	7, 6
I =	1, 4	J =	6, 7	K =	1, 1	L =	9, 5
M =	6, 1	N =	3, 9	O =	5, 5	P =	2, 10

Make sure that children understand that the order of the number pairs is important. The first number is from the horizontal or *x*-axis, and the second number is from the vertical or *y*-axis.

---

126 ☆ Multiply or divide?

Write + or – in the box.
$6 \times 5 = 30$ $18 \div 2 = 9$ $5 \times 10 = 50$

Write x or ÷ in the box.

$7 \times 5 = 35$	$10 \div 2 = 5$	$12 \div 2 = 6$
$30 \div 5 = 6$	$30 \div 10 = 3$	$9 \times 2 = 18$
$14 \div 2 = 7$	$35 \div 5 = 7$	$6 \times 10 = 60$
$40 \div 10 = 4$	$20 \div 4 = 5$	$5 \times 3 = 15$
$5 \times 6 = 30$	$3 \times 10 = 30$	$90 \div 10 = 9$
$50 \div 5 = 10$	$18 \div 2 = 9$	$15 \div 3 = 5$

Write the answers in the boxes.

A number divided by 4 is 10. What is the number?	40
I multiply a number by 6 and the answer is 30. What is the number?	5
A number multiplied by 10 gives the answer 10. What is the number?	1
I divide a number by 8 and the answer is 5. What is the number?	40
A number divided by 7 is 5. What is the number?	35
I multiply a number by 2 and the answer is 18. What is the number?	9
A number multiplied by 5 is 45. What is the number?	9
I divide a number by 2 and the answer is 1. What is the number?	2

Write x or ÷ in the box.

$7 \times 10 = 70$	$5 \times 5 = 25$	$10 \div 10 = 1$
$5 \div 5 = 1$	$9 \times 2 = 18$	$2 \times 2 = 4$
$15 \div 5 = 3$	$10 \times 10 = 100$	$50 \div 5 = 10$
$100 \div 10 = 10$	$2 \div 2 = 1$	$20 \div 5 = 4$

The second section requires children to perform the inverse operation to reach the answer. For the other sections, children should realize that if the answer is larger than the first number, they must multiply, and if it is smaller, they must divide.

---

127 Lines of symmetry ☆

Draw the line of symmetry on each shape.

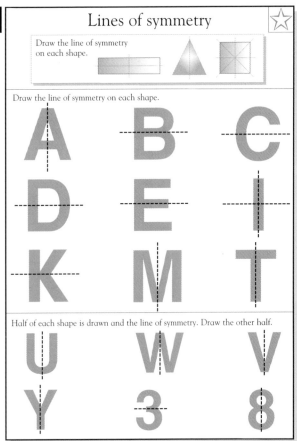

Draw the line of symmetry on each shape.

Half of each shape is drawn and the line of symmetry. Draw the other half.

If children pick an incorrect line of symmetry, you can use a small mirror to show them their mistake.

---

128 ☆ Counting by 3s, 4s, and 5s

Find the pattern. Continue each row.

Count by 3s.	9	12	15	18	21	24	27
Count by 4s.	8	12	16	20	24	28	32
Count by 5s.	55	50	45	40	35	30	25

Find the pattern. Continue each row.

0	3	6	9	12	15	18	21
8	12	16	20	24	28	32	36
38	41	44	47	50	53	56	59
40	45	50	55	60	65	70	75
63	67	71	75	79	83	87	91
85	90	95	100	105	110	115	120
6	10	14	18	22	26	30	34
21	18	15	12	9	6	3	0
68	65	62	59	56	53	50	47
85	80	75	70	65	60	55	50
43	40	37	34	31	28	25	22
49	45	41	37	33	29	25	21
71	67	63	59	55	51	47	43
83	78	73	68	63	58	53	48
39	34	29	24	19	14	9	4

Some of the patterns show an increase, while others show a decrease. Children should be able to complete these questions using mental math.

Multiples

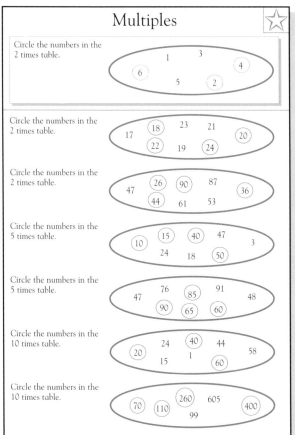

Circle the numbers in the 2 times table.

1   3   4   6   5   2

Circle the numbers in the 2 times table.

17   18   23   21   20   22   19   24

Circle the numbers in the 2 times table.

47   26   90   87   44   61   53   36

Circle the numbers in the 5 times table.

10   15   40   47   24   18   50   3

Circle the numbers in the 5 times table.

76   85   91   47   90   65   60   48

Circle the numbers in the 10 times table.

24   40   44   20   15   1   60   58

Circle the numbers in the 10 times table.

70   110   260   605   99   400

These questions test children's familiarity with the 2, 5, and 10 times tables.

Comparing and ordering

Write these numbers in order, starting with the smallest.

431   678   273   586   *273   431   586   678*

Write these numbers in order, starting with the smallest.

267	931	374	740	267	374	740	931
734	218	625	389	218	389	625	734
836	590	374	669	374	590	669	836
572	197	469	533	197	469	533	572
948	385	846	289	289	385	846	948
406	560	460	650	406	460	560	650
738	837	378	783	378	738	783	837
582	285	528	852	285	528	582	852
206	620	602	260	206	260	602	620
634	436	364	463	364	436	463	634
47	740	74	704	47	74	704	740
501	150	51	105	51	105	150	501
290	92	209	29	29	92	209	290
803	380	83	38	38	83	380	803
504	450	54	45	45	54	450	504

Make sure that children do not simply order the numbers according to the first digits.

Rounding

What is 327 rounded to the nearest 100?

300   310   320   330   340   350   360   370   380   390   400

300   327

What is each number rounded to the nearest 100?

478	500	231	200	147	100	687	700
342	300	812	800	973	1,000	439	400
639	600	108	100	374	400	752	800
418	400	639	600	523	500	446	400
857	900	560	600	299	300	809	800

What is 250 rounded to the nearest 100?

200   210   220   230   240   250   260   270   280   290   300

300   250

What is each number rounded to the nearest 100?

450	500	850	900	650	700	87	100
21	0	405	400	150	200	950	1,000
655	700	540	500	980	1,000	50	100
750	800	250	300	90	100	59	100
550	600	105	100	955	1,000	350	400

Children should recognize that amounts of 50 and above are rounded up, and amounts below 50 are rounded down. Make sure that children increase the hundreds digit by 1 when they round up.

Fractions

$\frac{1}{2}$ of 12 is *8* $\frac{1}{3}$ of 9 is *3* $\frac{1}{4}$ of 20 is *5*

What is $\frac{1}{2}$ of each number?

4	2	8	4	10	5	2	1
6	3	12	6	20	10	16	8
14	7	50	25	100	50	60	30

What is $\frac{1}{3}$ of each number?

6	2	12	4	18	6	9	3
3	1	15	5	21	7	30	10
24	8	60	20	27	9	33	11

What is $\frac{1}{4}$ of each number?

8	2	16	4	4	1	12	3
20	5	40	10	80	20	1	$\frac{1}{4}$

What is $\frac{1}{8}$ of each number?

16	2	8	1	24	3	40	5
32	4	48	6	80	10	56	7

What is $\frac{1}{10}$ of each number?

20	2	40	4	80	8	100	10
10	1	30	3	50	5	90	9

Each of the fractions on this page is a unit fraction—it has a numerator of 1. Children should realize that multiplying by these fractions is the same as dividing by the denominator.

Multiplying

Write the answer in the box.

7 x 3 = 21   9 x 5 = 45   6 x 10 = 60

Write the answer in the box.

2 x 3 = 6	7 x 4 = 28	4 x 3 = 12	6 x 4 = 24
9 x 5 = 45	8 x 3 = 24	6 x 3 = 18	10 x 9 = 90
3 x 2 = 6	9 x 4 = 36	7 x 5 = 35	5 x 4 = 20
0 x 3 = 0	8 x 4 = 32	4 x 10 = 40	0 x 4 = 0
5 x 3 = 15	4 x 4 = 16	9 x 3 = 27	8 x 5 = 40

Write the answer in the box.

Three times a number is 18. What is the number?   6

A child draws 8 squares. How many sides have to be drawn?   32

A box contains 4 cans of beans. A man buys 9 boxes. How many cans does he have?   36

A girl is given 3 stickers for every point she gains in a spelling test. How many will she receive if she gets 10 points?   30

A number multiplied by 4 is 36. What is the number?   9

Light bulbs come in packs of 3. Erin buys 6 packs. How many bulbs will she have?   18

Mari is given eight 5¢ coins. How much money is she given?   40¢

Four times a number is 24. What is the number?   6

A bottle holds 4 liters of soda. How much will 7 bottles hold?   28 liters

Six times a number is 30. What is the number?   5

Children should be able to answer all the questions on this page using mental math.

Dividing

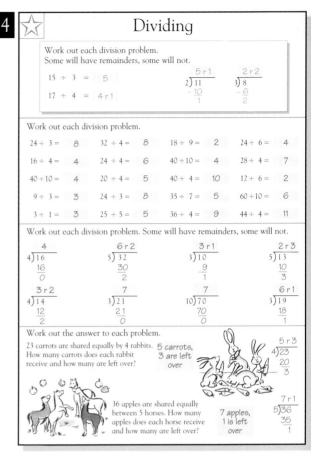

Work out each division problem. Some will have remainders, some will not.

15 ÷ 3 = 5

17 ÷ 4 = 4 r 1

```
      5 r 1          2 r 2
2)11           3)8
 -10            -6
   1             2
```

Work out each division problem.

24 ÷ 3 = 8	32 ÷ 4 = 8	18 ÷ 9 = 2	24 ÷ 6 = 4
16 ÷ 4 = 4	24 ÷ 4 = 6	40 ÷ 10 = 4	28 ÷ 4 = 7
40 ÷ 10 = 4	20 ÷ 4 = 5	40 ÷ 4 = 10	12 ÷ 6 = 2
9 ÷ 3 = 3	24 ÷ 3 = 8	35 ÷ 7 = 5	60 ÷ 10 = 6
3 ÷ 1 = 3	25 ÷ 5 = 5	36 ÷ 4 = 9	44 ÷ 4 = 11

Work out each division problem. Some will have remainders, some will not.

```
    4           6 r 2          3 r 1          2 r 3
4)16         5)32         3)10         5)13
 16           30            9            10
  0            2            1             3

  3 r 2         7            7            6 r 1
4)14         3)21        10)70         3)19
 12           21           70            18
  2            0            0             1
```

Work out the answer to each problem.

23 carrots are shared equally by 4 rabbits. How many carrots does each rabbit receive and how many are left over?   5 carrots, 3 are left over

```
  5 r 3
4)23
 20
  3
```

36 apples are shared equally between 5 horses. How many apples does each horse receive and how many are left over?   7 apples, 1 is left over

```
  7 r 1
5)36
 35
  1
```

Children should be able to answer all the questions on this page using mental math.

Bar graphs

Look at the bar graph. Then answer the question.

How many cherries does Robbie have?   6

Look at the bar graph. Then answer the questions.

Favorite seasons

This graph shows the favorite seasons of a group of children.

How many children were asked which season they liked best?   20

How many children liked autumn best?   6

Which season did four children like?   spring

Which was the favorite season?   summer

How many more children liked autumn than liked winter?   4

Look at the bar graph. Then answer the questions.

Favorite pets

This graph shows the favorite pets of a group of children.

How many children were asked about which pets they liked?   14

Which pet did eight children like?   guinea pigs

How many children liked rabbits?   3

How many children liked hamsters?   1

How many more children liked rabbits than liked hamsters?   2

If children need help reading bar graphs, show them how to read across and up from the axis labels. To answer some of the questions, children will need to add and compare data.

Symmetry

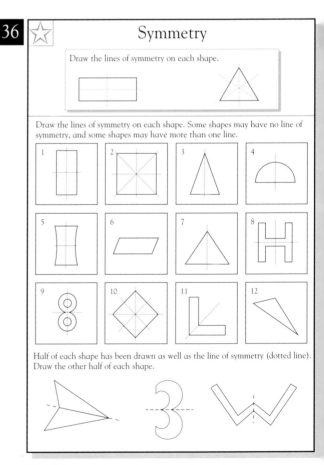

Draw the lines of symmetry on each shape.

Draw the lines of symmetry on each shape. Some shapes may have no line of symmetry, and some shapes may have more than one line.

1   2   3   4

5   6   7   8

9   10   11   12

Half of each shape has been drawn as well as the line of symmetry (dotted line). Draw the other half of each shape.

If children pick an incorrect line of symmetry, you can use a small mirror to show them their mistake.

Ordering

Write these numbers in order starting with the smallest.
670   760   607   706
607   670   706   760

Write these numbers in order starting with the smallest.

270	720	207	702
207	270	702	720

870	780	807	708
708	780	807	870

906	690	960	609
609	690	906	960

106	610	601	160
106	160	601	610

560	506	650	605
506	560	605	650

849	489	948	984
489	849	948	984

890	980	809	908
809	890	908	980

486	684	864	648
486	648	684	864

405	450	540	504
405	450	504	540

746	647	764	674
647	674	746	764

570	586	490	92
92	490	570	586

76	104	200	92
76	92	104	200

440	66	781	177
66	177	440	781

632	236	77	407
77	236	407	632

842	587	99	88
88	99	587	842

74	101	12	800
12	74	101	800

500	468	395	288
288	395	468	500

600	304	403	89
89	304	403	600

78	9	302	470
9	78	302	470

345	543	53	34
34	53	345	543

Make sure that children do not simply order the numbers according to the first digits.

Fractions of shapes

Shade half of each shape.

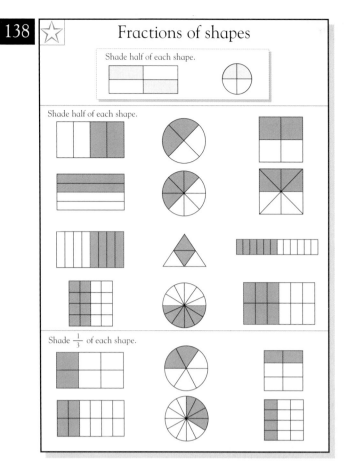

Shade half of each shape.

Shade $\frac{1}{3}$ of each shape.

Children may shade in any combination of the sections as long as the shaded area represents the fraction.

Choosing the operation

Write the answer in the box.

I add 25 to a number and the sum is 40. What number did I start with?   15

I subtract 13 and have 24 left. What number did I start with?   37

Write the answer in the box.

22 is added to a number and the sum is 30. What number did I begin with?   8

I subtract 14 from a number and end up with 17. What number did I start with?   31

I add 16 to a number and the total of the two numbers is 30. What number did I begin with?   14

When 26 is subtracted from a number, the difference is 14. What is the number?   40

After adding 22 to a number the total is 45. What is the number?   23

What number must you subtract from 19 to find a difference of 7?   12

I start with 29 and take away a number. The difference is 14. What number did I subtract?   15

35 is added to a number and the total is 60. What is the number?   25

I increase a number by 14 and the total is 30. What number did I start with?   16

After taking 17 away from a number I am left with 3. What number did I start with?   20

Paul starts with 50¢ but spends some money in a shop. He goes home with 18¢. How much did Paul spend?   32¢

Sue starts out with 23¢ but is given some money by her aunt. Sue then has 50¢. How much was she given?   27¢

Alice gives 20¢ to charity. If she started with 95¢, how much has she have left?   75¢

Jane has a 32-ounce bottle of orange soda. She drinks 12 ounces. How many ounces does she have left?   20 oz

A box contains 60 pins and then some are added so that the new total is 85. How many pins have been added?   25

A tower is made up of 30 blocks. 45 more are put on the top. How many blocks are in the tower now?   75

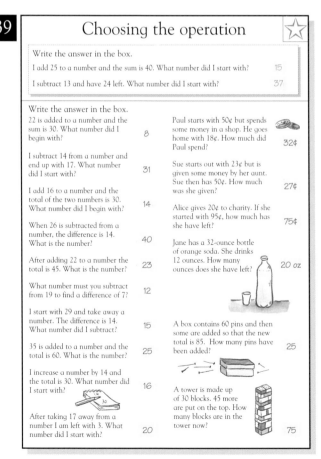

Children must choose between addition and subtraction to solve each problem. If they make an error, have them substitute their answer in the problem to help them understand why it is incorrect.

Choosing the operation

Write the answer in the box.

A number is multiplied by 8 and the result is 24. What is the number?   3

I divide a number by 4 and the answer is 9. What number did I begin with?   36

Write the answer in the box.

A number is multiplied by 6 and the result is 30. What is the number?   5

When a number is divided by 7 the result is 4. What is the number?   28

I multiply a number by 10, and the final number is 70. What number did I multiply?   7

After dividing a number by 8, I am left with 4. What number did I divide?   32

When 20 is multiplied by a number the result is 100. What number is used to multiply?   5

I divide a number by 3 and the result is 9. What is the number?   27

After multiplying a number by 5, I have 40. What was the number I started with?   8

When a number is divided by 10 the result is 3. What number was divided?   30

I multiply a number by 4 and the result is 40. What number was multiplied?   10

After dividing a number by 2, I am left with 30. What number was divided?   60

45¢ is shared equally by some children. Each child receives 9¢. How many children are there?   5

Each box contains 7 markers. I have 28 markers altogether. How many boxes do I have?   4

I share 80¢ equally among some children. Each child is given 20¢. How many children have shared the money?   4

A bag contains 10 chocolate bars. In all I have 100 chocolate bars. How many bags do I have?   10

50 peanuts are shared equally between 2 squirrels. How many peanuts does each squirrel receive?   25

I give $25 to each charity. I give away $200. How many charities did I give money to?   8

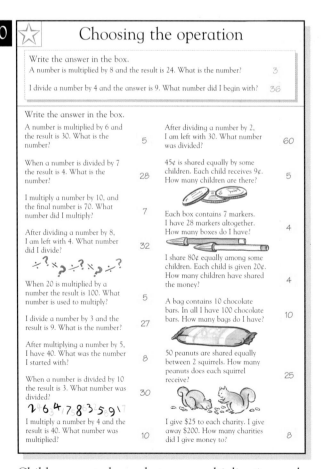

Children must choose between multiplication and division to solve each problem. If they make an error, have them substitute their answer in the problem to help them understand why it is incorrect.

Bar graphs and pictographs

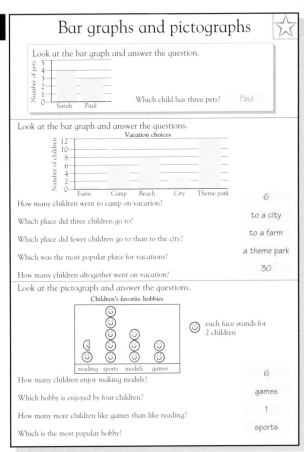

Look at the bar graph and answer the question.

Which child has three pets? **Paul**

Look at the bar graph and answer the questions.

Vacation choices

How many children went to camp on vacation? **6**

Which place did three children go to? **to a city**

Which place did fewer children go to than to the city? **to a farm**

Which was the most popular place for vacations? **a theme park**

How many children altogether went on vacation? **30**

Look at the pictograph and answer the questions.

Children's favorite hobbies

each face stands for 2 children

How many children enjoy making models? **6**

Which hobby is enjoyed by four children? **games**

How many more children like games than like reading? **1**

Which is the most popular hobby? **sports**

If children need help reading bar graphs, show them how to read across and up from the axis labels. To answer some of the questions, children will have to compare and add data.

Adding two numbers

Find each sum.

```
  2 7 1        4 8 3
+ 5 2 4      + 5 7 1
  7 9 5      1,0 5 4
```
Remember to regroup if you need to.

Find each sum.

```
  3 3 4        3 5 2        7 2 3        8 4 3
+ 2 6 5      + 1 2 7      + 3 4 5      + 2 9 1
  5 9 9        4 7 9      1,0 6 8      1,1 3 4

  3 8 5        3 6 3        5 3 5        3 9 2
+ 6 0 6      + 1 4 7      + 1 8 7      + 4 8 8
  9 9 1        5 1 0        7 2 2        8 8 0
```

Write the answer in the box.

213 + 137 = **350**   535 + 167 = **702**

Write the missing number in the box.

```
  3 6 2        2 5 6        7 2 1        7 3 9
+ 4 1 9      + 5 8 1      + 2 6 4      + 2 4 0
  7 8 1        8 3 7        9 8 5        9 7 9
```

Find each sum.

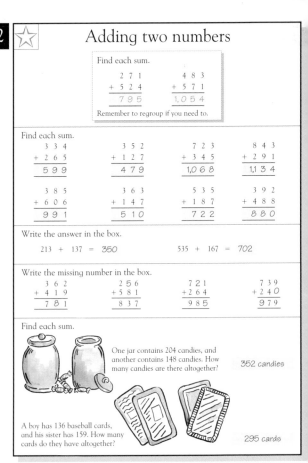

One jar contains 204 candies, and another contains 148 candies. How many candies are there altogether? **352 candies**

A boy has 136 baseball cards, and his sister has 159. How many cards do they have altogether? **295 cards**

The questions on this page involve straightforward addition work. If children have difficulty with the horizontal sums, suggest that they rewrite them in vertical form. Some errors may result from neglecting to regroup.

Adding two numbers

Find each sum.

```
  4, 3 2 1      3, 7 9 4
+ 2, 4 6 5    + 5, 3 2 5
  6, 7 8 6      9, 1 1 9
```
Remember to carry if you need to.

Find each sum.

```
  2, 6 4 2      4, 3 2 5      2, 4 7 1
+ 3, 2 4 1    + 2, 6 5 3    + 4, 2 3 8
  5, 8 8 3      6, 9 7 8      6, 7 0 9

  3, 7 4 9      5, 7 6 4      8, 4 8 2
+ 2, 4 7 1    + 3, 9 1 5    + 1, 3 4 9
  6, 2 2 0      9, 6 7 9      9, 8 3 1
```

Write the answer in the box.

1,342 + 1,264 = **2,606**   2,531 + 4,236 = **6,767**

2,013 + 3,642 = **5,655**   1,738 + 4,261 = **5,999**

Write the missing number in the box.

```
  3, 7 4 1      1, 6 5 2      3, 6 4 2
+ 2, 9 4 3    + 3, 2 7 4    + 4, 8 3 1
  6, 6 8 4      4, 9 2 6      8, 4 7 3
```

Find each sum.

5,621 people saw the local soccer team play on Saturday, and 3,246 people watched the midweek match. How many people saw the soccer team play that week? **8,867 people**

6,214 people went to the rock concert on Saturday night, and 3,471 people went on Sunday night. How many people saw rock concerts that weekend? **9,685 people**

This page is similar to the previous page, with larger numbers. If children have difficulty with the section on finding missing numbers, have them try various digits until they find the correct one.

Subtracting three-digit numbers

Write the difference between the lines.

```
  364         471 cm
- 223       - 252 cm
  141         219 cm
```

Write the difference between the lines.

```
  263         478         845         793
- 151       - 234       - 624       - 581
  112         244         221         212

  580 ft      659 m       850 yd      372 m
- 230 ft    - 318 m     - 740 yd    - 262 m
  350 ft      341 m       110 yd      110 m
```

Write the difference in the box.

365 − 123 = **242**   799 − 354 = **445**

$876 − $515 = **$361** $940 − $730 = **$210**

$684 − $574 = **$110** $220 − $120 = **$100**

Write the difference between the lines.

```
  363         484         561         394
- 145       - 237       - 342       - 185
  218         247         219         209

  937         568         225         752
- 719       - 209       - 116       - 329
  218         359         109         423
```

Find the answer to each problem.

A grocer has 234 apples. He sells 127. How many apples does he have left? **107 apples**

A store has 860 movie videos to rent. 420 are rented. How many are left in the store? **440 videos**

There are 572 children in a school. 335 are girls. How many are boys? **237 boys**

In some of these sums, children may incorrectly subtract the smaller digit from the larger one, when they should be subtracting the larger digit from the smaller one. In such cases, point out that they should regroup.

Subtracting three-digit numbers ☆

Write the difference between the lines.

415	711 m
− 152	− 392 m
263	319 m

Write the difference between the lines.

524 m	319 m	647 ft	915 yd
− 263 m	− 137 m	− 456 ft	− 193 yd
261 m	182 m	191 ft	722 yd

714	926	421	815
− 407	− 827	− 355	− 786
307	99	66	29

Write the difference in the box.

512 − 304 = 208   648 − 239 = 409

831 − 642 = 189   377 − 198 = 179

Write the difference between the lines.

423	615	312	924
− 136	− 418	− 113	− 528
287	197	199	396

Write the missing number in the box.

7 2 3	5 6 2	8 3 4	5 3 2
− 1 2 8	− 3 1 7	− 2 5 7	− 1 8 5
5 9 5	2 4 5	5 7 7	3 4 7

Find the answer to each problem.

A theater holds 645 people. 257 people buy tickets. How many seats are empty? 388 seats

There are 564 people in a park. 276 are boating on the lake. How many are taking part in other activities? 288 people

If children have difficulty with the section on missing numbers, have them use trial and error until they find the correct number. Encourage them to use addition and subtraction fact families to find the number.

☆ Multiplying by one-digit numbers

Find each product.

32	26	34
x 2	x 3	x 4
64	78	136

Find each product.

27	32	16	19
x 2	x 3	x 4	x 2
54	96	64	38

22	25	18	33
x 3	x 4	x 6	x 5
66	100	108	165

39	26	41	38
x 2	x 2	x 2	x 3
78	52	82	114

29	45	28	16
x 3	x 2	x 3	x 6
87	90	84	96

10	40	20	50
x 5	x 2	x 4	x 3
50	80	80	150

Find the answer to each problem.

Laura has 36 marbles, and Sarah has twice as many. How many marbles does Sarah have? 72 marbles

A ruler is 30 cm long. How long will 4 rulers be altogether? 120 cm

Errors made on this page generally highlight gaps in children's knowledge of the 2, 3, 4, and 5 times tables. Other errors can also result from neglecting to regroup.

Multiplying by one-digit numbers ☆

Find each product.

53	76	25
x 3	x 6	x 7
159	456	175

Find each product.

56	46	32	36	45
x 8	x 7	x 6	x 9	x 4
448	322	192	324	180

73	96	58	33	48
x 5	x 3	x 7	x 6	x 5
365	288	406	198	240

24	19	64	52	81
x 9	x 8	x 4	x 6	x 3
216	152	256	312	243

37	40	50	30	20
x 7	x 8	x 3	x 7	x 9
259	320	150	210	180

Find the answer to each problem.

A school bus holds 36 children. How many children can travel in 6 busloads? 216 children

Each of 28 children brings 7 drawings to school. How many drawings do they have altogether? 196 drawings

Errors made on this page generally highlight gaps in children's knowledge of the 6, 7, 8, and 9 times tables. As on the previous page, the other most likely error will result from neglecting to regroup.

☆ Division with remainders

Find each quotient.

5 r 1
3) 16
15
1

6 r 2
4) 26
24
2

Find each quotient.

17 r 1	11 r 2	7 r 1	9 r 4
2) 35	4) 46	3) 22	5) 49

14 r 2	12 r 3	7 r 2	12 r 2
4) 58	5) 63	5) 37	4) 50

25 r 1	14 r 3	18 r 4	16 r 3
3) 76	4) 59	5) 94	5) 83

49 r 1	18 r 3	15 r 2	18 r 1
2) 99	4) 75	5) 77	2) 37

Write the answer in the box.

What is 27 divided by 4? 6 r 3   Divide 78 by 5. 15 r 3

What is 46 divided by 3? 15 r 1   Divide 63 by 2. 31 r 1

Children may have difficulty finding quotients with remainders. Have them perform long division until the remaining value to be divided is less than the divisor. That value is the remainder.

Division with remainders

Find each quotient.

$$6 \overline{)34} \quad = 5\,r\,4 \quad \frac{30}{4}$$

$$7 \overline{)50} \quad = 7\,r\,1 \quad \frac{49}{1}$$

Find each quotient.

16 r 3	7 r 1	3 r 3	9 r 4
6)99	6)43	9)30	8)76

7 r 3	11 r 6	5 r 7	15 r 1
7)52	7)83	9)52	6)91

9 r 3	7 r 7	4 r 3	5 r 6
7)66	8)63	6)27	8)46

10 r 3	12 r 1	8 r 3	3 r 5
9)93	7)85	8)67	7)26

Write the answer in the box.

What is 87 divided by 7? 12 r 3

Divide 84 by 8. 10 r 4

What is 75 divided by 6? 12 r 3

Divide 73 by 9. 8 r 1

This page is similar to the previous page, but the divisors are numbers greater than 5. Children will need to know their 6, 7, 8, and 9 times tables to solve the problems.

Appropriate units of measure

Choose the best units to measure the length of each item.

inches	feet	yards
notebook	car	swimming pool
inches	feet	yards

Choose the best units to measure the length of each item.

inches	feet	yards
bed	bicycle	toothbrush	football field
feet	feet	inches	yards
shoe	driveway	canoe	fence
inches	feet or yards	feet	yards

The height of a door is about 7 feet .

The length of a pencil is about 7 inches .

The height of a flagpole is about 7 yards .

Choose the best units to measure the weight of each item.

ounces	pounds	tons
train	kitten	watermelon	tennis ball
tons	ounces	pounds	ounces
shoe	bag of potatoes	elephant	washing machine
ounces	pounds	tons	pounds

The weight of a hamburger is about 6 ounces .

The weight of a bag of apples is about 5 pounds .

The weight of a truck is about 4 tons .

Children might come up with their own examples of items that measure about 1 inch, 1 foot, and 1 yard, as well as items that weigh about 1 ounce, 1 pound, and 1 ton. They can use these as benchmarks to find the appropriate unit.

Real-life problems

Find the answer to each problem.

Jacob spent $4.68 at the store and had $4.77 left. How much did he have to start with?

$9.45

$$\begin{array}{r} 4.77 \\ + 4.68 \\ \hline 9.45 \end{array}$$

Tracy receives a weekly allowance of $3.00 a week. How much will she have if she saves all of it for 8 weeks?

$24.00

$$\begin{array}{r} 3.00 \\ \times \quad 8 \\ \hline 24.00 \end{array}$$

Find the answer to each problem.

A theater charges $4 for each matinee ticket. If it sells 360 tickets for a matinee performance, how much does it take in?

$1,440

$$\begin{array}{r} 2 \\ 360 \\ \times \quad 4 \\ \hline 1,440 \end{array}$$

David has saved $9.59. His sister has $3.24 less. How much does she have?

$6.35

$$\begin{array}{r} 9.59 \\ - 3.24 \\ \hline 6.35 \end{array}$$

The cost for 9 children to go to a theme park is $72. How much does each child pay? If only 6 children go, what will the cost be?

$8 per child
$48 for 6 children

$$9 \overline{)72} \quad = 8 \quad \frac{72}{0}$$
$$6 \times 8 = 48$$

Paul has $3.69. His sister gives him another $5.25, and he goes out and buys a CD single for $3.99. How much does he have left?

$4.95

$$\begin{array}{r} 1 \\ 3.69 \\ + 5.25 \\ \hline 8.94 \end{array} \quad \begin{array}{r} 7\ 18\ 14 \\ 8.94 \\ - 3.99 \\ \hline 4.95 \end{array}$$

Ian has $20 in savings. He decides to spend $\frac{1}{4}$ of it. How much will he have left?

$15

$$20 \div 4 = 5$$
$$20 - 5 = 15$$

This page provides children an opportunity to apply the skills they have practiced. To select the appropriate operation, discuss if they expect the answer to be larger or smaller. This can help them decide whether to add, multiply, subtract or divide.

Perimeters of squares and rectangles

Find the perimeter of this rectangle.

To find the perimeter of a rectangle or a square, add the lengths of the four sides.
6 in. + 6 in. + 4 in. + 4 in. = 20 in.
You can also do this with multiplication.
(2 x 6) in. + (2 x 4) in.
= 12 in. + 8 in. = 20 in.

6 in. 4 in. 20 in.

Find the perimeters of these rectangles and squares.

4 in. × 1 in. 10 in.

3 yd × 3 yd 12 yd

2 mi × 3 mi 10 mi

3 cm × 2 cm 10 cm

1 m × 1 m 4 m

4 ft × 2 ft 12 ft

4 in. × 4 in. 16 in.

4 cm × 3 cm 14 cm

2 km × 2 km 8 km

Make sure that children do not simply add the lengths of two sides of a figure rather than all four sides. Help children realize that the perimeter of a square can be found by multiplying the length of one side by 4.

Comparing areas

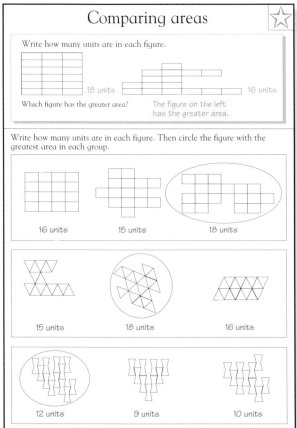

Write how many units are in each figure.

18 units   16 units

Which figure has the greater area?   The figure on the left has the greater area.

Write how many units are in each figure. Then circle the figure with the greatest area in each group.

16 units   15 units   18 units

15 units   18 units   16 units

12 units   9 units   10 units

Children may not realize that they can compare the areas of irregular figures. Make sure that they take care to count the units in each figure, rather than incorrectly assuming that the longest or tallest figure has the greater area.

Adding fractions

Write the sum in the simplest form.

$\frac{1}{8} + \frac{3}{8} = \frac{4}{8} = \frac{1}{2}$ $\frac{3}{5} + \frac{3}{5} = \frac{6}{5} = 1\frac{1}{5}$

Write the sum in the simplest form.

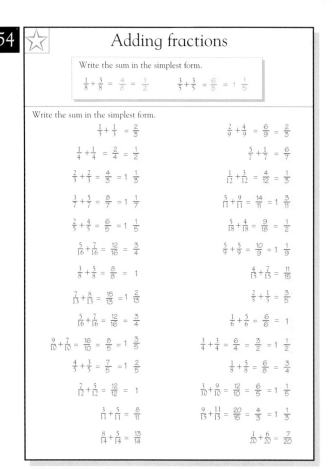

$\frac{1}{3} + \frac{1}{3} = \frac{2}{3}$ $\frac{2}{9} + \frac{4}{9} = \frac{6}{9} = \frac{2}{3}$

$\frac{1}{4} + \frac{1}{4} = \frac{2}{4} = \frac{1}{2}$ $\frac{5}{7} + \frac{1}{7} = \frac{6}{7}$

$\frac{2}{3} + \frac{2}{3} = \frac{4}{3} = 1\frac{1}{3}$ $\frac{1}{12} + \frac{3}{12} = \frac{4}{12} = \frac{1}{3}$

$\frac{3}{7} + \frac{5}{7} = \frac{8}{7} = 1\frac{1}{7}$ $\frac{5}{11} + \frac{9}{11} = \frac{14}{11} = 1\frac{3}{11}$

$\frac{2}{5} + \frac{4}{5} = \frac{6}{5} = 1\frac{1}{5}$ $\frac{5}{18} + \frac{4}{18} = \frac{9}{18} = \frac{1}{2}$

$\frac{5}{16} + \frac{7}{16} = \frac{12}{16} = \frac{3}{4}$ $\frac{5}{9} + \frac{5}{9} = \frac{10}{9} = 1\frac{1}{9}$

$\frac{3}{8} + \frac{5}{8} = \frac{8}{8} = 1$ $\frac{4}{13} + \frac{7}{13} = \frac{11}{13}$

$\frac{7}{13} + \frac{8}{13} = \frac{15}{13} = 1\frac{2}{13}$ $\frac{2}{5} + \frac{1}{5} = \frac{3}{5}$

$\frac{5}{16} + \frac{7}{16} = \frac{12}{16} = \frac{3}{4}$ $\frac{1}{6} + \frac{5}{6} = \frac{6}{6} = 1$

$\frac{9}{10} + \frac{7}{10} = \frac{16}{10} = \frac{8}{5} = 1\frac{3}{5}$ $\frac{3}{4} + \frac{3}{4} = \frac{6}{4} = \frac{3}{2} = 1\frac{1}{2}$

$\frac{4}{5} + \frac{3}{5} = \frac{7}{5} = 1\frac{2}{5}$ $\frac{1}{8} + \frac{5}{8} = \frac{6}{8} = \frac{3}{4}$

$\frac{7}{12} + \frac{5}{12} = \frac{12}{12} = 1$ $\frac{3}{10} + \frac{9}{10} = \frac{12}{10} = \frac{6}{5} = 1\frac{1}{5}$

$\frac{3}{11} + \frac{5}{11} = \frac{8}{11}$ $\frac{9}{15} + \frac{11}{15} = \frac{20}{15} = \frac{4}{3} = 1\frac{1}{3}$

$\frac{8}{14} + \frac{5}{14} = \frac{13}{14}$ $\frac{1}{20} + \frac{6}{20} = \frac{7}{20}$

Some children may incorrectly add both the numerators and the denominators. Demonstrate that only the numerators should be added when the fractions have the same denominators: $\frac{1}{2} + \frac{1}{2}$ equals $\frac{2}{2}$ or 1, not $\frac{2}{4}$.

Subtracting fractions

Write the sum in the simplest form.

$\frac{5}{6} - \frac{4}{6} = \frac{1}{6}$ $\frac{5}{8} - \frac{3}{8} = \frac{2}{8} = \frac{1}{4}$

Write the answer in the simplest form.

$\frac{2}{3} - \frac{1}{3} = \frac{1}{3}$ $\frac{7}{9} - \frac{4}{9} = \frac{3}{9} = \frac{1}{3}$

$\frac{1}{4} - \frac{1}{4} = 0$ $\frac{5}{7} - \frac{1}{7} = \frac{4}{7}$

$\frac{7}{12} - \frac{5}{12} = \frac{2}{12} = \frac{1}{6}$ $\frac{5}{11} - \frac{3}{11} = \frac{2}{11}$

$\frac{6}{7} - \frac{5}{7} = \frac{1}{7}$ $\frac{9}{12} - \frac{5}{12} = \frac{4}{12} = \frac{1}{3}$

$\frac{18}{30} - \frac{15}{30} = \frac{3}{30} = \frac{1}{10}$ $\frac{4}{5} - \frac{2}{5} = \frac{2}{5}$

$\frac{3}{6} - \frac{1}{6} = \frac{2}{6} = \frac{1}{3}$ $\frac{7}{8} - \frac{1}{8} = \frac{6}{8} = \frac{3}{4}$

$\frac{11}{16} - \frac{7}{16} = \frac{4}{16} = \frac{1}{4}$ $\frac{5}{9} - \frac{2}{9} = \frac{3}{9} = \frac{1}{3}$

$\frac{7}{13} - \frac{5}{13} = \frac{2}{13}$ $\frac{14}{15} - \frac{4}{15} = \frac{10}{15} = \frac{2}{3}$

$\frac{12}{13} - \frac{8}{13} = \frac{4}{13}$ $\frac{4}{5} - \frac{1}{5} = \frac{3}{5}$

$\frac{9}{10} - \frac{7}{10} = \frac{2}{10} = \frac{1}{5}$ $\frac{5}{6} - \frac{1}{6} = \frac{4}{6} = \frac{2}{3}$

$\frac{8}{17} - \frac{4}{17} = \frac{4}{17}$ $\frac{11}{18} - \frac{8}{18} = \frac{3}{18} = \frac{1}{6}$

$\frac{4}{5} - \frac{3}{5} = \frac{1}{5}$ $\frac{9}{11} - \frac{5}{11} = \frac{4}{11}$

$\frac{7}{8} - \frac{5}{8} = \frac{2}{8} = \frac{1}{4}$ $\frac{3}{16} - \frac{2}{16} = \frac{1}{16}$

$\frac{7}{12} - \frac{5}{12} = \frac{2}{12} = \frac{1}{6}$ $\frac{8}{14} - \frac{5}{14} = \frac{3}{14}$

$\frac{9}{10} - \frac{3}{10} = \frac{6}{10} = \frac{3}{5}$ $\frac{17}{20} - \frac{6}{20} = \frac{11}{20}$

On this page, children subtract fractions that have the same denominators. Some children may neglect to simplify their answers. Help them do so by finding common factors in the numerator and the denominator.

Volumes of cubes

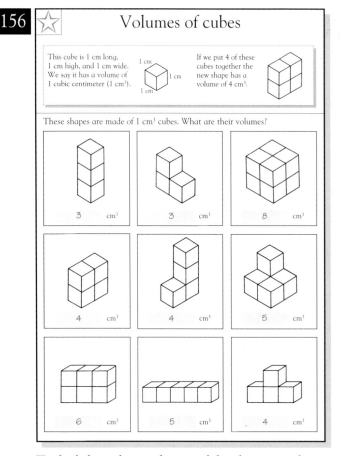

This cube is 1 cm long, 1 cm high, and 1 cm wide. We say it has a volume of 1 cubic centimeter (1 cm³).

If we put 4 of these cubes together the new shape has a volume of 4 cm³.

These shapes are made of 1 cm³ cubes. What are their volumes?

3 cm³   3 cm³   8 cm³

4 cm³   4 cm³   5 cm³

6 cm³   5 cm³   4 cm³

To find the volume of some of the shapes on this page, children will need to visualize how many blocks cannot be seen in the illustrations. For example, in the third and sixth shapes, there is one block that is not shown.